Sabine Gehm, Pirkko Husemann, ...
Knowledge in Motion

SABINE GEHM, PIRKKO HUSEMANN, KATHARINA VON WILCKE (EDS.)

Knowledge in Motion

Perspectives of Artistic and Scientific Research in Dance

[transcript]

Under the motto »Knowledge in Motion« the Dance Congress Germany took place from 20-23 April 2006 at the House of World Cultures in Berlin. The Dance Congress was a project initiated by the German Federal Cultural Foundation. Besides some of the lectures held at the Dance Congress the publication at hand includes further articles and interviews on the issue of the congress. Cf. also: http://www.tanzkongress.de

This publication is funded by the German Federal Cultural Foundation

Bibliographic information published by Die Deutsche Bibliothek
Die Deutsche Bibliothek lists this publication in the Deutsche National-bibliografie; detailed bibliographic data are available on the Internet at http://dnb.ddb.de

© **2007 transcript Verlag, Bielefeld**

Layout by: Kordula Röckenhaus, Bielefeld
Edited by: Sabine Gehm, Pirkko Husemann, Katharina von Wilcke
Translations from German: Bettina von Arps-Aubert –
  Interpretation and Translation
English Proofreading: Geoffrey Garrison, Ingrid Hagmeister
Cover photo: »water glass« from the education project BOCAL
  by Boris Charmatz, 2003/04.
Photo: © Alexander Ch. Wulz, http://www.wulz.cc
Typeset & Printed by: Majuskel Medienproduktion GmbH, Wetzlar
ISBN 978-3-89942-809-4

Distributed in North America by:

Transaction Publishers
New Brunswick (U.S.A.) and London (U.K.)

Transaction Publishers
Rutgers University
35 Berrue Circle
Piscataway, NJ 08854

Tel.: (732) 445-2280
Fax: (732) 445-3138
for orders (U.S. only):
toll free 888-999-6778

Content

Reception and Participation

Professional Education and Retraining in Dance

Dance Pedagogy and Cultural Work

Preface

HORTENSIA VÖLCKERS

For us, the Federal Cultural Foundation, who organised the first German dance congress in over fifty years in April 2006, the three legendary dancers' congresses held in Magdeburg and Essen in the 1920s and in Munich in 1930 were our role models. The DANCE CONGRESS GERMANY was therefore an attempt at a new start. It established conscious links to the dance congresses of the Weimar era, to which dancers, choreographers, dance pedagogues, critics, theatre producers, musicians and many others interested in dance flocked in their hundreds in order to discuss issues and problems in various programme formats. They triggered astonishing developments in the process. In 1927 in Magdeburg, to mention just one example, Adolf Loos spoke of the return of dance to its natural state: the feet needed no longer be placed crossways, but were allowed to be positioned in parallel in a completely natural stance. Oskar Schlemmer in his turn presented his TRIADIC BALLET and emphasised the significance of abstraction in dance: there was enough chaos being created at the time and it was therefore a matter of priority to revert to the laws of space, form and colour. And naturally the pioneers of modern dance used the congresses to proclaim their own agendas. Mary Wigman gave a rousing speech on »dance in its absolute form«.[1] No more theatrical dance, she demanded, but »conquering the entire theatre by means of a dance-like gesture!«, this »grandiose play and mirror reflecting life!«[2]

---

1 | Mary Wigman: »Der neue künstlerische Tanz und das Theater«, in: Hedwig Müller/Patricia Stöckemann (eds.): ... jeder Mensch ist ein Tänzer. Ausdruckstanz in Deutschland zwischen 1900 und 1945, Gießen: Anabas 1993, p. 77.

2 | Ibid., p. 82.

This means that at the time, in addition to solidly uniting all dancers within a professional organisation, the focus was on dance as a means of liberation from strait-laced conventions, of comprehending a chaotic world through a new, danced order and asserting the autonomy of dance as an art form. However, the dance congresses soon came to a halt. At the beginning of the 1930s the NSDAP set a new course: no more dance revolutions, no unleashing of corporeity and liberation from forms that had become hollow, no emancipation of the body, but rather state rule over the body through mass parades, decreed folkloristic attitudes, formal rigidity in dance performance and ultimately ›mechanisation‹ of the body in an all-out war. Dance therefore always bears the hallmark of its era and the inconsistencies of this era and the same also applies, of course, to the questions the respective society puts to dance.

Knowledge in motion was the motto of the Dance Congress Germany and is also the title of the resulting book presented here. Dance as a culture of knowledge was and is the thematic focus. Dance and knowledge – this raises many questions: What do we want and what does society want to learn from dance? What does the individual need to know in order to dance? What do we know when we dance? But also, and this seems the most interesting aspect to me: what does dance know about us that we do not know or only have a vague idea of or have forgotten? How can we convert this knowledge held by dance itself into motion?

The American philosopher Nelson Goodman, an expert in dance, said about the perception of art that there is more to seeing than meets the eye. This applies in a similar form to dance and is one of the reasons for the interest in dance recently shown by neurophysiology. The neuroscientist Wolf Singer is a case in point. His visits to the choreographies of William Forsythe motivated Singer to investigate the question of the physiological conditions of our perception of dance in neural terms. The answer is astonishing: watching dance causes our brain to simulate the range of movement we see on stage. Our brain participates in the motor performance of the dancers. This creates a process of interplay between those who move and those who watch the movement. Singer calls this resonance looping between dancers and audience »dynamic excitation patterns«.

The inference from this is that dance is infectious. It requires effort and it is virtually impossible not to react to expressive gestures, not to dance, at least internally, when others are moving. The separation of thinking and feeling from the movement of the body must be practiced in an enforced learning process and cannot fully succeed because our thinking is linked to our body.

Dancers have always been aware of this. Now science has followed suit. Advanced neuroscience has departed from the rationalism propagated by the French philosopher René Descartes and the rigid body-soul dualism, which has led our thinking (and our bodies) towards progress since the Enlightenment and finally pushed them into a corner. It has dispensed with a notion of reason which, being a hegemonic instrument of control, excludes the body as an organ capable of knowledge. It focuses its attention on the body as a store of experience, as a place where pleasure and pain leave their marks and influence habits and the shape of life. At the end of scientific modernity our knowledge about knowledge starts moving again.

Brain research today, with all its sophisticated equipment and methods, follows the historical avant-garde of modern dance. Rudolph von Laban, Mary Wigman and Gret Palucca took, like Frederick Matthias Alexander or Moshe Feldenkrais, the first few practical steps towards rediscovering the body as a source of knowledge. They were pioneers who positioned dance against the ideologically adjusted body concepts of their time. They wanted to obtain harmony between body and mind. They were driven by a productive obsession, which included dance, theory and the desire for social reform in equal measure. And with the Berlin DANCE CONGRESS, too, we set ourselves the aim of enlightening minds through the body and of calling into question the dominance of one-dimensional rationality through the movement of our bodies.

But how can we learn more about the knowledge that is imprinted in our bodies? How do we overcome the chronic illiteracy of our ›age of reason‹ in understanding our body language? How can we discover and how can we use the semiotic richness that helps us to communicate, long before and long after ›words have been exchanged‹ and symbols produced?

The film RHYTHM IS IT! documented in an extremely moving way the spectacular effect the dance project organised by the Berlin Philharmonic Orchestra in conjunction with British choreographer Royston Maldoom had on teenagers from ›socially marginalised areas‹. Why was that? Firstly, simply because Royston Maldoom did not have to start exporting dance to Berlin-Neukölln, it had already been there for a long time! On music videos, on the Hip-Hop-scene and throughout popular culture dance has been a central medium of expression for young people for decades, irrespective of whether they have a German, Turkish, Nigerian or Polish family background. But then something important was added: namely that choreographers and dancers insisted on discipline, perfection and perseverance, in short: on work, which is an absolute prerequisite for creating a new common form.

Dance – the film can also be interpreted in this way – has a positive impact on the growing-up process. This has also been supported by research, which has shown that young people less often stray off the straight and narrow if they dance on a regular basis and that learning to dance also promotes the acquisition of school-based knowledge. Should this, i.e. the inadvertent dialectic triggered by the learning difficulties and concentration problems revealed in the Pisa survey, after all be the way to realising the old dream of dance as a school subject, as a means of educating people? As early as the 18th century the Swiss educationalist Johann Heinrich Pestalozzi had already tried in vain to gain acceptance for his plans for reform among his contemporaries.

Opening of Dance Congress Germany, 20 April 2006 at House of World Cultures, Berlin

Photo: Thomas Aurin

I very much welcome the educational alliances which are currently being formed in many places across Germany in order to promote the integration of dance into the curriculum in our schools. However, dance should not be reduced to the role of ›sweeper‹ in educational reform strategies. Dance is more than an exercise designed for getting top marks for good behaviour and more than a treatment for hyperactivity. It is not an all-purpose educational weapon for disciplining poorly integrated teenagers. Children who are able to walk backwards become better students of mathematics – that would be a positive effect of dance programmes. However, I shudder at the thought of including movement exercises in mathematics teaching. Dance as an art form, which is what it is in the first place, must remain unimpeded. Re-socialising young people or improving their achievements should not take priority, because in dance bodies learn about the ground under their feet and the effect of gravity. They learn about their freedom and their individual ability to overcome gravity, to jump, fly, flow and join forces in moving with others. They learn to find a form for their desire, their pain, their social drive and their impulse to place themselves in or against the world.

By promoting dance in the context of the »Tanzplan Deutschland« initiative[3] the German Cultural Foundation aims at creating spaces for such experiences. We want to give artists and cultural activists the opportunity to work freely, in the hope that they will provide us with all the material and knowledge necessary to better understand the world in order to find an answer to the question ›Where do we want to move?‹.

It is about keeping our knowledge in motion and, by doing so, being involved in a more comprehensive and more stimulating education. Not only is this our way out of the »self-inflicted mental immaturity« as Immanuel Kant said, but also the way out of »self-imposed inertia«. As quoted in Denis Diderot's Large Encyclopaedia of the Enlightenment Period:

Dance and song are as natural to humankind as gestures and voice. Ever since there have been human beings on Earth, there has doubtless been song and dance, people have sung and danced from the start of creation to the present day and it is more than likely that people will go on singing and dancing until the human race dies out completely.[4]

Translation from German

References

Wigman, Mary: »Der neue künstlerische Tanz und das Theater«, in: Hedwig Müller/Patricia Stöckemann (eds.): ... *jeder Mensch ist ein Tänzer. Ausdruckstanz in Deutschland zwischen 1900 und 1945*, Gießen: Anabas 1993, pp. 77–82.

Online References

www.kulturstiftung-des-bundes.de/media_archive/1146062396597.pdf.
www.tanzplan-deutschland.de.

---

3 | The »Tanzplan« is a five-year funding programme for dance in Germany. In addition to the DANCE CONGRESS GERMANY, which marked the beginning of this initiative, the programme includes »Tanzplan local« projects in eight German towns and cities as well as the »Tanzplan educational programme«. Cf. *www.tanzplan-deutschland.de* from 11 May 2007.

4 | Cf. *www.kulturstiftung-des-bundes.de/media_archive/1146062396597.pdf* from 11 May 2007.

Introduction

SABINE GEHM, PIRKKO HUSEMANN
AND KATHARINA VON WILCKE

The DANCE CONGRESS GERMANY was held under the motto KNOWLEDGE IN MOTION at the House of World Cultures in Berlin from 20 to 23 April 2006. A total of 1,700 international participants representing a highly diverse range of occupational and research fields addressed all manner of practical and theoretical issues relating to dance. The unexpectedly high attendance rate is testimony to the increased interest in dance as an independent art form and culture of knowledge. The exceptional response is also partly due to the fact that, in the same year, the Federal Cultural Foundation launched its »Tanzplan« initiative. As a result, the focal point of the DANCE CONGRESS was the significance of dance within the context of cultural and education policy as well as the emerging dance studies, which are developing rapidly at present. In the hope of not only engaging academics in dialogue with each other but also with practitioners and theorists, we as the curators from the very beginning focused on the issue of knowledge production in and about dance. Consequently the title KNOWLEDGE IN MOTION, which was chosen both for the congress and this publication, comprises two fundamental working hypotheses: executing a dance movement entails specific knowledge. At the same time, dance requires and facilitates extraordinary processes of understanding.

In addition to a selection of the lectures held at the DANCE CONGRESS, the book, which is published both in English and German, contains additional essays and interviews that provide in-depth insights into these theses on KNOWLEDGE IN MOTION. At the same time, the contributions made during the congress have, above all, been supplemented by comments and articles from the artists. As a consequence, the knowledge of dance as described in this publication is mainly based on the perceptions and concepts of dancers and choreographers. To them, talking about KNOWLEDGE IN MOTION as embodied thinking is second nature. For this reason, we wanted to clarify how this type of knowledge production is perceived and carried out in art practice: what defines body and movement knowledge? How and through which means is it generated and passed on? How are practical cognitive processes reflected? Is there such a thing as artistic research in dance alongside scientific research about dance? How can the division of labour between science and art, which remains especially rigid in Germany, be resolved?

All of these questions formed the starting point for collecting heterogeneous opinions from all manner of perspectives, which we have divided into seven topics. These roughly reflect the programme of the DANCE CONGRESS, with the economic and structural aspects of dance production being replaced by a separate focus on artistic research. One particular feature of this anthology is the combination of a variety of trains of thought, modes of speech and writing styles which we have consciously juxtaposed and contrasted. Organised in this way, KNOWLEDGE IN MOTION is not available at a glance, but must instead be sought between the lines, in the cross-references and along the lines of flight of the articles in this book. The text formats and levels of reflection have deliberately been changed to keep the reader in motion. As a result, reading becomes an active discovery. To breathe even more life into these contributions, we recommend the following exercise devised by choreographer Boris Charmatz: Try to read this book by placing it on the ground and standing on it without touching the floor. Anyone watching you doing this will be able to draw initial conclusions from your reading behaviour about your habitual movement patterns: Do you usually work at a desk or primarily in a dance studio?

The issue of the existence of such inherent habits in the body is raised at the very beginning of the first chapter, which is entitled »*Dance as Culture of Knowledge*«. Gabriele Klein addresses the role of dance in the knowledge society. Fleetingness and mobility form a paradigm of modernity in which the subjects have to adjust and constantly reinvent themselves. In this regard, dance as a metaphor fosters social development that needs to be cautiously monitored. At the same time, however, it presents a challenge to the scientific and academic world. Since movement cannot be translated into language offhand, a language needs to be found to express the dynamic processes. Just what form such a notation might take is illustrated by Gabriele Brandstetter: the perception of movement can best be written when the language used to do so is also set in motion. In doing so, the scientific world is venturing into an uncontrollable and unpredictable area.

Proof that such ventures can also extend beyond the field of rhetoric is provided through the contributions made by Bojana Cvejic and Peter Stamer. Both deal with dialogical formats of knowledge production that were tested during the course of the DANCE CONGRESS. As a participant in Hannah Hurtzig's BLACKMARKET FOR USEFUL KNOWLEDGE AND NON-KNOWLEDGE – /me, Cvejic analyses the installation as a public and at the same time unofficial user room where knowledge is mainly passed on orally. Stamer's retrospective look at his SANS PAPIERS laboratory deals less with the status of the illegal people than with the question of the type of knowledge production in a workgroup that needs to get by without paper. In a metalogue, he asks himself about the peculiarities of a work situation in which the main idea is to generate questions.

Consequently, the first chapter introduces both the concept of knowledge culture as well as the scientific and artistic formats of knowledge production. The second chapter addresses the difficult relationship between science and art, honing it down to the debate surrounding the term »*Artistic Research*«. Henk Borgdorff initially discusses the question of whether and to what extent research conducted in art is comparable with scientific research. Discussing the European guidelines for scientific research to be applied in the academic establishment, he draws two conclusions: either art does not constitute research or the definitions of the term »research« need to be rethought. Marijke Hoogenboom illustrates this using an artist-in-residence programme at the Amsterdam School of the Arts as an example and in doing so brings to the fore both the context pertaining to science policy and the concrete research processes in dance.

Dancers and choreographers largely define their own practical experience as research when it has to do with archiving and teaching movements and composition principles. This becomes apparent both in the »living archive« designed by choreographer Emio Greco and presented by Hoogenboom and in the »interactive score« by William Forsythe. This latter project, going by the working title MOTION BANK, is presented by a trio of authors, Scott deLahunta, Rebecca Groves and Norah Zuniga Shaw as a vision of a new form of »dance literature«. The role played by thinking and watching in improvisation is made clear by choreographer João Fiadeiro in his comments on his self-developed method for REAL-TIME COMPOSITION. Jeroen Peeters in turn outlines in his notes on a salon organised and held at the DANCE CONGRESS by André Lepecki and Myriam Van Imschoot how improvisation techniques can also be used for verbal conversation.

If salon participant Thomas Lehmen caused some confusion through his statement that choreography is a form of worldmaking, he is confirmed in his belief by the first contribution found in the third chapter entitled »*Body Knowledge and Body Memory*«. From a philosophical point of view, the TUNING SCORES of choreographer Lisa Nelson can be compared with Wittgenstein's language games as they allow people to access and design their environment with the help of perception. Alva Noë's perspective is extended to include the considerations provided by choreographer Meg Stuart. For her artistic practice, it is not so much the logically recordable perception processes that are of interest but the uncontrollable exceptional circumstances of the body. Stuart not only reflects on her methods of generating movement material but also on the processes for modulating physical states.

A state of raised sensory attention also forms the starting point of Irene Sieben's historical abstract on the »pioneers of movement studies« in dance. Using the example of kinaesthetic researchers such as Frederick Matthias Alexander and Moshe Feldenkrais, Sieben explains that neuroscience was by no means the first to discover body knowledge but that it was actually discovered at the beginning of the 20th century with the help of movement analysis. As a consequence, work with the kinaesthetic motion sense has meanwhile also become a natural element of contemporary dance techniques. Dieter Heitkamp illustrates this in conversation with Gabriele Wittmann using the skin's function in Contact Improvisation as an example. Closing this chapter, dance doctor Eileen Wanke discusses the consequences of disregarding the body memory and the risks involved in various dance techniques.

The fourth chapter, »*Dance History and Reconstruction*«, opens with a personal review by Jason Beechey who not only backs up his experiences through reconstruction work on choreographies by George Balanchine but also through his awareness of a variety of ballet traditions and the subjectivity of his own recollection. Each reconstruction is associated with construction on a wide variety of levels. This fact forms the starting point for Claudia Jeschke's comments on the reconstruction of Nijinsky's L'APRÈS-MIDI D'UN FAUNE, which alternate between theories of the cultural and body memory on the one hand, and practical work with dance notations on the other. The role played by dancers in conveying choreographic heritage is explained by Norbert Servos on the basis of Pina Bausch's concept of keeping the repertoire up to date. In order to keep her choreographic heritage alive, Bausch combines every new production with the revival of an older piece.

Yvonne Hardt discusses the potentials and impossibilities of reconstruction in a retrospective evaluation of a panel discussion on Dore Hoyer's AFFECTOS HUMANOS involving Susanne Linke, Waltraud Luley and Martin Nachbar. In an interview conducted by Alexandra Baudelot, dancer Julia Cima talks about the aspect of interpretation and incorporation of dance history using her production VISITATIONS as an example. Inge Baxmann rounds off this topic with her comments on the body as an archive using the Archives Nationales de la Danse as an example. As far back as the 1930s, the conferences organised in Paris used presentation formats which we today describe as lecture performances: not just a lecture or a performance alone, but both at the same time.

Choreographer Felix Ruckert's work on completely different types of hybrid formats is the opening contribution for the fifth chapter entitled »*Reception and Participation*«. Ruckert's pamphlet for a theatre of sensuous participation involving actors and the audience is complemented by Erika Fischer-Lichte's reception-aesthetic comments on the exceptional circumstances surrounding liminal experiences. In contrast, Rudi Laermans addresses artistic strategies which divert the attention of the audience to the constituting achievements of the performance situation without actually removing the separation existing between the stage and the auditorium.

Choreographer Hooman Sharifi in turn – in his productions for children and adults – plays with the expectations of the audience which are dependent on their cultural context. He believes that there is not only participation in the interaction on stage but also seeks to find it in a wide variety of motives of the social community. That contemporary dance always more or less explicitly reflects its cultural field is confirmed by the comments provided by Constanze Klementz on the subject of understanding art criticism and criticism by artists. In the light of choreographers exercising practice-immanent criticism in their productions, it is impossible for dance critics to uphold their exclusive claim to maintaining a professional distance.

However, the barrier between critics and artists is not the only one gradually disappearing. A similar situation can be found between such pairings as artists and teachers, and lecturers and students. For this reason, the sixth chapter entitled »*Professional Training and Retraining in Dance*« not only focuses on innovative training models but also on learning and teaching concepts. Taking his one-year BOCAL school project as an example, choreographer Boris Charmatz formulates his vision for unconventional dance training. That the study of movement is based on both physical and verbal communication processes is backed up by the comments of fellow artist Thomas Lehmen. In the course of his teaching practice throughout the world, Lehmen has specialised in establishing a common level of communication with his students.

BOCAL by Boris Charmatz

Photo: Alexander Ch. Wulz

To illustrate his methodology, dance pedagogue Kurt Koegel does not so much resort to linguistic as to architectural concepts: in order to guide dancers and choreographers in their own kinaesthetic research, he has developed a comparative model for the classification of dance techniques, which he explains using the example of »Partnering« in Contact Improvisation. Koegel, who holds a professorship for contemporary dance pedagogy in Frankfurt a.M., now fills one of the positions created as part of the »Tanzplan local«. The developments that have emerged in German education institutes since the beginning of the programme are summarised by Ingo Diehl in his report on a series of meetings held with representatives of German dance colleges and universities. In her contribution entitled »Dance Careers in Transition«, Cornelia Dümcke looks beyond job-orientated dance education and points to the acute need for action to be taken with respect to the retraining of dancers.

The book closes with four interviews on the subject of »*Dance Pedagogy and Cultural Work*«. In response to the question posed by Edit Boxberger to choreographer Royston Maldoom on the methods employed within his cultural work with socially disadvantaged children and young adults, Maldoom states that he does not have a method as such but does pursue a philosophy. Sylvia Stammen in turn conducted interviews with the pioneers of the »Tanz in Schulen« and »TanzZeit« initiatives. While Linda Müller from the Regional Office for Dance in North Rhine-Westphalia primarily focuses on the organisational and structural aspects of the cooperation with schools, Livia Patrizi looks back at the first teaching year in Berlin and provides an initial evaluation of her more artistic than educational programme.

In the meantime, the level of cooperation between school teachers and dance teachers in social hotspots has become especially close and the use of team teaching in teams consisting of dancers and teachers has stood the test. Finally, Elisabeth Nehring talks with Hanna Hegenscheidt and Jo Parkes in an interview about the influence of teaching experiences on artistic practice. Both regard the confrontation with people and situations they would not normally face in an art context as a productive challenge. Frequently, creative potential emerges especially during those moments when teachers are forced to admit to the pupils that they do not know what to do next. In this respect, the pupils ultimately also bring art up to speed.

As this summary of the numerous different contributions from scientific and artistic practice shows, the field of dance is not at all about accumulating knowledge just for the sake of it. If a formula was to be created for the form of knowledge production practiced in and through dance, it would come down to this: dance trains sensory perception and heightens awareness for dealing with others. This sensitisation in turn allows experiences to be made within a specific socio-cultural context. As such experiences can ultimately be converted into knowledge, they are of value in everyday work.

Knowledge is therefore not systematically acquired merely for the sake of accumulating knowledge about dance itself but is acquired with a view to being applied. In doing so, dance art provides practical access intelligible via the senses to understanding those processes and contexts of experiences that generate knowledge and make it accessible. Those aware of the potential behind such areas of opportunity, who are both prepared and in a position to actively and reflectively move within its bounds can easily make use of it. In this respect, dance – with its orientation function – is also of social and political relevance outside art. Making this potential tangible and applicable requires having a wide variety of processes and approaches some of which we would like to present in this book.

Translation from German

Dance as Culture of Knowledge

BLACKMARKET FOR USEFUL KNOWLEDGE AND NON-KNOWLEDGE by Hannah Hurtzig, DANCE CONGRESS GERMANY 2006, Photo: Thomas Aurin

Dance in a Knowledge Society

Gabriele Klein

What do you need to know to be able to talk about knowledge? And how can dance-based knowledge be made to ›talk‹, made accessible to discourse, dance being considered a specific, physical kind of knowledge? These questions touch upon a knowledge theory of dance or perhaps a physical theory of knowledge defined by subjects such as knowledge and experience, knowledge and education, physical and instinctive knowledge, the exchange of knowledge, knowledge archives and knowledge transfer which outline dance as culture of knowledge. These are major themes that refer to a long and complex history of interdisciplinary academic discourse.

The social-science perspective, which I would like to contribute, makes it possible to narrow down the extremely wide-ranging subject of ›dance knowledge‹ although – due to the very sophisticated sociological theories of its history – I am only able to outline a few ideas for a social-science theory of dance knowledge here.

What is special about the social-science perspective on dance knowledge is the fact that it considers the relationship between the practice of dance and social and cultural contexts, as well as asking what contribution dance knowledge makes to societal knowledge. The point is not, therefore, to show *what* dance knowledge is, but rather, *how* this knowledge is acquired and used[1]: how do we know what we know about dance? This article aims to shed light on this question from the perspective of social theory by looking at social and cultural frameworks for the production and dissemination of dance knowledge, as well as the conditions for its acceptance within society. Just like any other type of knowledge, dance

---

1 | Cf. Karin Knorr-Cetina: *Wissenskulturen. Ein Vergleich naturwissenschaftlicher Wissensformen*, Frankfurt a.M.: Suhrkamp 2002.

knowledge cannot be regarded as innate, as something one possesses or as a mental or physical state of a subject. Dance knowledge is developed within social practice and, accordingly, can only be examined within this field of reference, which may be termed »culture of knowledge«. Hence, dance as knowledge of culture means the practices of validating, disseminating and making use of dance knowledge.

The Social Status of Dance Knowledge

In the globalised world of the 21st century, knowledge is considered the key to prosperity, influence and power. The idea that knowledge and power are closely intertwined is, however, not a new one. People have always relied on knowledge in all societies and cultures. Knowledge is fundamental to our world view, to communication between people and, finally, to the establishment of fundamental social, political, cultural, and economic relations. And while it has always been true that those who have control over knowledge also have power, they are not necessarily the people who actually ›know‹. Rather, the history of the power of knowledge shows that control is essential for the production of knowledge and its dissemination. This is illustrated, for example, by the power of the Church in the Middle Ages, the machinery of power employed in dictatorships and, albeit in a different way, by the media in globalised media societies.

It is also true for all societies that knowledge does not remain static, but is in a permanent state of flux. The constant process of change in societies gives rise to ever new forms of knowledge which, in turn, replace the old ones. As a new form of knowledge gains in social significance, it helps new forms and distributions of power develop and become established within state and society. This close relationship between knowledge and the organisation of society can, for instance, be seen in the Renaissance[2], when modern knowledge established itself along with the foundations of the modern world during a period of great upheaval. Today, we are in the midst of a similar upheaval of knowledge structures as we undergo the transition from an industrial, work-based society to a knowledge-based society and media.

The Congress under the motto KNOWLEDGE IN MOTION called for dance to be placed within the context of the current debate on the place of knowledge, so that dance may gain and secure a place in the political, social and aesthetic discourses within our knowledge-based society. This is a particularly urgent requirement; those in the dance community have always had a hard time – and to some extent made it hard for

---

2 | Cf. Richard van Dülmen/Sina Rauschenbach (eds.): *Macht des Wissens: die Entstehung der modernen Wissensgesellschaft*, Köln etc.: Böhlau 2004.

themselves – making a case for the social and political significance of their art. This has had the disastrous cultural and political consequence of marginalising dance as an art form and a popular form of movement. One might say, provocatively, that dance has a communication problem. More than any other artistic discipline, the field of dance consists of a relatively closed section of the population. In his well-known postdoctoral thesis on the structural change of the public sphere, the sociologist and philosopher Jürgen Habermas[3] made out a transformation of bourgeois »salon culture« to a media-based public culture and identified this transition as the beginning of modern media society – a society, according to Habermas, that is based on a fundamentally different, more abstract and alienated communication structure. However, the dance community has always preferred to keep its distance from this medial public culture. This detachment has been explained as either a form of culture critique – in which dance is conceived of as a form of opposition to the trend towards alienation in contemporary society – or as a fundamental disassociation of dance knowledge from the rest of societal discourse. While a certain degree of scepticism towards medial public culture is certainly justified, the result has been that dance has largely remained a kind of bourgeois »salon culture« and is rarely taken into account in the realms of politics, science and the media – even less so than other art forms. To date, the vast amount of knowledge accumulated by those in the dance community has played a rather marginal role in public debate in these spheres.

The limited presence and representation of dance in politics, academia and the media is even more surprising in light of the fact that dance has always been regarded as a very special form of art and movement. More than any other medium, it was always also the physical expression of a society's experience of an era: you might say the body ›knew what it was doing‹ when it acted out the exhilarating experience of speed and transcending distance made possible by the construction of railways in the 19th century in the waltz; when couples jazz-dancing in the early 1920s disengaged in a powerful symbol of new-found individuality and female emancipation; when John Travolta, in his unforgettable appearance as Tony Manero in SATURDAY NIGHT FEVER, portrayed the Narcissus of the 1970s with its ›look at me! society‹, becoming the ultimate icon of post-modern society all over the world; when ravers dancing to techno in the 1990s attempted to transcend their physical limit, or when break-dancers played previously unthinkable games with their bodies' axes and centres of gravity, in a physical expression of the fragmented and flexible nature of the citizens of post-industrial society.

---

3 | Cf. Jürgen Habermas: *The Structural Transformation of the Public Sphere: An Inquiry into a Category of Bourgois Society*, Cambridge, Massachusetts: MIT Press 1991.

While these sorts of physical diagnoses of a time happen more or less intuitively in popular dance culture, artistic dance conducts them on an aesthetic, reflective level. In modernity, the aesthetic level also always incorporated a critique of traditional aesthetic concepts and of society and culture in general. Whereas *Ausdruckstanz* (expressionist dance) of the 1920s was a bourgeois criticism of the mechanisation, fragmentation and alienation of a society in the throes of industrialisation, and dance theatre in the 1970s drew its strength from the condemnation of the distribution of power in society, contemporary dance in the early 21st century is positioned within the context of a knowledge-based society. The aesthetic concepts are correspondingly disparate: while *Ausdruckstanz* called for a return to nature and postulated the organic experience of the body as a social alternative, dance theatre in the 1970s was more concerned with portraying the penetration of body and power. Contemporary dance from the 1990s on has been, much like modernity, self-reflective and interested in issues such as presence and representation, identity and cultural differences, body and language, by means of which it sounds out not only the principles of the medium itself but also its social and cultural context.

But the knowledge which is so crucial for our collective cultural memory and which has been and is being created in these aesthetic productions, has rarely attained the status of a »legitimate form of knowledge« recognized by society, as formulated by the sociologist Pierre Bourdieu[4], and dancers have rarely ascended to the ranks of »authorized spokespersons«, i.e. artists recognized and acknowledged by society, like artists in other disciplines. Why is this? Does this marginalisation of dance knowledge, discrimination against dance as a profession and the limited recognition accorded to dance knowledge have something to do with the specific form of knowledge that dance contains?

Production of Dance Knowledge

Just as theories on modern art generally see the physical medium of dance as a ›the other‹ of modernity, dance knowledge is also considered ›another type of knowledge‹ – a form of knowledge whose physical nature prohibits discourse about it. This view is problematic in various ways. If we talk about dance knowledge as ›another type of knowledge‹, we are assuming that a ›proper‹ form of knowledge exists. This normative positioning of knowledge follows the modernist concept, since this ›proper‹ knowledge is knowledge gained through reason, understanding and rationality. Seen from this perspective, dance knowledge can only ever

---

4 | Pierre Bourdieu: *Was heißt sprechen? Die Ökonomie des sprachlichen Tausches*, Vienna: Braumüller 1990.

be the negation of modern knowledge. Consequently, dance knowledge is characterised as a specific, distinct type of knowledge which cannot be regarded as discursive (i.e. accessible through language) knowledge. From the perspective of cultural critique this knowledge is labelled as authentic knowledge that has merely been buried by civilisation. This labelling is an attempt to protect it and leads to its exaltation to a quasi-mythological status.

Traditionally, modern concepts of dance have defined dance knowledge as a physical, transient, non-classifiable type of knowledge, bound more to experience than to cognition. The argument, postulated by Mary Wigman, that dance must remain a pure medium and that the experience of dance has nothing to do with dialogue about it, was prototypical and persisted throughout the history of dance in the 20th century. However, this position ignores the levels of communication and the public: the perception and experience of the spectator as well as the public reception of dance that gives dance a ›place‹ within contemporary artistic and cultural discourse. Furthermore, the idea of ›pure‹ dance poses a major problem: that of assigning dance a self-ascribed ahistorical quality. For how can dance knowledge be saved, how can experiences of dance be entered into history, if they are not incorporated into other media, texts and images? And how can dance attain cultural and social relevance over the long term without transferring dance movements to other media in order to save them as knowledge and place them within other contexts?

The idea of dance knowledge as direct, physical, practical knowledge has always contributed to the myth of dance, and also to dance being either marginalised as ›the other‹ (something separate from society or culturally irrelevant) or idealised precisely because of its emotionality, irrationality and physicality. In other words, it has always been defined as something outside of society.

In addition, being volatile and transient, experienced and physical is not unique to dance; music, for instance, or any everyday situation also display these qualities. Indeed, everyday life also centres around practical knowledge – and practical knowledge is physical knowledge. Almost 90 percent of everyday actions are carried out using intuitive knowledge. This kind of knowledge is sometimes called ›automated‹ knowledge because the body can access it without the need for any cognitive processes. It is only thanks to this kind of internalized knowledge that we are able to, for instance, turn on the coffee-maker, brush our teeth without thinking about it and, as the sociologist Erving Goffman[5] illustrated so impressively with the example of interaction in traffic situations which can sometimes turn into ritualistic little dances, communicate by means

---

5 | Cf. Erving Goffman: *Interaction Ritual: Essays on Face-to-Face Behavior*, Garden City, New York: Anchor Books 1967.

of body language and gestures. The sociologist Pierre Bourdieu[6] has termed this type of quasi-automatic knowledge »sens pratique«, a ›practical sense‹, describing everyday situations as »structured improvisations« or social choreographies.

The fact that being volatile and transient, experienced and physical is actually not that specific to dance after all, is also demonstrated by the new-found attention dance is enjoying in today's knowledge-based society.

Dance as Metaphor for the Knowledge Society

The notion of a knowledge society is one of the most influential ideas circulating today. It is one of a series of social concepts used to diagnose time periods which neither claim to define the nature of contemporary societies nor attempt to present a critical social theory inspired by philosophy in emulation of Marx and the proponents of Critical Theory. Social diagnosticians tend to focus on individual aspects of society and devise a trenchant – and thus inevitably exaggerated – label for them.[7]

The concept of the knowledge society emphasises the close link between modernisation and mechanisation.[8] Thus, information and communication technologies have not only been the motor behind accelerated knowledge production and global knowledge dissemination, they have also fostered the transformation of knowledge: knowledge in knowledge-based societies is fast-moving and transient – just like dance. It is generated and disappears rapidly; we only need to think of websites. The sociologist Zygmunt Bauman[9] described transience as the key metaphor for our times. Everything previously stable and reliable dissolves in this »liquid modernity«. It floats by, as Bauman says:

Fluids travel easily. They ›flow‹, ›spill‹, ›run out‹, ›splash‹, ›pour over‹, ›leak‹, ›flood‹, ›spray‹, ›drip‹, ›seep‹, ›ooze‹ [...]. The extraordinary mobility of fluids

---

6 | Cf. Pierre Bourdieu: *Distinction: A Social Critique of Judgement of Taste*, Cambridge/Massachusetts: Havard University Press 2007.

7 | Cf. for example: Ulrich Beck: *Risk Society. Towards a New Modernity*, London/ Newbury Park, California: SAGE 1992; Gerhard Schulze: *Erlebnisgesellschaft. Kultursoziologie der Gegenwart*, Frankfurt a.M./New York: Campus 1992; Peter Gross: *Die Multioptionsgesellschaft*, Frankfurt a.M.: Suhrkamp 1994; Norbert Bolz: *Die Sinngesellschaft*, Düsseldorf: Econ 1997.

8 | Cf. for example: Uwe H. Bittlingmayer/Ullrich Bauer (eds.): *Die ›Wissensgesellschaft‹: Mythos, Ideologie oder Realität?* Wiesbaden: VS-Verlag 2006.

9 | Cf. Zygmunt Bauman: *Liquid Modernity*, Cambridge: Polity Press 2000.

makes us associate them with the idea of ›lightness‹. [...] We associate ›lightness‹ or ›weightlessness‹ with mobility and inconstancy [...].[10]

It may sound wonderfully dance-like, but is cause for concern when seen from a sociological point of view. Expressed less metaphorically, transience and liquidity mean the disappearance of social security, state provision, settled communities, social integration and mutual obligations in favour of a lack of commitment, loss of ties, nomadic lifestyles and social disintegration.

For the people involved this means that the social context becomes more fluid: more flexibility, dynamism, self-initiative and self-sufficiency. Life-long, self-directed learning and the end of the ›normal curriculum vitae‹ are, accordingly, the key phrases of the knowledge society.

The knowledge society's new »technologies of the self« (Foucault) have long been an everyday experience for dancers; the neo-liberal model of providing and being responsible for oneself is practised daily in the world of dance. It is thus that the figure of the flexible, footloose, wandering subject, living by his/her wits found its prototype in the ›freelance artist‹ back at the dawn of modernity. However, in contrast to other artistic disciplines, the dancer's artistic existence seldom lasts a lifetime. Once they are in their mid-30s, many dancers know that their artistic existence is coming to an end and that they will go on to practice one or more further professions. Many retrain as computer specialists, for example. There is no chance for dancers to have a normal CV, i.e. practise a single profession throughout their entire working lives. In this respect, the life of a dancer also represents the sobering flip side of the flexibility discussed by the sociologist Richard Sennett[11] and the interpretation of the move towards a knowledge society as an enthusiastically welcomed move towards modernisation, seen as offering the opportunity to speak a new language, develop new economic structures and new, flexible skills.[12]

Consequently, whosoever looks for the value, the social location or the conditions governing the production and dissemination of dance knowledge will always have to examine the structures of a society, its ideologies, goals and role models. In a knowledge-based society, these aspects are geared towards movement, transformation and transience. Dance is a suitable metaphor here – with all the political problems which the metaphor contains.

---

10 | Ibid., p. 2.

11 | Cf. Richard Sennett: *The Corrosion of Character. The Personal Consequences of Work in the New Capitalism*, New York: W.W. Norton 1998.

12 | Cf. Adrienne Goehler: *Verflüssigungen. Wege und Umwege vom Sozialstaat zur Kulturgesellschaft*, Frankfurt a.M./New York: Campus 2006.

Dance as Hybrid Culture of Knowledge

But it is not enough to attempt to deal with the meaning of dance within knowledge societies on a merely metaphorical level. Dance does not only represent movement and transformation. Dance knowledge can also get things moving and have a transformative effect.

The philosopher Jean-François Lyotard distinguished between two different forms of knowledge: »narrative knowledge« based on what one is told and which implicitly legitimises itself, and »discursive knowledge«, which is a knowledge form specific to modernity, primarily created by science and requiring explicit legitimisation.[13] For dancers, dance knowledge is a type of knowledge based on a physical experience which conveys itself inter-subjectively – in this case via bodily communication. This sort of knowledge could be identified as a specific type of narrative knowledge. Specific insofar as the narration is conveyed via the body and the body cannot speak. The body does not speak, it displays. This process of displaying ideas does not work according to the either/or logic of the spoken language. Communication via the body, as media specialist Dieter Mersch persistently emphasises, means the »non-identical«.[14] And this has undoubtedly not been taken seriously enough in the language-dominated scientific discourse.

The fact that the body displays its message presents the emerging science of dance with a range of big cognition theory problems since science produces discursive knowledge via the medium of the spoken language, unlike the practice of dance itself. Discursive knowledge must be able to be checked and reproduced. It is the type of modern knowledge which made a significant contribution to the Enlightenment, but also to the disenchantment of the world. This ambivalence of modern knowledge, something the sociologist Max Weber did a lot of work on, is fundamental to the development of modern knowledge.

The ambivalence of enlightenment and disenchantment is also an irresolvable aspect of discursive dance knowledge, which must not only be able to make statements about a transient phenomenon, but also speak and think it.

»Thinking movement«[15], i.e. finding a language for dynamic processes, has always been a challenge for those creating knowledge, a challenge which is doomed to failure, because discursive knowledge always

---

13 | Cf. Jean-François Lyotard: *The Postmodern Condition. A Report on Knowledge*, Minneapolis: University of Minnesota Press 1984.

14 | Cf. Dieter Mersch: *Ereignis und Aura*, Frankfurt a.M.: Suhrkamp 2002.

15 | Cf. Gabriele Klein: »Bewegung denken. Ein soziologischer Entwurf«; in: idem (ed.): *Bewegung. Sozial- und kulturwissenschaftliche Konzepte*, Bielefeld: transcript 2004, pp. 131–154.

has to avail itself of the medium of the spoken word. From this perspective, the science of dance is a critique of science as it is opposed to a form of knowledge which attempts to grasp dynamic processes through static concepts. In this respect dance knowledge is in good company: viz. all those sociological theories which experienced this very problem of the dynamic and the transient many years ago with regard to social situations. They tried to develop the appropriate terms, concepts (like Elias' concept of »figuration«) and methods to deal with the problem. It is no coincidence that dance is given special attention in those areas of scientific discourse which look at how cultural and social phenomena become practical reality, as is the case in body and performance theory. Dance research of this kind can make a significant contribution to the re-enchantment of science. But it could also disenchant by helping remove the myth of dance knowledge as a ›different sort‹ of knowledge.

In a knowledge society, playing off one kind of knowledge in dance against another no longer makes sense. Such binary concepts have become obsolete. Science and art have long been converging towards each other – though they can and should never merge completely; rather, they should enter into a dialogue. In her foreword, Hortensia Völckers so emphatically stated that dance must remain free. The same holds true, I might add, for academic discourse. Both are creative endeavours *par excellence* and beget what the curator Adrienne Goehler has termed the »creative classes«.[16] However: science is not art and vice versa. Science and art are two distinct social fields. Each has its own, very different culture of knowledge; each produces different forms of knowledge; each employs different practices and techniques of generating and disseminating knowledge; and finally, each is very different in regard to the authority at their disposal and access to knowledge. Nonetheless, science and art are cross-referenced. They both need each other, and each needs the other to define their place in society. Just as a science of dance would be absurd if it made no reference to dance itself, dance has no relevance in society if it is not communicated and placed into a meaningful context and thus acquires a powerful position as a culture of knowledge.

Consequently, dance might be described as a hybrid culture of knowledge, in which different forms of knowledge are at odds with one another. Knowledge can only arise out of a collective effort, and it grows in and through controversy and debate.[17] One of the major challenges of the future will be to develop a »culture of conflict«[18] in order to go beyond

---

16 | Cf. Goehler: *Verflüssigungen*, l.c., pp. 78ff.

17 | Cf. Wolf-Andreas Liebert/Marc-Denis Weitze (eds.): *Kontroversen als Schlüssel zur Wissenschaft. Wissenskulturen in sprachlicher Interaktion*, Bielefeld: transcript 2006.

18 | Cf. Lyotard: *The Postmodern Condition*, l.c.

the metaphorical meaning of dance and establish it as a relevant force in cultural policy as well as society and culture as a whole.

What sociologist Niklas Luhmann wrote in 1995 on modern knowledge ultimately applies to dance knowledge as well: »Modern knowledge must put up with explanations. How well does it manage?«[19]

Translation from German

19 | Niklas Luhmann: »Die Soziologie des Wissens: Probleme ihrer theoretischen Konstruktion«, in: idem: *Gesellschaftsstruktur und Semantik: Studien zur Wissenssoziologie der modernen Gesellschaft*, Vol. 4, Frankfurt a.M.: Suhrkamp 1995, p. 151.

References

Bauman, Zygmunt: *Liquid Modernity*, Cambridge: Polity Press 2000.

Beck, Ulrich: *Risk Society. Towards a New Modernity*, London/Newbury Park, California: SAGE 1992.

Bittlingmayer, Uwe H./Bauer, Ullrich (eds.): *Die ›Wissensgesellschaft‹: Mythos, Ideologie oder Realität?*, Wiesbaden: VS-Verlag 2006.

Bolz, Norbert: *Die Sinngesellschaft*, Düsseldorf: Econ 1997.

Bourdieu, Pierre: *A Social Critique of Judgement of Taste*, Cambridge/Massachusetts: Havard University Press 2007.

Bourdieu, Pierre: *Was heißt sprechen? Zur Ökonomie des sprachlichen Tausches*, Vienna: Braumüller 1990.

Goehler, Adrienne: *Verflüssigungen. Wege und Umwege vom Sozialstaat zur Kulturgesellschaft*, Frankfurt a.M./New York: Campus 2006.

Goffman, Erving: *Interaction Ritual: Essays on Face-to-Face Behavior*, Garden City, New York: Anchor Books 1967.

Gross, Peter: *Die Multioptionsgesellschaft*, Frankfurt a.M.: Suhrkamp 1994.

Habermas, Jürgen: *The Structural Transformation of the Public Sphere: An Inquiry into a Category of Bourgois Society*, Cambridge, Massachusetts: MIT Press 1991.

Klein, Gabriele/Zipprich, Christa (eds.): *Tanz Theorie Text. Jahrbuch Tanzforschung* Vol. 12, Hamburg/London: Lit 2002.

Klein, Gabriele: »Bewegung denken. Ein soziologischer Entwurf«, in: idem (ed.): *Bewegung. Sozial- und kulturwissenschaftliche Konzepte*, Bielefeld: transcript 2004, pp. 131–154.

Knorr-Cetina, Karin: *Wissenskulturen. Ein Vergleich naturwissenschaftlicher Wissensformen*, Frankfurt a.M.: Suhrkamp 2002.

Liebert, Wolf-Andreas/Weitze, Marc-Denis (eds.): *Kontroversen als Schlüssel zur Wissenschaft. Wissenskulturen in sprachlicher Interaktion*, Bielefeld: transcript 2006.

Luhmann, Niklas: »Die Soziologie des Wissens: Probleme ihrer theoretischen Konstruktion«, in: idem: *Gesellschaftsstruktur und Semantik: Studien zur Wissenssoziologie der modernen Gesellschaft*, Vol. 4, Frankfurt a.M.: Suhrkamp 1995, pp. 151–180.

Lyotard, Jean-François: *The Postmodern Condition. A Report on Knowledge*, Minneapolis: University of Minnesota Press 1984.

Mersch, Dieter: *Ereignis und Aura*, Frankfurt a.M.: Suhrkamp 2002.

Pongs, Armin (ed.): *In welcher Gesellschaft leben wir eigentlich?*, München: Dilemma 1999.

Schulze, Gerhard: *Erlebnisgesellschaft. Kultursoziologie der Gegenwart*, Frankfurt a.M./New York: Campus 1992.

Sennett, Richard: *The Corrosion of Character. The Personal Consequences of Work in the New Capitalism*, New York: WW. Norton 1998.

van Dülmen, Richard/Rauschenbach, Sina (eds.): *Macht des Wissens: die Entstehung der modernen Wissensgesellschaft*, Köln etc.: Böhlau 2004.

Dance as Culture of Knowledge

Body Memory and the Challenge

of Theoretical Knowledge

GABRIELE BRANDSTETTER

Dance and knowledge: do these terms not mutually exclude each other? What qualifications – in terms of knowledge – are linked to the cultural patterns of movement we call ›dance‹? »Why,« asked Noa Eshkol, founder of the Eshkol-Wachman-Movement-Notation,

[...] why are we such illiterates when it comes to movement?« [...] We have a musical notation system, so why has culture not created a suitable movement notation, a way to think movement, to conceive it? We also have a body, not just a voice?[1]

And she gives a second answer – in addition to the notation she developed: »We change all the time. So how can you make a notation about change ...?«[2]

Why are we illiterates when it comes to dance and passing on records of movement? Rudolf von Laban also asked this question when presenting his concept of kinetography to the general public during the first German dancers' congress, held in Magdeburg in 1927. The second dancers' congress took place in Essen in 1928; over one thousand dancers took part in a plenary assembly in which fierce discussions preceded the adoption of a resolution to found a »Hochschule für Tanz« (Academy for Dance) and create a »Scientific Sociological Research Centre for Movement«. The

---

1 | Katarina Holländer: »Noten des Tanzes. Vom Versuch, das Tanzen mit Worten und Zeichen festzuhalten. Und ein Besuch in Noa Eshkols Werkstatt der Verschriftlichung«, in: du. Zeitschrift für Kultur 765, April 2006, p. 68.

2 | Ibid., p. 69.

following resolution regarding the burning question of a binding dance notation was unanimously adopted: »In general, the dancers' congress recognises the importance and necessity of a dance notation, and values the choreography created by Rudolf von Laban as a first-rate intellectual achievement and recommends it as a practical dance notation method«.[3]

Admittedly, this unanimous resolution, which amounted to a ›victory‹ for Labanotation was surrounded by numerous controversies. They resulted from competing notation concepts, for example the G. I. Vischer-Klamt system, and to a greater extent from a fundamental controversy involving a group of dancers whose spokeswoman was Mary Wigman. This group was against dance notation as a matter of principle and felt that passing on and producing choreographies were linked to the ever-present body in motion. The foundation of a quarterly journal with the programmatic title SCHRIFTTANZ (Written Dance) in 1928 documented the euphoria that captured wide sections of artists and ›amateurs‹ as a result of the upsurge of dance in the context of the physical culture movement of the 1920s. SCHRIFTTANZ, was focused on archiving *and* producing choreographies, a means of dance analysis, and »dance education« as well as »dance research«. It was meant to be a medium to canonise dance and at the same time an instrument to institutionalise it: »The goal is written dance«[4] – stated the programmatic introduction, written dance as a means to allow a wide distribution and a democratisation of dance *works* through reproduction in notation.[5] However, the programme of a general introduction of this comprehensive SCHRIFTTANZ model to culture and education remained utopian. The quarterly only appeared until the end of 1932. The enforced political conformity of dance culture during the National Socialist period »unter dem Hakenkreuz«[6] (under

---

3 | *Schrifttanz. Eine Vierteljahresschrift*, 1. year. October 1928, Issue 2, Universaledition Vienna, p. 33

4 | Ewald Moll: »Die neue Tanzschrift«, in: *Schrifttanz 1928, Mitteilungen der Deutschen Gesellschaft für Schrifttanz*, p. 16.

5 | It becomes clear how the ›work character‹ of dance – in terms of notation heritage and canonisation – is meant; the problematic nature of the attempt that was controversial at the time also becomes apparent: »Written dance is the only thing that can help single out the worthwhile from the worthless. To create a tradition and possibilities of comparison. Because old or new dance do not exist. There is only worthwhile dance art or worthless surrogates. The same applies to the dance education methods, ballroom dancing and folk dances.« (Ewald Moll, »Die neue Tanzschrift«, l.c., p. 16)

6 | Cf. Lilian Karina/Marion Kant (eds.): *Tanz unterm Hakenkreuz. Eine Dokumentation*, Berlin: Henschel 1996, and Hedwig Müller/Patricia Stöckemann (eds.): »*... jeder Mensch ist ein Tänzer.« Ausdruckstanz in Deutschland zwischen 1900 und 1945*, Gießen: Anabas 1993.

the swastika), put a caesura that remained visible and perceptible in post 1945, and brought about a different development of dance in Germany.[7] On the one hand, it had recourse to ballet and, on the other hand, new forms of modern dance and the dance theatre emerged.

A comparison between the endeavours of the dancers' congresses of the Weimar Republic and the situation of today, which has put a multi-faceted dance scene in motion and – with films such as RHYTHM IS IT! (2004) – has triggered a wide public debate about the knowledge of dance and its importance in education would be worth of a more detailed study. The cultural situation has changed and is not comparable; however, similarities can yet be discerned – regarding the questions of institutionalisation as well as education.

Today, evidence of illiteracy in the field of dance and movement would hardly result in the establishment of a universal dance script and to a distribution monopoly. In fact, since then a practice of choreology has evolved, although it is limited to a narrow field of experts and not a script system comparable with that of music notation, which is part of our educational curriculum. But above all, there are other means of documentation; even though neither choreographers nor researchers have any illusions regarding the usability of videos as a medium for storing dance archives: the vast importance of the media, the digitalisation of movement have nowadays become indispensable to dance. This also means that amongst others the questions regarding the preservation of dance movement are treated differently today. The possibilities to record and also digitally generate movement and space scenarios have brought about manifold effects for the contemporary performer and researcher, as demonstrated for example by the reception of »analytical tools« in William Forsythe's model IMPROVISATION TECHNOLOGIES.[8] Conversely, dance in particular, with its transient space-time form, makes us aware that the traditional concept of cultural memory is static, architectonic, quantitative and encyclopaedic; the performance aspect, the *movement* inherent in any active recollection is often cut off. Dance on the other hand, especially in view of the fact that it is *missing* from the art and cultural archives, reveals that the presumably static, encyclopaedic knowledge systems of standardised recollection in culture are also dynamic: contingent, in motion and thus not easy to grasp.

---

7 | Cf. Hedwig Müller/Ralf Stabel/Patricia Stöckemann (eds.): *Krokodil im Schwanensee. Tanz in Deutschland seit 1945*, Frankfurt a.M.: Anabas 2003.

8 | William Forsythe: *Improvisation Technologies. A Tool for the Analytical Dance Eye*, Ostfildern: Hatje Cantz 1999.

CITY OF ABSTRACTS by William For-
sythe, Alaunstraße, Dresden-Neustadt
2006

Photo: Julian Richter

Dance as culture of knowledge: what knowledge lies in the movement of dance? What do we know about and through (this) movement? And conversely: how does movement work and what effect does it have on our knowledge and in anthropological research? The first question is exciting and widely ramified – dancers and choreographers as well as phenomenologists and neuroscientists ask: what is the specific knowledge of dance? A *different* kind of knowledge from what we generally accept as rational, technical or discursive knowledge. The scene for this different kind of knowledge is set in the moving body. The knowledge that becomes apparent and is transferred in dances and choreographies is dynamic: physical, sensuous and implicit knowledge. It is conveyed in a kinetic and kinaesthetic manner. Can this be called knowledge at all? These doubts arise time and again; and although we live in a society where highly different and contradictory forms of knowledge exist side by side, the question of accepting a knowledge model that carries such seemingly subjective and emotional connotations is controversial. Where does the resistance against such a physical and performative idea of knowledge come from, causing us to adhere to our familiar oppositions of theory and practice, of rationalism and emotionality, of body and mind? Despite the fact that body knowledge and the knowledge of the dancer as movement researcher have long been discussed in many ways – as indicated by formulations such as »The Thinking Body«[9] by Mabel E. Todd or »Tanzdenker« (dance thinker).[10] Is it lack of passion to ›know‹ more about this ›dynamic‹ and transient body-related knowledge? Or fear of disenchantment?

This leads to the second question directed at the subject – and it is equally controversial: because if dance is a ›culture of knowledge‹, i.e. appears and is accepted as a setting for a different type of sensuous, dynamic knowledge, this cannot remain without impact on our general understanding of knowledge and science. Dance would then shift the boundaries of what we consider to be knowledge and science and in doing so begin to set our understanding of knowledge in motion; for example, if we – proceeding on the assumption that dance as the object under investigation cannot be fixed like an immobile object – realise that object blurriness and a temporary structure also affect those artefacts, monuments or test set-ups of knowledge that were presumed to be secure; that a dynamic and contingent relationship between scientist and object of investigation is also being established in other scientific research areas and is changing in the research process: also in disciplines that deal with seemingly fixed objects and reliable results. The notion of truth, the verifiability of test arrangements is put to the test if dynamic reflections inspired by dance touch on or even violate the parameters of scientific perception: for example, by acknowledging that the physical movement, the sensuousness, the researcher's emotion influence the process.[11]

The philosopher Thomas S. Kuhn described »The Structure of Scientific Revolutions«[12] using the term »paradigm shift«. According to his theory, there is no (as had been assumed since the Enlightenment) linear development in the progress of knowledge. On the contrary, any novelty, e.g. a discovery, stands out in the field of the accepted scientific norms like some foreign matter. A new paradigm of knowledge can only assert itself through a crisis in the existing paradigm and in a long social process of acceptance (i.e. the discussion, for instance, in periodicals or

---

9 | Mabel E. Todd: *The Thinking Body. A Study of the Balancing Forces of Dynamic Man*, New York: Dance Horizons 1937.

10 | Forsythe: *Improvisation Technologies*, l.c., p. 16.

11 | Cf. Gabriele Brandstetter: »Zu einer Poetologie des Medienwechsels. Aufführung und Aufzeichnung – Kunst der Wissenschaft?«, in: idem: *Bild-Sprung. TanzTheaterBewegung im Wechsel der Medien*, Berlin: Theater der Zeit 2005, pp. 199–210, and idem: »Inventur: Tanz. Performance und die Listen der Wissenschaft«, in: Sybille Peters/Martin Jörg Schäfer (eds.): *Intellektuelle Anschauung. Figurationen von Evidenz zwischen Kunst und Wissen*, Bielefeld: transcript 2006, pp. 295–300.

12 | Thomas S. Kuhn: *The Structure of Scientific Revolutions*, Chicago: University of Chicago Press 1962.

at congresses as knowledge politics). This is not aimed at – that much is clear today – establishing exclusive control for a single knowledge model. In fact, the predominant paradigm competes against and is intertwined with various approaches. Modern cultures – not least under the influence of the so-called globalisation – have different models of knowledge and science, based on different images of humanity, coexisting side by side: for example, the technologically highly developed Western style of medicine alongside the older traditions of natural medicine as well as traditional Chinese medicine, which can today also be found in the West.

Can a pattern comparable to the paradigm shifts described in the history and theory of science be transferred to dance? More precisely: to dance as an *art* form of body motion in space and time? This is an awkward question because it is aimed exactly at the previously mentioned shifting of boundaries between what we regard as knowledge and science and what we subsume in a different system ›beyond‹ it. Traditionally, art is perceived as such a field. Art and aesthetics have – thus the traditional and accepted opinion – no place in the field of knowledge and science. And vice versa. How can dance enter the stage as a separate form of knowledge in this field of art and anthropology? Often it is not the performance but rather the creative process of developing a dance piece that opens a situation for experimentation – for instance, in the question rituals and improvisation exercises in the wake of Pina Bausch's *Tanztheater*; or in the film sessions and the psychiatric research carried out by Meg Stuart. The uniqueness of such a physical knowledge of dance is apparent in its contextualisation: not only within the history of dance, but equally so in the assessment of the broader context of cultural history. Thus tangible knowledge may be gained in and through dance about new notions of time, with dance reinterpreting the known process of time by means of the movement syncope; or about the amount of freedom experienced in taking away the rigidity of the body axes; and about how much potential for variation can be derived from the transformation of symmetrical into asymmetrical movement and interaction processes. A very broad historical and cultural terrain provides evidence for ways in which aesthetic, ethnic and sexual *difference* can be expressed in dance.

Science and art both convince each in its own way by means of perception[13]; even if the scenarios and the effects of this perception differ: cognitive but yet not *only* cognitive in the case of science; sensory but nevertheless *also* cognitive in the case of art. Hypotheses, experiments, argumentation strategies and discourse make up the scenario for perception (of knowledge) in the sciences. Whereas in art, it is the perception of the aesthetic illusion[14]; and this is (or: this renders) speechless. There

---

13 | Cf. Peters/Schäfer (eds.): *Intellektuelle Anschauung*, l.c.
14 | Cf. Martin Seel: *Ästhetik des Erscheinens*, Munich/Vienna: Hanser 2000.

are certainly all kinds of supplementary discourse here as well. From pro-grammatic writings and artists commenting on their own productions to reviews and catalogues, the actual performance of dance attracts a wealth of information, opinions and interpretations from various fields of exper-tise. The question what one has to know (or not to know) to understand dance, is – as in other art forms – to all intents and purposes obsolete, because hardly any art form, and dance even less so, exists without this *text margin*: whether this is due to the fact that modern art needs to be explained (*Kommentar-Bedürftigkeit,* as Arnold Gehlen put it) or rather to the fact that everybody feels compelled to comment?! In the end it is the artists – just recently for instance Tino Sehgal[15] –, whose consistent refusal to accept the prescriptions and transcriptions regulating per-formance have made the question of the perception of art as perform-ance, as ›dance‹ a subject of discussion again. The aesthetic experience – the perception of art – takes place in a realm beyond informational knowledge *about* art – although it may not be quite unrelated because the complexity of the experience is made up of an individual mixture of memory, knowledge, perception, anticipation, and desire. However, the aesthetic experience is primarily sensuous and emotional – and there-fore activates a different knowledge than, for example, the solution of a mathematical problem. Dance has a special power of evoking moments of enchantment, enthusiasm or shock that render ›speechless‹ in certain respects; on the other hand, this experience of speechlessness often supports the prejudice that it cannot involve knowledge. However, the knowledge in question is a different kind of knowledge: sensual, erotic and unstable – and it goes without saying, also cognitive; knowledge that touches on the boundaries of knowledge and zones of non-knowledge (also and in particular of ›not-knowing-oneself‹). One of these bounda-ries is indicated by the absence of language for this knowledge gained through experience.

Talking about movement. Finding a language for experience and perception is a challenge that can never be met. However, accepting the challenge is worthwhile because it is the only way of expressing the dif-

---

15 | Cf. for example his contribution in the German Pavilion at the 51. Bien-nale in Venice 2005; the catalogue comment by Julian Heynen: »Tino Sehgal (born in 1976) has developed a specific form of art that takes shape only at the moment of one's encounter with it. His works are performed by interpreters (such as museum attendants) and consist of movements, spoken words, song or communication with the visitor. Sehgal replaces the production of objects with works related to the body, space and time [...]. [T]hey consist only as a situation, conversation, in transformation, in memory and in the past.« (La biennale di Venezia: *Participating countries – collateral events,* Vol. 3, Germany, Venice: Marsilio 2005, p. 46)

ferent experiences and knowledge forms and putting them in a relation in which tension, contradictions, gaps and boundaries become visible.

This is the stage, the liminal stage between performance and observation, where a dialogue begins. It is an experiential space in which not only the events on the dance stage (meaning all the spaces and processes of a performance) become perceptible. No, this is not a one-sided gift, it is reciprocated. The inter-est of the spectators, their concentration invests in the process. In so far the experiential space of ›knowledge‹ doubles or multiplies even further in size: a space in which the dance scenography is superimposed on the attention span of the viewer/listener.

›Somehow‹ all this is self-evident; and yet exactly this productive, creative situation has recently become the topic of intense research. Neurophysiological research is interested in the relationship between movement and neural activity in the brain, in the concentration processes, in the link between affective and cognitive processes. Philosophy, in particular phenomenology, and from other perspectives Theatre and Dance Studies are interested in the theoretical and aesthetic problems in these situations of encounter and experience. And the choreographers and performers are also shifting the field of their interest to the investigation of this zone of concentration between performance and observation: for example, the work of Felix Ruckert; or the group She She Pop, who in every performance of their production WARUM TANZT IHR NICHT? (»Why don't you dance?«) engage in a new and different dialogue and interaction with the audience, and allow space for fundamental questions relating to dance: for the wishes ›in motion‹ as well as for the inhibitions about dance; for the questions regarding the ›right step‹ as well as the decisions about ›belonging‹ or ›not participating‹ and the consequences.

The frequently asked question ›What should, what does one have to know to understand dance?‹ fades into the background here. It could be elaborately unfolded for dance as for other art forms and other fields of coded movement in our culture – for example sport: one of these questions would be whether one ›understands better‹ and perceives better if one (as for instance in the Japanese Nô play or in traditional ballet classics or in modern dance technique) knows something about the ›system‹ of movement scenography, for instance, the rules of the production, the poetry of the choreography, comparable to the knowledge about the measures of a poem or the rules of a music composition. It goes without saying that dance, like other art forms, has a history and various performance theories, with their respective transformations and inconsistencies. The fact that this aspect of knowledge has been allotted less space in our culture than in other art and science fields has often been mentioned. And it is currently the subject of numerous debates about education in schools and universities. Is there a marginalisation of knowledge about dance? Yes, there is and the reasons are manifold.

But they are also partially rooted in dance itself. For, however important it may be that dance achieves a wide basis in educational and formative institutions, not only as an appendage to sports or gymnastics classes, but rather as ›theory of dance and choreographic art forms of movement‹, it is even more important to make the potential of dance stand out as a challenge to our established concepts of knowledge and science. The research of dance, its scenographies of knowledge do not simply consist of finding forms of movement or in media-supported experiments with the visibility of the body.

CITY OF ABSTRACTS by William Forsythe, Pinakothek der Moderne, Munich 2006

Photo: Julian Richter

Transformations in dance, in the movement patterns or in the structures of choreographic composition, implicitly incorporate a paradigm shift of knowledge. Under this auspice of a different physical knowledge, how would, for instance, contact improvisation as movement interaction be understood? As an open system of a consistently shifting balance of power?

With the transformation of body and composition structures the position of the observer also changes. And consequently also the position of the expert. The knowledge parallelogram shifts. In the process, the recurring question ›how one can understand dance‹ becomes a central theme; and breaks away from the rules of hermeneutic art interpretation. The place of ›knowledge‹ is taken over by different forms of experience, especially if the goal of a dance performance does no longer consist in following a specific, *prescribed* pattern of movements or code.

If the system of traditional dance forms or styles – e.g. ballet, modern dance or ballroom dancing – is opened up or discarded, what remains of the *movens* of the performance, what knowledge does it transport? And how can the observer perceive the processes as research in and through movement? The philosopher Bernhard Waldenfels defines the relationship between knowledge and aesthetic perception – with recourse to phenomenological theories – as balance between »recognising« and »seeing« vision.[16] Recognising vision establishes itself in what has been seen. It transfers the crossing fields of knowledge, of (dance) discourse, for instance dancer biographies, history of dance, into the performance event and reads what is already available as knowledge, as information or as context. »Seeing vision«, on the other hand, reacts to the sensuous, physical experiences in the process of seeing. It is a vision that tries out new ways of seeing, that »goes beyond the scope«[17] and describes incompatible structuring. This would be the perceptive condition that is open to the respective dance performance seen at the time as kinaesthetic experience, as scenography of a different knowledge. This opens up a very free dialogue space of awareness: non-hierarchical, different from the dance performances that require the expert audience (although we know that this competence does not say anything about the seeing or rather kinaesthetic perception). With the autonomy of the dancers and the openness in the structural flow of the dance, the observer also acquires his own autonomy: the freedom to endow what he has seen and perceived ›as dance‹ in his own way with images and experiences belonging to his own knowledge. William Forsythe recently gave an interview in which he spoke about the authorisation, indeed the productive meaning of these inconsistencies in the fields of knowledge, and about the freedom of the observer: »I remember how a man once came to me after a performance. He had clearly enjoyed it, and he wanted to tell me about his interpretation. He gave me a knowing look and said: »›Seagulls!‹ I nodded of course.«[18]

Dance allows space for association. And in this scenography the limitations and fallibility of knowledge as well as the boundlessness of our ignorance both become apparent.

Dance and choreography as body movement in space and time configure a situational knowledge: the kinaesthetic alignment of the body,

---

16 | Cf. Bernhard Waldenfels: *Sinnesschwellen*, Frankfurt a.M.: Suhrkamp 1999.

17 | Ibid., p. 139.

18 | William Forsythe in dialogue with Wiebke Hüster: »Interview. Tanzdenker William Forsythe im Gespräch mit Wiebke Hüster«, in: *du. Zeitschrift für Kultur* 765, April 2006, p. 18.

its balance, its bearing, its dynamism. This alignment knowledge of dance is admittedly no more application-oriented or translatable than scientific research about dance. This is precisely what makes it political. For the implications of knowledge experienced in dance can act as interruptions and disturbances in the presumably self-evident fields of knowledge. Dance and choreography explore problems of alignment in and through the moving body, a knowledge that is an important issue in other contexts such as control engineering, the complexity theory and neurophysiology and lastly in politics. The potential for innovation and creativity – everything we think and know about it today – is closely connected to it. Choreographers and dancers today cannot be interested in an affirmative transfer, however. Like the experts they are in their field of alignment knowledge, they deliberately place their test labs on the boundaries of alignment: disruption, collapse, failure represent the challenge. It is certainly no coincidence that in recent years numerous choreographers have tackled the collapse of movement systems, have dealt with the subject of disasters (like chaos, war, tumult and tsunami principle), taking every conceivable approach as, for example, seen in Berlin in the most recent choreographies by Sasha Waltz (GEZEITEN, 2005), Meg Stuart (REPLACEMENT, 2006) and William Forsythe (THREE ATMOSPHERIC STUDIES, 2006).

It is a venture into areas that can no longer only be comprehended in terms of controllable and operationalised knowledge – the field of the unforeseeable, the unknowable, the uncontrollable as a challenge for a different experience and a different political commitment. This is where the publicity, the visibility of such scenographies of knowledge is perhaps most demanding and most significant – on the boundary of knowledge, a different knowledge about non-knowledge.

Translation from German

References

»Interview. Tanzdenker William Forsythe im Gespräch mit Wiebke Hüster«, in: *du. Zeitschrift für Kultur* 765, April 2006, pp. 16–18.

Brandstetter, Gabriele: »Inventur: Tanz. Performance und die Listen der Wissenschaft«, in: Sybille Peters/Martin Jörg Schäfer (eds.): *Intellektuelle Anschauung. Figurationen von Evidenz zwischen Kunst und Wissen*, Bielefeld: transcript 2006, pp. 295–300.

Brandstetter, Gabriele: »Zu einer Poetologie des Medienwechsels. Aufführung und Aufzeichnung – Kunst der Wissenschaft?«, in: idem: *Bild-Sprung. TanzTheaterBewegung im Wechsel der Medien*, Berlin: Theater der Zeit 2005, pp. 199–210.

Forsythe, William: *Improvisation Technologies. A Tool for the Analytical Dance Eye*, Ostfildern: Hatje Cantz 1999.

Holländer, Katarina: »Noten des Tanzes. Vom Versuch, das Tanzen mit Worten und Zeichen festzuhalten. Und ein Besuch in Noa Eshkols Werkstatt der Verschriftlichung«, in: *du. Zeitschrift für Kultur 765*, April 2006, pp. 65–74.

Karina, Lilian/Kant, Marion (eds.): *Tanz unterm Hakenkreuz. Eine Dokumentation*, Berlin: Henschel 1996.

Kuhn, Thomas S.: *The Structure of Scientific Revolutions*, Chicago: University of Chicago Press 1962.

La biennale di Venezia: *Participating countries – collateral events*, Vol. 3, Germany, Venezia: Marsilio 2005.

Moll, Ewald: »Die neue Tanzschrift«, in: *Schrifttanz 1928, Mitteilungen der Deutschen Gesellschaft für Schrifttanz*, p. 16.

Müller, Hedwig/Stabel, Ralf/Stöckemann, Patricia (eds.): *Krokodil im Schwanensee. Tanz in Deutschland seit 1945*, Frankfurt a.M.: Anabas 2003.

Müller, Hedwig/Stöckemann, Patricia (eds.): »*... jeder Mensch ist ein Tänzer.*« *Ausdruckstanz in Deutschland zwischen 1900 und 1945*, Gießen: Anabas 1993.

Schrifttanz. Eine Vierteljahresschrift, 1. year. October 1928, Issue 2, Universaledition Wien.

Seel, Martin: *Ästhetik des Erscheinens*, Munich/Vienna: Hanser 2000.

Todd, Mabel E.: *The Thinking Body. A Study of the Balancing Forces of Dynamic Man*, New York: Dance Horizons 1937.

Waldenfels, Bernhard: *Sinnesschwellen*, Frankfurt a.M.: Suhrkamp 1999.

Trickstering, Hallucinating and Exhausting Production

The Blackmarket for Useful Knowledge and Non-Knowledge[1]

BOJANA CVEJIC

There are projects that inaugurate a curated topic, and they act as and are looked upon as the curatorial markers of a period; for instance, the documenta XII in Kassel or the cancelled Manifesta 6 School in Nicosia both draw political relevance from the topics of education and knowledge production. And there are projects that develop an autonomous practice over a longer period of time, and though they are not conceived in reaction to or anticipation of a trend, their appearance is amplified at times by current curatorial interest.

Such is the BLACKMARKET FOR USEFUL KNOWLEDGE AND NON-KNOWLEDGE, emerging from a series of projects that Hannah Hurtzig has created since 1995 in order to experiment with the forms of knowledge production and transfer in constructed public spaces. For a brief account of the history of the BLACKMARKET, the Mobile Academies should be mentioned (Bochum 1999, Berlin 2001 and 2004, Warsaw 2006).

Even if they are now lumped together with other summer schools and academies, which have been burgeoning all over since 2004, Hurtzig's projects were the first to hybridise (un-)disciplined workshops and lectures, cultural fieldwork and political activism in events that create their own imaginary community.

Out of the FAKELORE Academy that took place in Berlin in 2004 sprang the first official BLACKMARKET FOR USEFUL KNOWLEDGE AND NON-KNOWLEDGE as a »hallucinated community college of the Mobile Academy with 100 experts from Berlin«. An attempt at an encyclopaedic

---

1 | Apropos of an ENCYCLOPAEDIA OF DANCE GESTURES AND APPLIED MOVEMENTS IN HUMANS, ANIMALS AND MATTER presented at the DANCE CONGRESS GERMANY, House of World Cultures in Berlin on 20th April, 2006.

systematisation of »terms and topics that played an important part in the past Mobile Academies«², it was a wild taxonomy of cultural, artistic, scientific, jargonised, practical and common-sense based, disciplinary and non-disciplinary, acknowledged and clandestine areas of knowledge – 42 topics from A for »Aeronautics« to U for »Urbanism« in languages (or dialects) such as Arabic, Bengali, Chinese, German, English, French, Greek, Hindi, Italian, Japanese, Dutch, Low German, Portuguese, Russian, Swedish, Urdu and Viennese.

Out of three elements already set out in the first event – including a one-on-one talk between an ›expert‹ and a ›client‹ for one euro, lasting 30 minutes, with an audience offered the possibility to listen in on six talks via headphones – a model crystallised that could be a topic of discussion for several days. The reason why I would like to talk about the BLACKMARKET is to analyse the specifics of its format and effects vis-à-vis new forms of knowledge production and their politics. I will examine element by element the particularities that produced the BLACKMARKET as a new autonomous model, using as an example the ENCYCLOPAEDIA OF DANCE GESTURES AND APPLIED MOVEMENTS IN HUMANS, ANIMALS AND MATTER, created for the opening of the DANCE CONGRESS GERMANY 2006.

E: When we go to the studio, and especially when it comes to improvisation, how is it possible to carry out a movement that we don't know? Oftentimes, the choreographer says, ›surprise me!‹ Then we know of course that we can't but fail. But how can we make a movement that we are not capable of, neither technically nor in our imagination? If we say that every movement has been made before, how can we have a new dance emerge by changing just a small thing? There must be some way for something new to sneak in [...] I am not interested in abducting anybody, but in being abducted. When you get abducted, the only thing an abductor can't cope with is the hostage saying: ›I'll lie down and die‹. The Stockholm syndrome implies absolute surrender, no responsibility; for the abductor will always keep me alive. Situation-induced dedication to something we can't control. It's the only possibility to create something new; how can I abduct myself in the process of creating a dance?³

---

2 | All quotations of Hannah Hurtzig date from a conversation that took place in March 2006 in Berlin.

3 | The following paragraphs in italics are excerpts from the ENCYCLOPEDIA OF DANCE GESTURES AND APPLIED MOVEMENTS IN HUMANS, ANIMALS AND MATTER. ›E‹ stands for the ›expert‹ and ›C‹ for the ›client‹. I deliberately omit the names of experts (and clients' names I could only guess in some cases) so as to imitate the buzzing noise of voices from which the fragments of conversa-

*Blackmarket for Useful Knowledge
and Non-Knowledge by Hannah Hurtzig,
Dance Congress Germany 2006*

Photo: Thomas Aurin

Machinising Public Space

What distinguishes Blackmarket from the artistic interventions that critique public spaces as being closed, controlled and dominated by marketplace consumerism is its proactive approach: not to discover, display or import the ready-made exhibit of a museum, theatre or academy, but to construct a public space in the city that is not officially dedicated to the production of knowledge. Hurtzig explains that her resources were

[...] archives and reading rooms in libraries, stock exchanges and rooms with a special function in non-European countries, for instance offices in Zimbabwe, where illiterate persons can have their story or knowledge written down in form of a letter, an advertisement or any other type of message to be recorded on paper.

The type of public space the Blackmarket is aiming for is a *Benutzerraum*, a user-oriented space. What it shares with the theatre is the reference to the antique public forum and being a mixture of performance and event. It is a performance in so far as each expert takes the position of a savant = performer, self-appointed by means of the speech-act, employing all techniques of performing. This does not refer to the acting techniques, but the linguistic skill of making, fulfilling or betraying a

---

tions loomed. Doing so, I also avoid authorizing information and opinion by disclosing the names under citations.

promise of knowledge. BLACKMARKET is less a performance than an event in that it does not present itself in confrontation with an audience that seeks consensus in reception.

There are no spectators to watch and react to a performance, but all participants – experts, their clients and the listeners passing-by – are users involved in shaping the event to a varying degree. The intimacy of the encounter at each table-unit requires people to speak at a low voice, to whisper and maybe even to mumble – so the view from above onto a room filled with 100 tables has very little significance in the sense that the scene resembled, represented or spoke for something/someone. BLACKMARKET is therefore only an installation in technical terms, in its set-up, rather than in the genre it displays. It is more an autonomous machine that *puts* a space *into motion* in an open, uncontrolled, unrestrained production, dissemination and infiltration of knowledge. For now I will use the word ›knowledge‹ for want of a more adequate term, I will, however, make suitable allowance for its intrinsic complexities.

E: [...] Does something happen between the people who are deliberately look-ing at the same thing at the same time? Is there some kind of communication taking place which could turn them into a community for a short while and thus prompt maybe them to participate in something completely different? [...] Why are these questions being asked at all?

Because there is a widespread notion in the Western World today [...] that art and culture perform along the principles of parliamentary democratic representation – representing all people etc. The hidden agenda behind this idea is that the model of democratic representation should be applied to the cultural sphere as well. The question is, however, whether politics cannot learn something from the cultural sphere it did not know before.

Storytelling

Storytelling is the technology that explicitly distinguishes knowledge transfer in the BLACKMARKET from all other learning situations. Telling a story immediately detaches the object of knowledge transfer from any academic discipline. This is another reason why the BLACKMARKET is an event: BLACKMARKET is not about recording new or different ideas (the political mission of recording knowledge), not about detecting or archiv-ing erased traces. Even if it produces a certain abundance, profusion and surplus of meaning it is still a place to trade and not to exchange gifts and rewards. Selling one's story mirrors a fundamental social contract: it puts the storyteller in the exposed position of having to ›perform or else‹, in which he has to provide a service, and the client in a position to claim provision of this service. Narrative leads away from the academic methods of analysing, contextualising, commenting on and verifying information. In fact it separates knowledge from information and defines it somewhere between what is known as the object of knowledge, research, and any discipline (*savoir*), and what makes up the subject, i.e. experiencing or encountering (*connaissance*). The savant in this definition is not someone who has a love for knowledge and whose knowledge is necessarily legitimated by an institution, but savants can be tricksters, who not only betray the ruling regimes, but also take possession of territories that do not belong to them, or do not exist yet and are, therefore, invented.

E: If you single out an instance of communication in a performance, for example, and compare it to the way we are talking here, I think you can see one big difference. If I say something and you misunderstand it, the way you react to what I said will show me that there has been a misunderstanding.
C: I will let you know one way or another.
E: Exactly. I think one of the particular features you're faced with when creating art is that you're cut off from interaction, which means that you can't correct the misunderstanding [...].

BLACKMARKET FOR USEFUL KNOWLEDGE
AND NON-KNOWLEDGE *by Hannah Hurtzig,*
DANCE CONGRESS GERMANY 2006

Photo: Thomas Aurin

Subjectification and Expertise

If subjectification is not just tracing or interpreting elements of one's own experience, but always already includes a process of transformation, appropriating something by embellishing it, by ›messing‹ it up, giving it one's own body, then expertise means reaching a generally achievable condition or a condition conducive to general understanding: there is always something one knows. The question is not so much what one knows, but how one knows, what constitutes ability to know and passing on that knowledge to other people. Subjectification is all about partiality and partial insights, which in fact, enable participation on a contingent basis. Partiality should also be read in opposition to »being impartial«, i.e. objective, unbiased or dispassionate. Now BLACKMARKET's mission is not to empower humankind by making it realise its own capabilities, but to explore the potentials that lie in the vague and less visibly circulating aspects of knowledge: assumptions, beliefs, opinions, habits, facts, information, methods etc. Talk is an encounter that correlates knowledge and non-knowledge, activates learning and unlearning, explores the difference and the distance between ignorance, or opinion respectively, and what is idealised as its opposite – namely knowledge. Hurtzig refers to Niklas Luhmann by saying that the BLACKMARKET should be understood pragmatically as a »tool to find problems for already existing solutions«.

E: *We are trying to find something out about masses. What's your interest in swarms?*
C: *What's my interest? Uuuh ...*
E: *Are you all right?*
C: *I'm a conductor, and I'm very interested in large numbers of energetic bodies and what they can do collectively and how they can make group decisions.*
E: *I love your approach.*

Topics and Experts

The ENCYCLOPAEDIA of the DANCE CONGRESS organised its ›entries‹ in the following abecedarian sequence: ABSENCE, AGE, ANIMALS, BODY TECHNIQUES, CHOREOGRAPHERS, CONCEPTUAL DANCE, DANCE STYLES, EDUCATION, FILM, IMAGE, INTERPRETATION, MACHINE MAN, MARKET, MEMORY, MIGRATION, MOVEMENT, NOTATION, PARTICIPATION, PERCEPTION, SENSATION, SOLO, SPORTS, TRANSITION, TRAVEL, VISUAL REGIME, NO CATEGORY. Listing all categories serves to show that the heterogeneity was not choreographed from above (i.e. as a pool of topics to choose from and respond to), but that the themes were the result of an *a posteriori* grouping of the talks, as they were formulated by the experts. The wording represents a variety of strategies and tactics of self-determination, they range from canonical expert knowledge (e.g. »How to Reconstruct a Dance Piece by Mary Wigman?« by Waltraud Luley) to an alternative technique (»How to Move As Effortlessly As Possible With Minimum Input – On the Reversibility of Movement in Feldenkrais« by Irene Sieben) to the know-how of performers or maxims of everyday-life (»Alternative Techniques for Remembering Physical Actions and Movements« by Thomas Conway, »Frame-Dragging. Perceptual Shifts While Dancing, Travelling and Having Sex« by Siegmar Zacharias), exposing opposite political sides and positions (»What Are the Right Communication Strategies to Follow, and How Do I Formulate a Dance Project for Cultural Politicians to Understand It and to Find It Worthy of Funding« by Barbara Kisseler, »Global Market and Local Authorities: About the Hidden Structures of the Artistic Production Process« by Eszter Salamon); the notion of movement was extended beyond the art of dance to non-human bodies (»Finding the Way Without Markers: the Sky Compass of Desert Ants« by Bernhard Ronacher, »Dance of the Chromosomes. Short Introduction to Cell Biology« by Helmut Höge), to cultural practices (»The Grotesque Formation of Dance Couples in Competitive Dance or the Dance Sports and Its Effects on Gay-Lesbian Ballroom Dancing« by Christoph Neumann, »On Wall of Death, Pogo and Mosh – Hard Core Music and Dance« by Volkan) or investigation of movement in perception (»What Are the Raised Hands of Students Not Called Up Doing in the Airspace of the Classroom? From Sketching the Glance to the Movement of Thought: Camera Ethnography as Movement Research with the Senses« by Elisabeth Mohn) to intriguing mismatches between profession and proclaimed competence (»1. Applied Movements on Board: Struggling with Cargo from Mopti to Timbuktu 2. How to Travel Around Armenia Without a Car« by dance and theatre critic Renate Klett) and sparklingly humorous or bizarre contributions (»Why I Hate the Scenic Poetry of Dance Theatre or: The Late Revenge of Pantomime – Images in Dance Theatre« by Florian Malzacher). These titles clearly show how BLACKMARKET responds to an invitation like the one issued by the DANCE CONGRESS. The BLACKMARKET on the DANCE CONGRESS does not serve the purpose of illustrating the whole *spectrum* of dance, but rather of trying to describe new approaches to dance by expanding the field to those registers current practice overlooks, ignores or misjudges. The BLACKMARKET adds a new element to the DANCE CONGRESS: a reality-check of the scene with its political edginess, and its moods of silliness, laziness or useless invention.

E: I was very surprised when they contacted me, because what I do has nothing to do with dance or art.
C: That's quite okay with me.
E: [...] the goal of the project is to develop a so-called brain-computer interface: the user can control a computer application or any device by mental activity only. You can sit motionless while a certain mental activity is going on. [...] a paralysed patient, for instance, who wants to control a word-processing system, may think of a word which will then appear on screen [...].

Cutting across Society

There are certain procedures and aims that need to be followed in preparing a topic to become the area of research. However, by not imposing a particular theme on a particular context with the interpretative arrogance of a ›this is good for you‹, Hurtzig does not set a certain *telos* as ultimate purpose of the artwork, nor specified preferences and criteria: »As I'm not a talented person, I work on the basis of ›deficit and deficiency‹. I search for what I think we're in lack of.« In the Blackmarket held in Warsaw in 2005, for instance, the topic of Ghostly or Invisible Knowledge made connections between people, knowledge and experience from before and after the regime change in Poland, and presented different ways of deciphering and reading the process of political and economic transition and its concomitant circumstances. The thematic guideline for this Blackmarket was a quote by Heiner Müller: »The phantom of the market economy has replaced the ghost of communism.«

Another example illustrates how the Blackmarket team proceed now that the model has become popular, when they receive commissions or invitations on particular topics. Having been asked recently to carry out a Blackmarket on the topic of »Aging in Germany«, Hurtzig says:

Searching for what could be interesting apart from old people speaking about their life, which isn't particularly exiting, I came across the strange phenomenon of aged ›researchers‹, i.e. people who specialise in ›small‹ topics after their professional career has ended. For instance, a woman who had spent 15 years since her retirement on researching the irregular shapes of cherries. These are people who decided to do something they couldn't do before, and as they are now self-determined and not linked to any institution, these researchers are driven by a passion to obtain knowledge, without knowing whether this knowledge will be of use to anybody.

The process of research resembles a »rehearsal process identical with its result – a communication process of two to three months, in which different sources are consulted that help re-hallucinate a context.« To achieve this, Hurtzig and her collaborators perform a kind of cut across society, which is fundamentally different from what is commonly referred to as interdisciplinary research. An interdisciplinary approach presupposes that a topic crystallises as a kind of event from the enriching influence of joining and mixing generally accepted disciplines. In the case of Blackmarket this mixing of disciplines looks rather monstrous: something known, established or invariable is combined with something that does not possess these qualities; the aim thus seems to be to mix discipline-based, alternative, parallel, amateur, practical, technical, conventional, experience-based registers of articulating knowledge as something one has, one is capable of, one uses, one can teach, one can learn or one can only name. In short, this means »make the scientist meet the man next door«. In this way you first of all avoid having only ›the usual suspects‹ or »discourse leaders« (*Diskursstatthalter*) represented and, second, there is never only one result or distinguishing feature vis-à-vis the established or dominant notion. The outcome will therefore never be a coherent, unified or homogeneous catalogue of expert knowledge, but always irreproducible connections between people, places, memories and interests.

Where to Go and What to Do

Today, when theory has become yet another superstructure of late capitalism, which applies to the rhetoric of the arts as well as to the creative industries and business management, it actually takes some art to de-instrumentalise theory from producing an added intellectual value. Even if it explicitly focuses on making knowledge transfer an event, BLACKMARKET is not conceived to reclaim the function of art in contemporary society as a particular form of knowledge production. If it does seem to invest in the current curatorial debate on education, it is not its by-product or side effect. »I am interested in the situations where there is a collective moment of learning that people aren't aware of and which, potentially, could lead to action, arousing enthusiasm and hallucination with the impossible.«

Not having primarily critical aspirations, BLACKMARKET presents itself as a field for experimentation against a speculative and pragmatic backdrop. It operates with possibilities and potentialities of concrete situations, topics/research projects or areas/fields in particular contexts (like cities), and in particular moments (like »Tanzplan« or Poland entering the EU). It satisfies the curiosity of experiencing the places one happens to be in more intensely.

What is an Artistic Laboratory?

A METALOGUE BETWEEN PETER STAMER

I'm excited. – *What about?* – Whether we'll get anywhere. – *With what?* – With this conversation. – *What is our conversation supposed to be about?* – About finding out what an artistic laboratory is. Or, more precisely, about the conditions and attributes of knowledge production. – *And why do you need me in your text?* – Well, because I feel that the dialogue form is similar to an artistic laboratory in its approach to producing knowledge. I speak with you and answer your questions, which are, after all, my own questions. – *It sounds a bit like Xavier Le Roy's SELF-INTERVIEW[1] from 1999, if I may say so. In it, he converses with his own voice, which he has recorded on a cassette recorder, about the background to his project E.X.T.E.N.S.I.O.N.S. By bouncing thoughts against his own voice, he reflects on how one of his projects came about and presents reflection as a performance. A laboratory of thought, in actu. By the way, it was interesting that one of the voices began every reply with »I don't know«, as if it didn't know what it should contribute to the conversation. Pretended ignorance.* – I remember. At least it knows that it knows nothing. And that reminds me of the Socratic dialogues, where Plato brought together his mentor Socrates and his fellow student Theaetetus. The two converse about the possibilities of knowledge in general until Socrates suddenly confronts the younger man with the question »That's exactly what I am uncertain about and what I cannot really understand: what actually is knowledge?«[2] The discussion partners do not come to a conclusive answer to the question, although for over 100 pages they do nothing but debate

---

1 | To read the interview go to: *www.insituproductions.net/_eng/framesetl.html* from 14 May 2007.

2 | Cf. *www.e-text.org/text/Platon%20-%20Theaitetos.pdf* from 25 April 2007.

the possibilities of being able to know. Socrates' mind, which functions as a midwife to other people's thoughts, gives birth to endless pages of considerations, but cannot capture the ultimate knowledge about what knowledge is. – *What fascinated me about the dialogue was that although the speakers could not find a final solution to the ›How of knowledge‹, at least they knew how to approach their desire to know. Namely, through the medium of dialogue; they know that they need to pose question after question. In this way, the dialogical element of reflection becomes important in* THEAETETUS, *but even more important is the reflection on the dialogical approach, contemplation about the How which itself becomes a type of knowledge with epistemological significance.* – The anthropologist Gregory Bateson proposed the term metalogue for such self-reflective conversations. He wrote: »A metalogue is a conversation about a problematic topic. The participants in this conversation shouldn't only discuss the problem – the structure of the conversation as a whole should also be relevant for precisely this topic.«[3]

SANS PAPIERS, DANCE CONGRESS
GERMANY 2006

Photo: Thomas Aurin

The dialogue itself is not only a fixed textual format which attempts to hold the contents like a vessel, it also triggers discourse itself. – *By the way, the word discourse is derived from the Latin word* discurrere, *which*

---

3 | Gregory Bateson: *Ökologie des Geistes. Anthropologische, psychologische, biologische und epistemologische Perspektiven,* Frankfurt a.M.: Suhrkamp 1994, p. 31.

roughly means running to and fro. – Right. That's why I chose you to be my discursive running partner, someone I would like to make this journey with together. Incidentally, in his book »Ökologie des Geistes« (»Steps to an Ecology of Mind«), Bateson dedicates an entire chapter to metalogues between ›father‹ and ›daughter‹. In one of them, the girl asks her dad how much he knows.[4] He at first claims that knowledge cannot be measured, but the longer he thinks about this question, and the more points of view he takes, the clearer it becomes how much ›Daddy‹, or the author of Daddy's statements, does know after all. For example, he knows a great deal about how contemplation can only lead to results within an overall system. »What we have to think about is how the pieces of knowledge are connected,«[5] says Daddy, and thus addresses a cultural understanding of knowledge ... – ... *one which the sociologist Karin Knorr Cetina also refers to in her book »Wissenskulturen« (»Cultures of Knowledge«), which endeavours to find out »how we know what we know«.[6] In the book, she defines epistemic cultures as »cultures within a knowledge context«[7] which can be differentiated specifically into epistemic cultures.[8] How something can be known is dependent on the respective context in which the knowledge is created and practiced. Knorr Cetina's understanding of culture draws upon the work of the anthropologist Clifford Geertz, who states that culture is »a system of inherited conceptions, expressed in symbolic forms, by means of which people communicate, perpetuate and develop their knowledge about and attitudes towards life«.[9] Here, being able to know is less an ability of an intelligent subject but rather a condition of the cultural possibilities available. What can be known and how it can be known depends on the conditions under which a possible item of knowledge is capable of being accepted as truth. These conditions structure the knowledge and the experiences of a culture, which, however, the respective speakers, theoreticians or scientists are not aware of.* – Within the social weave of the culture, which all speakers in a period of time share, there are various fine differentiations – namely these epistemic cultures – which Knorr Cetina speaks of when she investigates the modes of knowledge of the laboratory culture in the field of microbiology and high-energy physics. Scientific laboratories create their epistemic efficacy from the differences between them and the environment around them.[10]

---

4 | Cf. ibid., p. 53.

5 | Ibid., p. 54.

6 | Karin Knorr Cetina: *Wissenskulturen. Ein Vergleich naturwissenschaftlicher Wissensformen*, Frankfurt a.M.: Suhrkamp 2002, p. 11.

7 | Ibid., p. 19.

8 | Cf. ibid., p. 18.

9 | Clifford Geertz: *Dichte Beschreibung. Beiträge zum Verstehen kultureller Systeme*, Frankfurt a.M.: Suhrkamp 1983, p. 46.

10 | Knorr Cetina: *Wissenskulturen*, l.c., p. 65.

– *By the way, in her book, Karin Knorr Cetina attempts to address the same question as you, which I would now like to pass on to you: »What is a laboratory?«*[11] – The very first question one needs to think about when conceiving, visiting, designing, implementing an artistic laboratory. The first question, that is, after the methodological foundations, which are not so easy ... – *This sounds dangerously like the »I don't know« game in Le Roy's* SELF-INTERVIEW, *which, I must admit, I don't find particularly satisfying. If you had to explain to someone who didn't know anything about it, how would you answer the question ›What is an artistic laboratory?‹* – But I am not entirely convinced by the question, because there is no such thing as a total lack of knowledge, an absolute ignorance. For if it is true that the interlinking of cultural contexts determines how and what we can know about something, then everyone brings their own prior knowledge and thus some kind of preconception into the discussion. If I say that an artistic laboratory is an important research tool for contemporary dance, then I have already made more than *one* proposition. For example, I need to have an idea of what it is that I have, for simplicity's sake, called »contemporary dance«. Therefore I am always already within a certain context, one in which I first have to make myself understood, in order to be able to explain the special characteristics of epistemic culture, as represented in contemporary dance, in my opinion. – *Can't you then maybe try to explain what you understand by research into contemporary dance?* – That, too, I can only do by comparing the differences between various characteristics. First and foremost, I understand research as a mentality and an attitude to work which begins with interest in gaining knowledge, whatever this may be like. I have to have a question which occupies my mind, which dogs me constantly, which informs the way I see the world and determines my behaviour. – *Can you give me an example of such a question?* – Wait. The real question is: what are the tools we need to tackle this question? I could try to find an expert to help me answer my questions. Or I could try to answer my questions myself by constantly trying out possible answers until I find the right one. These would be the familiar knowledge strategies of the workshop and the rehearsal. – *In a workshop a teacher communicates his knowledge, in a rehearsal the focus is more on trying out solutions.* – Both approaches emphasise finding out an answer. In a workshop, the teacher demonstrates how ›it‹ is done. Dancers in a rehearsal, on the other hand, are trying to find an answer to their artistic questions through performance. But how can they find the answer if they don't know what it looks like? – *After all, every question formulates its own answer.* – And so, right from the beginning, I already have the answer which, at bottom, I don't even need to look for because it is already embedded within the question. I would, however, say that the research paradigm

---

11 | Ibid., p. 45.

of contemporary dance looks for answers which the question does not, to all intents and purposes, take into account. Impossible answers to possible questions. Consequently, each question always results in another question, not in order to make the original question more precise with regard to possible answers, but rather to make the question a sharper tool with which to gain knowledge. Contemporary research is not defined by a search *for* something, the *search* becomes the object in itself. – *That sounds a little esoteric, to be honest.* – Do you know the story about the discovery of the post-it? – *The notes you stick on things?* – The story is that a certain Spencer Silver set out to invent a superglue but all he managed to create in the lab was a gooey mass. Although this product could be used to make light materials stick, they could easily be peeled off again. A few years later, one of his colleagues was looking for a way to stick notes in his songbook without gluing up the whole page. He remembered Silver's unsuccessful invention, had another close look at it, and the post-it was born.– *Chance favours the prepared mind, as bacteriologist Louis Pasteur is supposed to have said once.*[12] – But the idea should actually be attributed to Spencer Silver. He discovered something which he didn't mean to discover, a ›Columbus effect‹ which opened up a whole new world. This effect is called »serendipity«, namely a form of knowledge which is not the result of focussed research, but rather a by-product of a supposedly flawed experiment or an unsuccessful answer, which only comes to be valued at a later date. – *And so in order to question my own question: the question ›What is a laboratory?‹ is epistimically productive precisely if it is not answered. But then, how can a question like that be research-oriented?* – Precisely because it questions the question. Maybe I need to expand a little more. In 1999, the two curators Hans Ulrich Obrist and Barbara Vanderlinden set up an exhibition project in Antwerp which they called LABORATORIUM.[13] During their events, they examined a wide range of public workplaces such as official departments, police stations, the harbour, even the zoo, as places in which social knowledge is produced. They then opened them up to artistic intervention, choreographic rehearsals or playful experimentation.[14] The authors prefaced the catalogue which accompanied the project with a semi-ironic, semi-paradoxical motto: »Laboratorium is the answer. What is the question?«[15] They meant that a laboratory does not provide the final answer, but, first and foremost, allows questions to be asked. The laboratory represents the framework of

---

12 | Cf. Bruno Latour: *Die Hoffnung der Pandora*, Frankfurt a.M.: Suhrkamp 2002, p. 143.

13 | Cf. Hans Ulrich Obrist/Barbara Vanderlinden (eds.): *Laboratorium*, Antwerp: DuMont 2001.

14 | Cf. ibid., pp. 19f.

15 | Cf. ibid., no page designation.

conditions; it is, in the best sense of the word, an epistemic armoury, without which questions could not even be posed. – *So asking questions here is equivalent to research, whose context, in the case of LABORATORIUM, is the social interweaving of the production of art and knowledge. Accordingly, questions which art throws up are also relevant from a social point of view.* – And, conversely, the way social processes and negotiations work are also undergoing closer examination with regard to questions concerning art. The group or social fabric in which art is produced is not neutral, it is steeped in the culture from which it originates. And these are the experiences which are fed back into artistic processes in LABORATORIUM. – *Where do research and the laboratory meet in contemporary dance? Because as far as I understand, the Antwerp LABORATORIUM was an urban exhibition project and not a research event.* – Choreographers such as Meg Stuart and Xavier Le Roy also took part in the Antwerp project. Whereas Meg Stuart invited people to conduct several weeks of movement research in her CHOREOGRAPHIC LABORATORY, Le Roy worked on his experimental project E.X.T.E.N.S.I.O.N.S. – *And as Le Roy is considered to be one of the leading exponents of contemporary dance, and as he demonstrated in his lecture performance PRODUCT OF CIRCUMSTANCES that he experienced an epistemic connection between his training to become a doctor in microbiology and his training to become a dancer, his biography is a perfect example of the connection between research and the Laboratorium. Once a researcher, always a researcher.* – As a consequence, Le Roy was always seen as an authority when it came to emphasising the importance of research in contemporary dance. – *Once in the laboratory, always in the laboratory.* – Suddenly, at the end of the 1990s, dance became intellectual, started to produce its own knowledge and was even able to externalise this knowledge. On the threshold between artistic practice and the production of knowledge, the laboratory as a research format has come onto the scene at just the right time. Contemporary dance is already well on the way to becoming a separate epistemic culture within the knowledge society. – *And the DANCE CONGRESS under the motto KNOWLEDGE IN MOTION has now bestowed this consecration upon dance.* – A well-meant concept of the laboratory as a »truly free space for artists« which »breaks down the boundaries between production and presentation«,[16] thus allowing unlimited knowledge to be produced is currently in circulation. – *Well-meant because this concept of freedom is based on an idea of scholarliness which suggests that only research performed within the isolation of the laboratory theatre can be called scientific?* – And because it implies an understanding of the laboratory which could be seen as outmoded. Even in the natural sciences, the laboratory can no longer be considered a neutral place dedicated to the pure joy of discovering

---

16 | Quote taken from an unpublished Tanzquartier Wien mission statement made at its opening in 2001.

knowledge, in which research geniuses freely undertake fundamental research with no kind of obligation to action. On the contrary, Karin Knorr Cetina in her book »Wissenskulturen« emphasises the importance of the researcher's body, which is only able to perceive through its social and corporeal nature.[17] The point is that scientific laboratories are not separate from social orders, but rather in their very midst, they renegotiate them, integrate them into their work and have to deal with them in it. – *To what extent does the metaphor of the free space hold if we take it literally? Is the free space provided by the laboratory a place in the spatial sense of the word?* – To answer that, I have to come back to LABORATORIUM. The Antwerp project understood the production of knowledge as being attached to a locality. It is »situated«, to use a term coined by the feminist natural scientist Donna Haraway.[18] Each respective social laboratory produces knowledge in places »where knowledge *and* culture are made,«[19] which, correspondingly, feeds one of the basic ideas of the artistic laboratory. The decisive step is therefore the attempt, not only to artistically and discursively localise the place in which knowledge is produced but also, inversely, to determine the underlying concept of knowledge topographically. If we adopt this method, we can say that a laboratory is not just a place in which researchers produce knowledge under the given social circumstances, but that it is much rather a black-boxed ›thinking space‹ located within the researcher's body.[20] – *That means that this thinking space is enclosed within the body of the researcher.* – The thinking space is not possible without a body, simple as that may sound. This understanding of research as contained within the body is, however, in no way an attempt to authenticate the truth of the bodies. In fact, the bodies negotiate with each other about those truth conditions which are possible in a given culture. Because the bodies taking part in the research have been infiltrated with all of the social discourses and practices which they bring into the laboratory with them. They share with others the same epistemes,[21] as Michel Foucault called the sets of conditions which allow discourses to be considered true. They share the same cultural knowledge with other bodies although each of them processes it in a different way. Knorr Cetina also calls this knowledge »tacit knowledge«,[22] which initially

---

17 | Cf. Knorr Cetina: *Wissenskulturen*, ibid., pp. 138f.

18 | Cf. Donna Haraway: *Die Neuerfindung der Natur. Primaten, Cyborgs und Frauen*, Frankfurt a.M./New York: Campus 1995.

19 | Obrist/Vanderlinden (eds.): *Laboratorium*, l.c., p. 17 (emphasis P.S.).

20 | Cf. Knorr Cetina: *Wissenskulturen*, l.c., pp. 138f.

21 | Cf. Michel Foucault: *Die Ordnung der Dinge*, Frankfurt a.M.: Suhrkamp 1974, p. 24; Idem: *Die Ordnung des Diskurses*, Frankfurt a.M.: Fischer 1998, pp. 15ff., and Pravu Mazumdar: *Foucault*, Munich: DTV 2001, p. 533.

22 | Knorr Cetina: *Wissenskulturen*, l.c., p. 144.

remains unspoken but then has to be shared as a result of knowledge interests formulated as questions. – *I don't quite understand.* – Whilst bodies with the same cultural experiences and modes of knowledge come together in the thinking space which the laboratory provides, the question of how they deal with these experiences and knowledge is decided by the individual protagonists. This individual way of dealing with the knowledge located and, until now, concealed within the body cannot be communicated until it has to be put into words. The question is not whether this silent knowledge can be verbalised, but rather, what kind of negotiations the laboratory participants enter into *in order* to communicate it. These intentions to impart knowledge, these correspondences or attempts to communicate situate knowledge within the laboratory. – *Meaning, research only becomes a laboratory, a place, a thinking space, when it is shared by several people who are constantly reformulating questions.* – To give you an example: for the DANCE CONGRESS I suggested we set up a laboratory for the investigation of knowledge production issues over three days. Besides myself, Karin Knorr Cetina, Franz Anton Cramer, Tino Sehgal, Christine Standfest and Christina Thurner took part. Our aim was to discuss the »epistemological foundations and discursive conditions under which the other modules of the congress should create and present knowledge«.[23]

SANS PAPIERS, DANCE CONGRESS GERMANY 2006

Photo: Thomas Aurin

Our real-time working format was entitled, admittedly somewhat problematically, SANS PAPIERS. What interested me about this working format was the idea of speaking literally ›without paper‹, without written references or the safeguards afforded by footnotes. This was made even more difficult by the fact that every minute of our shared thinking within the

---

23 | Cf. event announcement of the SANS PAPIERS laboratory in the handout of the DANCE CONGRESS GERMANY.

laboratory was public. The six of us were sitting at a table whilst the audience were sitting against the wall and listening. – *Couldn't the people in the auditorium join in the discussion? Didn't they end up experiencing your dialogue as a kind of performance?* – One of the two agreements which SANS PAPIERS made was that communication would take place solely within the group. It's possible that this led to the impression of a performance – a performance, however, which was entirely improvised, which was fed by nothing but the knowledge embodied in the participants, their *tacit knowledge* that is. This separation of speakers and listeners had yet another consequence, however. The audience watched us draw closer to our thoughts. Their gaze laboratised the set-up to a certain extent because these people, like scientists, watched us in our negotiations. – *And, in doing so, they saw the contributions made by the participants, the search for and experimentation with knowledge as an epistemic object in itself, through which knowledge is made visible. What was the second agreement?* – As I said, that we would literally speak without recourse to paper. There wasn't a single sheet of paper on the table, nobody was allowed to make notes to fall back on as a memory aid. The object of our investigation, if you will, was the congress, its fundamental assumptions about knowledge and the »images of knowledge«[24] reflected in those assumptions. At the same time, however, we had not decided on a method for investigating this object – apart from using a form of speech whose rules we, again, negotiated within the group by means of speech itself: how should we talk to each other? How should I address the others? What questions would I put *to them?* All this represents the ethics of dialogue; the research methodology is born of this social interaction. – *The way I understand it, the connection between aesthetic and ethical, perceived and verbalised qualities, no longer needed to be described, for example by looking at a certain topic and trying to describe it precisely, but that the dialogue itself constituted the topic.* – In speaking *the laboratory,* we implicitly talked *about* it, about its modes of knowledge, knowledge-finding strategies, within our own epistemic culture. – *To me that sounds a bit like a curious appendage to the reference function of speech. Are you familiar with Jonathan Swift's satire on science in »Gulliver's Travels«? In the third book, Gulliver visits the Grand Academy of Lagado, where he meets scientists who want to abolish language altogether, the reason being that, since language merely provides words for things, communication would be easier if people carried the actual things around with them, thus replacing the words with the things. Swift mockingly describes how Gulliver meets two sages on the streets of the island, who are almost crushed by the weight of their bundles of words. For the more somebody*

---

24 | Yehuda Elkana: *Anthropologie der Erkenntnis. Die Entwicklung des Wissens als episches Theater einer listigen Vernunft,* Frankfurt a.M.: Suhrkamp 1986, p. 19.

knows, the more they have to say, the greater the burden they must carry. – So the academy is a research institution which works to make people's lives more difficult rather than making them easier? – *Precisely. With every extra letter, the weight of the ›word things‹ increases and the burden of the words grows. In the case of* SANS PAPIERS, *it seems to me that you carried the words around as if they were things which gained weight in the laboratory. A weight of words under which the users stagger, totter backwards and forwards and begin to talk.* – The etymological origin of the word laboratory comes from the Latin *laborare,* which does, in fact, mean ›to stagger under a heavy load‹. How many tottering metres in this metalogue have we put behind us in questioning the original question ›What is an artistic laboratory?‹ – *I think we've come quite far. By means of our metalogue we have negotiated a methodology, which, on the one hand, takes dialogue seriously as a knowledge-creating process, and, on the other, examines dialogue as a knowledge format itself. And during the drift of our dialogue, fully trusting the serendipity principle, during our discursive driftage on coincidence in knowledge theory, via a small detour into ethics in negotiating social protocols, we have unnoticeably come across a new term which seems to be at work in the laboratory. Namely work which is less geared to productivity than to deferring it.* – You mean because SANS PAPIERS didn't produce any utilisable results which could have been written down? Because the laboratory as a working format tills the fields of knowledge without reaping a harvest? – *It seems that the relationship between input and output, which is used as an indicator for economic work efficiency, does not apply to this format. While productivity in terms of economics and business management discourse refers to the creation of added value, in the laboratory, knowledge work seems to be most productive when it concentrates all its efforts on its own utility value.* – You mean on knowledge that applies at that moment and is relevant for that very moment of contemplation. – *And the success of these work processes can no longer be measured according to its immediate efficiency, but in terms of its long-term effects. The success is delayed. This delay, for which the work researcher Manfred Füllsack suggests the term »delayed productivity«[25], is based on the thought of an investment which is only amortised at a much later, unknown point in time. According to the ›delayed productivity‹ principle, the exchange in the laboratory is based on artistic, social, collaborative contributions of thought ...* – ... whose accumulated knowledge is incalculable by its very definition, to stay with your parlance. So a laboratory would be a place where knowledge is produced in ever new ways, necessitating the question of methodology to be constantly reformulated, to enable coin-

---

25 | Cf. Manfred Füllsack: *Delayed Productivity. Erkundungen zur Zeitlichkeit ›produktiver Arbeit‹,* unpublished lecture script 2007; cf. also: Idem: *Zuviel Wissen? Zur Wertschätzung von Arbeit und Wissen in der Moderne,* Berlin: Avinus 2006, pp. 307ff.

cidental knowledge. But if something worth knowing may perhaps have been discovered, the participants themselves remain unaware of this. – *Or to put it in another way: the laboratory is nothing but a self-circling, self-birthing metalogue ...*

Translation from German

References

Bateson, Gregory: Ökologie des Geistes. Anthropologische, psychologische, biologische und epistemologische Perspektiven, Frankfurt a.M.: Suhrkamp 1994.

Elkana, Yehuda: Anthropologie der Erkenntnis. Die Entwicklung des Wissens als episches Theater einer listigen Vernunft, Frankfurt a.M.: Suhrkamp 1986.

Foucault, Michel: Die Ordnung der Dinge, Frankfurt a.M.: Suhrkamp 1974.

Foucault, Michel: Die Ordnung des Diskurses, Frankfurt a.M.: Fischer 1998.

Füllsack, Manfred: Delayed Productivity. Erkundungen zur Zeitlichkeit ›produktiver Arbeit‹, unpublished lecture script 2007.

Füllsack, Manfred: Zuviel Wissen? Zur Wertschätzung von Arbeit und Wissen in der Moderne, Berlin: Avinus 2006.

Geertz, Clifford: Dichte Beschreibung. Beiträge zum Verstehen kultureller Systeme, Frankfurt a.M.: Suhrkamp 1983.

Haraway, Donna: Die Neuerfindung der Natur. Primaten, Cyborgs und Frauen, Frankfurt a.M./New York: Campus 1995.

Knorr Cetina, Karin: Wissenskulturen. Ein Vergleich naturwissenschaftlicher Wissensformen, Frankfurt a.M.: Suhrkamp 2002.

Latour, Bruno: Die Hoffnung der Pandora, Frankfurt a.M.: Suhrkamp 2002.

Mazumdar, Pravu: Foucault, Munich: DTV 2001.

Obrist, Hans Ulrich/Vanderlinden, Barbara (eds.): Laboratorium, Antwerp: DuMont 2001.

Online References

www.e-text.org/text/Platon%20-%20Theaitetos.pdf.
www.insituproductions.net/_eng/framesetl.html.

Artistic Research

Rehearsals for Where Does The Light Go When It's Gone
by João Fiadeiro, Photo: João Fiadeiro

The Mode of Knowledge Production
in Artistic Research

Henk Borgdorff

The standard model of scientific research, which distinguishes between basic or fundamental research, applied research and experimental development, still holds sway in the world of higher education and research. It also serves as the basis for statistical comparisons of governmental efforts in research and development, such as those conducted by the Organisation for Economic Co-operation and Development (OECD) and delineated in its »Frascati Manual«.[1] The same threefold distinction is encountered (always in the same hierarchy) in the mission statements of national and supranational research organisations that monitor research quality. The League of European Research Universities, for instance, is »[...] committed to the creation of new knowledge through basic research, which is the ultimate source for innovation in society.«[2] The Royal Netherlands Academy of Arts and Sciences states in its mission paper (which is »to ensure the quality of scientific research in the Netherlands«) that »the fundamental research carried out today will provide a basis for the applied research of tomorrow and, in turn, for the practical application of science in the future.«[3] And the Union of the German Academies of Sciences and Humanities devotes special attention to the support and coordination of fundamental research.[4]

---

1 | OECD: *Frascati Manual – Proposed Standard Praxis for Surveys on Research and Experimental Development*, Paris: OECD 2002.

2 | *www.leru.org* from 10 March 2007.

3 | *www.knaw.nl* from 10 March 2007.

4 | »The chief aim of the academies having organised themselves in a standing Conference is to coordinate their activities, notably in the field of basic research.« (Retrieved from the European Science Foundation website, *www. esf.org* from 4 March 2007)

The standard model as set out in the »Frascati Manual« has attracted criticism from various quarters. Research on the history of science and on science policy has shown that the factors now important to technological advancement and economic growth are more complex and multifarious than the standard model would lead us to believe. The intellectual and social organisation of the sciences in the early 21st century is likewise highly diversified, and different types of knowledge are generated in different specific contexts.[5]

In their book »The New Production of Knowledge«[6] from 1994, Michael Gibbons and his co-authors sparked a considerable debate with their proposed amendment to this standard research model. They described how »*Mode 1*-science« must now make increasing room for »*Mode 2*-knowledge production«. *Mode 1* refers to traditional, discipline-bound research that takes place in academic contexts (mostly universities); it is characterised by organisational homogeneity, uniformity and stability. The quality of *Mode 1* research – which is primarily focused on the finding of truths or the justification of beliefs – is assessed and controlled within each discipline by a peer review system, in which largely individual contributions are assessed by colleagues who are considered competent to judge quality by virtue of their own previous individual contributions.

Mode 2 research, in contrast, is said to take place in the »context of application«. It is interdisciplinary or trans-disciplinary, involving both academics and other parties. Research is not conducted exclusively in homogeneous, uniformly structured universities, but is more localised in heterogeneous, diversified, often transitory configurations, made up of universities, governmental agencies, industrial research centres, non-governmental organisations and other players that assemble around a particular set of problems. Specific attention is given to whether the outcomes are socially, economically or politically relevant, competitive or feasible. The quality of the research is assessed and audited by the various parties involved. Both »peers« from the respective faculties and other stakeholders critically examine research questions and priorities as well as findings. This »extended peer review« is one of the attributes that distinguish *Mode 2* knowledge production, in conjunction with the imperative of social robustness and reflexivity, organisational diversity, and the problem-focused teamwork that transcends disciplines.

The Frascati Manual defines six fields of science: natural sciences,

5 | Cf. Richard Whitley: *The Intellectual and Social Organisation of the Sciences*, Oxford/New York: Oxford University Press 2000, p. ix.

6 | Michael Gibbons/Camille Limoges/Helga Nowotny (eds.): *The New Production of Knowledge – The Dynamics of Science and Research in Contemporary Societies*, London/Thousand Oaks/New Delhi: Sage 1994.

engineering and technology, medical sciences, agricultural sciences, social sciences and humanities. The first five areas dominate the science debate. Although Gibbons and his co-authors did pay some heed to the status and role of the humanities in the academic system, they focused mainly on new developments in such areas as biomedical sciences, information technology and environmental studies. This makes it difficult to determine *whether*, and if so *how*, an activity like artistic research might be understood within the entire realm of »knowledge production«. The growing institutional and intellectual autonomy of scientific research vis-à-vis academic research in the humanities[7] has sharpened the contrast between ›scientific‹ knowledge and other types of knowledge and understanding, thus further complicating any comparison. Artistic research has only just begun its ›academic career‹, and much of this research still takes place in arts colleges that are organisationally and intellectually rather segregated from the rest of the academic and university world. Furthermore, its claim to have a unique research object, a specific kind of embodied knowledge and a distinct methodological framework[8] has kept artistic research outside the debate from the very beginning. On closer inspection, artistic research does not even readily fit into the *Mode 1/Mode 2* dichotomy of knowledge production as proposed by Gibbons. With a bit of goodwill, artistic research can sometimes be understood within the frameworks of traditional *Mode 1* academic research, and at other times as a prime example of *Mode 2* knowledge production – depending on which topics, questions, objectives and methods of research have been chosen. In the discussion that follows I will examine to what extent the five characteristics of *Mode 2* knowledge production – context of application, trans-disciplinary orientation, heterogeneity and diversity, accountability and reflexivity, and extended peer review – may be pertinent to artistic research.

Owing to its close ties with the art world and with art criticism, artistic research is not primarily an academic (university) matter, but is carried out in what Gibbons calls the »context of application« in his description of *Mode 2*. The research questions and topics, the methods, and the means of documenting and communicating the research are often motivated by what seems appropriate within art practice – a practice which, since it transects the realms of knowledge, morality (politics), beauty and daily life, has its own dynamics and logic that cannot be corralled into traditional academic structures. Yet all this notwithstand-

---

7 | Cf. Richard Whitley: *The Intellectual and Social Organisation of the Sciences*, l.c., p. 278.Whitley opposes here »scientific« research – increasingly accommodated in autonomous research institutes – to »academic« research in universities.

8 | Cf. Henk Borgdorff: »The Debate on Research in the Arts«, in: *Dutch Journal of Music Theory* 12, 1 (January 2007), pp. 1–17.

ing, artistic research can sometimes very well be understood as purely disciplinary experimental research into the aesthetic and formal qualities and universal regularities of elements that constitute an artwork or creative process. Materials research is one example, and so are the more conceptual research practices in traditions like fundamental art, experimental theatre or electronic music.

If multidisciplinary research is understood as collaboration between different disciplines around a particular topic, leaving the theoretical premises and working methods of the separate disciplines intact (typical of many art-science collaborations), then interdisciplinary or trans-disciplinary research is characterised by a partial interpenetration of practice, theory and method, in response to research questions arising from highly specific, local contexts. Especially the type of artistic research that combines the aesthetic project and the creative process with questions and topics from broader areas of life (such as globalisation, identity, gender or mediality, to mention some common ones) may be characterised as trans-disciplinary research if the synthesis achieved in the artwork has something additional (or different) to offer, both conceptually and perceptually, to the outcome that would have resulted from a single-discipline approach. Such trans-disciplinary research is characterised by a relinquishment of the specific (epistemological or aesthetic) foundations of one's own discipline (which were non-existent anyway), a continual adaptation of the recursive research process based on the input from the various fields of activity, and a certain pragmatism and diversity in the choice of concepts and methods. In the creation of images, sounds, narratives and experiences, the research delivers context-related knowledge and understandings of the areas of life it touches upon. But, as pointed out above in relation to the research context, *intra*-disciplinary research (research operating within the frameworks defined by a particular discipline) is also very common in the realm of the arts. For instance, research *in* performance practice *on* the performance practice of historical music, or choreographic research *in* and *on* specific movement potentials, often cannot be, and does not wish to be, understood as research that transcends disciplines. Hence, trans-disciplinary orientation, the second attribute of *Mode 2* knowledge production, is also not wholly compatible with what we understand by artistic research.

The remarkable growth in the number of collaborative ventures involving artists and scientists, artists and civic organisations or communities, artists and businesses, seems to point towards a heterogeneous, diversified organisation of artistic research. Research no longer takes place exclusively in studios, rehearsal rooms and workspaces, but also ›on site‹ – in the communities and settings where the collaboration arose. Many of the research findings, too, are disseminated beyond theatres, concert halls and museums. Nevertheless, heterogeneity and

organisational diversity are still not distinguishing characterist
artistic research. The bulk of the creation and transfer of knowledg
understandings which are articulated in artistic research still occi
settings built or fitted out for artists – in places like studios, theatres,
film houses, music venues, performance spaces and galleries, which,
for all their differences, are characterised by a certain organisational
homogeneity and similarity. Obviously there are also ›alternative provid-
ers‹: creative workspaces, informal art spaces and organisations, fringe
venues and other locations. But such organisations and venues in the
margins of the art world demarcate the mainstream. The institutional
and social partitions between art practice, scientific practice and moral
practice, which arose in the 18th century, can still be seen today in the
relative homogeneity and uniformity of the organisations and spaces
where these practices are carried out.

Social accountability and reflexivity – that is, an awareness of the
impact that research has (or might have) on the public sphere, and the
associated feedback that may influence the choice of research topic, the
direction of the research, and the interpretation and communication of
the findings – are further characteristics of the type of research that Gibbons and his co-authors call *Mode 2*. If the aim (to use Karl Marx's words)
is not just to interpret the world but to change it, then the research agenda
is determined not only by the challenges arising within a discipline, but
by the demands of the surrounding contexts as well. Yet the agenda of
artistic research seems to run counter to this kind of accountability and
reflexivity. Art often takes an antithetical stance towards the existing
world, and it delivers the unsolicited and the unexpected. This is its very
strength. At the same time, commitment and reflexivity are inseparably
bound up with the production of art – not in the form of demand and
supply, but in the conveyance of a ›narrative‹ in the materiality of the
medium which can be understood as a commentary on the existing
world and an opening to the other, the unknown. This applies equally to
textual theatre as to the most abstract kinds of music. The performative,
world-constituting and world-revealing power of art lies in its ability to
disclose to us new vistas, experiences and insights that bear upon our
relationship with the world and with ourselves.

As to the assessment of quality in artistic research, the following
developments can be observed. Just as peer review is the basis of quality control in the scientific world, the art world also conducts its own
form of »peer review«. The prominent role played today by mediators
like curators, programmers and critics might make us forget that the
artists themselves ultimately also belong to the ›forum of equals‹ that
determines what matters and what does not, what has quality and what
does not. As we have seen, *Mode 2* research is subject to extended peer
review – the value and quality of the research is judged by the stakehold-

ers involved in the research process. To a certain extent, the same is true of artistic research, albeit mainly where collaboration with others takes place or where the research is carried out on behalf of or commissioned by a third party. And in activities like doctoral research, the tendency is to involve academics as well as artists in evaluating the artistic research, since they have already attained the necessary qualifications to assess the merits of the discursive practice that accompanies the research. This is not the right place to discuss this type of extended peer review. By and large, though, the quality of artistic research is judged by the art field itself, as is customary in *Mode 1*. The fact that artists use other channels for this than academic articles in top-ranking journals does not alter this principle.

The five characteristics of *Mode 2* knowledge production – context of application, trans-disciplinary orientation, heterogeneity and diversity, accountability and reflexivity, and extended peer review – thus apply to artistic research only some of the time, and usually not at all or only partially. What can we learn from this? On the one hand, it could give support to the argument that artistic »research« was kept out of the »Frascati Manual« for good reason.[9] If it really does differ so much from *Mode 2* research (and from *Mode 1* research as well), then one might be justified in asking whether it is even research in the real sense of the word at all. Its context is entirely different – the context of the art world, not that of science or technology. Academic research *on* art (as performed in the meanwhile well-established humanities disciplines) is certainly a respectable undertaking, but even though sports sciences and political sciences also have their own places in the university system, no one would dream of elevating sports or politics *per se* to the status of research activities. Mutatis mutandis, this should apply to the arts as well, however reflexive or exploratory their practices might be. Hence, the interdisciplinary or trans-disciplinary nature of many artistic practices, their organisational diversity, their involvement in other areas of life, and their quality assessment procedures would not be sufficient grounds in themselves for lifting »artistic research« to the level of academic or scientific research.

A second, opposing conclusion may also be drawn. The *sui generis* nature of artistic research practices can actually be seen as casting a critical light on the very dichotomy between *Mode 1* and *Mode 2* as put forward by Gibbons. That dichotomy has already been criticised by various parties as excessively rigid.[10] It does insufficient justice to the divergent ways

---

9 | Artistic research is explicitly excluded from the Distribution List of Fields of Science and Technology in the »Frascati Manual«. Cf. OECD: *Frascati Manual*, l.c., p. 67.

10 | Cf. f.ex. Richard Whitley: *The Intellectual and Social Organisation of the Sciences*, l.c., p. 278.

in which knowledge and understanding are defined, generated and disseminated in the widely different domains of research and development. The dissimilarities between academic disciplines like biotechnology, economics, historiography and law are so great in terms of epistemology, methodology, internal dynamics and social organisation that it is hard to identify either *Mode 1* or *Mode 2* research there. From this point of view, artistic research practice does not differ any more from the practices in laboratories or cultural historiography than the latter differ from econometrics or architecture. There are therefore no good reasons to exclude artistic research from the broad domain of academic and technological endeavour, or of research and development in the sense of the »Frascati Manual«. In fact, even though artistic research may not always be easy to incorporate into existing discipline or academic structures, its distinctive ontological, epistemological and methodological framework, its social and intellectual organisation, and its specific forms of commitment, talent development and quality assurance all serve to highlight what academic research could also potentially be – a thorough and sensitive investigation, exploration and mobilisation of the affective and cognitive propensities of the human mind in their coherence, and of the artistic products of that mind. This means that artistic research, through its quest for fundamental understanding, is equally dedicated to broadening our perspectives and enriching our minds as it is to enriching our world with new images, narratives, sounds and experiences.

References

Borgdorff, Henk: »The Debate on Research in the Arts«, in: *Dutch Journal of Music Theory* 12, 1 (January 2007), pp. 1–17.
Gibbons, Michael/Limoges, Camille/Nowotny, Helga (eds.): *The New Production of Knowledge – The Dynamics of Science and Research in Contemporary Societies*, London/Thousand Oaks/New Delhi: Sage 1994.
OECD: *Frascati Manual – Proposed Standard Praxis for Surveys on Research and Experimental Development*, Paris: OECD 2002.
Whitley, Richard: *The Intellectual and Social Organisation of the Sciences*, Oxford/New York: Oxford University Press 2000.

Online References

www.esf.org.
www.knaw.nl.
www.leru.org.

Artistic Research as an Expanded Kind of Choreography Using the Example of Emio Greco|PC

The last five years have witnessed interesting developments in education policy in the Netherlands. Hopefully, the positive effect of these
developments will not be limited to academies and art schools, but will
also spread to affect artists and the arts in general.

Alongside traditional teaching practice, a series of research groups
(or *lectorate* as they are known in Dutch) are being funded. The express
purpose of these groups is to expand and regenerate existing educational practice at art schools with current artistic research projects.
The resulting initiatives – and particularly the work undertaken by
my own group Art Practice and Development – do not in any way
aim to imitate traditional academic models. Rather, a great variety
of artists are invited to further develop their practical proposals and
test out their individual methods at the Amsterdam School of the
Arts.[1]

It is no secret that these new opportunities for artistic research
projects were been initiated or even called for by the artists themselves. The *lectorate* scheme is a pure state intervention, which was
introduced in the Netherlands around five years ago. (This development, incidentally, is not limited to the Netherlands; Flanders is
also experiencing an intensive process of academisation; in Switzer-

---

1 | The working group »Art Practice and Development« was founded at the end
of 2003. It operates on an inter-faculty basis, and with no fixed boundaries
between the school and its professional environment. Besides individual
research projects, it runs an artist-in-residence programme and a great many
joint projects with venues, festivals and faculties. Cf. *www.lectoraten.ahk.nl*
from 25 March 2007.

land too, public funding policy has now been very closely linked to research.)[2]

This is due to a worrying development at art schools and technical colleges, which are increasingly defining themselves according to the current labour market and dedicating too much of their application-oriented teaching to concrete job-training. To take the example of theatre, this means that courses in directing, acting, dance or dramaturgy become stuck in traditional occupational images, barely contributing to contemporary developments or provoking innovative art forms. Teaching is based on what has already proved its value and therefore belongs to the canon of knowledge generally accepted as necessary to practising a certain profession or discipline within familiar contexts. In the worst case scenario, students' abilities are only judged according to vocational rather than artistic practice, a minor distinction which in my opinion is of fundamental significance in the reinterpretation of higher education in the arts.[3]

This development was of particular concern to the Ministry of Education and Science because:

- it has led to an alarmingly increasing distance to the academic discourse within Holland's dual education system (i.e. the strict separation of universities on the one hand, and art schools and technical colleges, on the other);
- art schools and technical colleges may not be able to stand up to the qualitative comparison within Europe required by the »Bologna Agreement«;
- publicly funded teaching is restricted to the predominant professional operating systems and only makes a negligible contribution to social innovation.

The fear was of a downright paralysis of educational practice, insufficient ties to the contemporary art scene, widespread isolation from international developments as well as alienation from a social, economic and cultural reality undergoing dramatic change.

---

2 | The most prominent institutions in Flanders are the IvOK (Institute for Practice Based Research in the Arts) at the K.U. Leuven and the Arts Platform at the Universitaire Associatie Brussel (University Association of Brussels). Cf. *http://associatie.kuleuven.be/eng/ivok/index.htm* from 25 March 2007 and *www.vub.ac.be/english/infoabout/associatie/platform.html* from 25 March 2007.

3 | Ute Meta Bauer's collection of essays on new artistic approaches to higher artistic education is still very topical: Ute Meta Bauer (ed.): *Education, Information, Entertainment. Neue Ansätze künstlerischer Hochschulbildung*, Vienna: edition selene 2001.

Accordingly, the aim of the later research offensive was formulated very firmly and established as an ›engine of innovation‹ in a dynamic mix of teaching, research and practice. (Although I restrict myself to the arts here, this measure naturally applied to the entire spectrum of technical colleges and the most varied faculties from the fields of technology, economics, education science, health, the media etc.).[4] This forced the art schools to undergo comprehensive ›upgrading‹ (though they still do not have the right to award doctorates, a privilege reserved for the universities) and they are now well on the way to developing a very specific alternative which is slowly beginning to present a challenge to academic activity: for in the lively debate regarding applied or artistic research, we have deliberately refrained from following the Anglo-Saxon model and made a conscious effort to maintain the differences between the education systems, preferring a productive coexistence of differing approaches.

The debate focuses on the mode of research (and its relationship to art) as well as its knowledge content (and its distinctiveness) in the light of existing and generally accepted research methods. When, the question is asked, can artistic practice be considered research? And what is the subject of this research – the result or the process? Does not all art – or do not all creative processes – inherently have a research quality? Must this process, for instance, have the scientific qualities of being systematic, integrated within a context, methodologically comprehensible and verifiable? And must (textual) publication make it accessible to the general public? Or is this objectification replaced by a certain subjectification, shaped by the experience of the artist whose work it is?

The argument is repeated when it comes to the issue of knowledge. Again, the distinction is made between theoretical and practical knowledge, with synonyms for practical knowledge such as embodied, tacit or implicit knowledge. Knowledge, anyway, which presupposes a fundamentally different way of understanding. But does that also mean that this type of cognition cannot be compared with other disciplines or supplemented with other approaches? Should artistic research even get involved in a debate on exclusivity (of differences)?[5]

Does not dance in particular (especially the improvisational dance practices of the last 30 years) focus on the complex relationship between

4 | For a complete overview of related research projects at art schools and technical colleges in the Netherlands see *www.lectoren.nl* from 25 March 2007.

5 | My colleague Henk Borgdorff, who leads the »Art Theory and Research« working group at the Amsterdam School of the Arts, has provided a very comprehensive account of the international debate on artistic research and the meta-theoretical discourse.
Cf. *www.ahk.nl/lectoraten/onderzoek/debate.pdf* from 25 March 2007.

body and mind, theory and practice? The tension between conscious thought and sensuous movement is a subject the American dancer and choreographer Steve Paxton always comes back to:

When we use body/mind we are just trying to deal with the fact that there seems not to be a word which contains both consciousness and all of sensation and the ability to move and create sensation or to move yourself and create sensations by the way you are dancing [...] [Then] the mind can be seen as being partly consciousness and partly physical.[6]

The »Art Practice and Development« working group is specifically concerned with the questions, methods and themes that artists approach us with when they wish to combine them with research opportunities. We assume that artists have long had their own, equivalent means of knowledge production, that they have appropriated research practices and that they should not necessarily be subjected to the conditions of the knowledge system prevalent in the academic establishment.

From the first »Bureau de Recherche« set up by the Surrealists, to Peter Brook's »Centre International de Recherche Theatrale« (CIRT), from Brecht's VERSUCHEN to James Lee Byars' WORLD QUESTION CENTER[7] there is a long tradition of lively artistic research which continues to this day, a testament to the need of artists to learn more about their own practice and to make their findings available to others. Artistic research has its own history, present and future. Correspondingly, as cultural critic Sarat Maharaj concluded in a detailed essay on Artistic Research: »Many of us must feel we've been doing ›artistic research‹ for years – without quite calling it that.«[8]

The dance theatre ensemble Emio Greco|PC is an interesting example, as over the last few years it has consciously expanded its work beyond the production or re-staging of old pieces. The ensemble has, on the one hand, already significantly contributed worldwide to public debates about contemporary dance in its so-called »Dance & Discourse Salons« (initiated parallel to their international guest-performances). It has done

---

6 | Steve Paxton op. cit. Sophie Lycouris: *Destabilising Dancing: Tensions between the Theory and Practice of Improvisational Performance*, dissertation, University of Surrey, September 1996, p. 91.

7 | As part of a ritual performance James Lee Byars incessantly asks fellow artists what question they ask themselves: »What question contributes to your own evolving sense of knowledge?« Cf. *www.edge.org/questioncenter.html* from 25 March 2007.

8 | Sarat Maharaj: »Unfinishable Sketch of ›An Unknown Object in 4D‹: scenes of artistic research«, in: Annette W. Balkema/Henk Slager (eds.): *Artistic Research*, Amsterdam/New York: Lier & Boog 2004, p. 39.

so for a long time and on an international basis. But on the other hand, EG|PC has now been around for ten years: veteran protagonist Bertha Bermudez has left the stage (but not the ensemble), and the choreographer and dancer Emio Greco also no longer wants to perform in all the pieces. The group now has to decide whether and in what way it can pass on its work to a younger generation and how it can maintain its repertoire. This is a problem the group shares with many contemporary choreographers and dancers.[9]

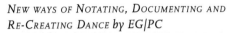

New ways of Notating, Documenting and Re-Creating Dance by EG|PC

Photo: Chris Ziegler

As artists-in-residence at the Amsterdam School of the Arts, EG|PC 2004–05 finally got the long-sought-after opportunity to examine the topic of »transfer« in an educational environment. This involved teaching their own methods of training and parts of their significant choreographies as well as discussing all the issues bound up with the subject in three consecutive salons with national and international theorists, dramaturges, critics and students. Direct results of this collective undertaking include the current research project New ways of Notating, Documenting and Re-creating Dance, and the Accademia Mobile – the company's mobile training centre – which has been on tour since 2006.

---

9 | The acronym PC stands for the director/choreographer Pieter C. Scholten, also a founding member and, along with Greco, artistic director of the ensemble right from the start. The work of Emio Greco|PC, their salons and the newly founded Accademia Mobile are fully documented. Cf. *www.emiogrecopc.nl* from 25 March 2007.

For EG|PC, the question of imparting practice and the need to gain an objective view of one's own art is indissolubly bound up with the dilemma of dance as an ephemeral art, the material nature of human presence and its continual disappearance. As dance theorist André Lepecki already asked in the very first salon: »Where does dance come to rest after it has been done? Where does dance move to and how is it revived in the memory during writing?«[10]

If the memory of and the search for the traces left by experiencing dance are to go beyond the written word, other media have to be applied and the debate needs to include the actual performance as well as the artistic process involved in its creation, which is even less perceptible than the final product.

Once the performance is over, all that is at stake in the process of making, all investment in the process as well as the post-production life of the work, tends to fall into oblivion. Neither festivals nor theatre venues make the effort of presenting the work besides the performance as its actualized product. The knowledge acquired, the tools developed in the working process and in collaboration, artists carry on with themselves. Rare are the opportunities where the knowledge of the artists themselves, rational and methodological as well as subjective and experiential, can be shared with a wider public.[11]

NEW WAYS OF NOTATING, DOCUMENTING AND RE-CREATING DANCE is an attempt to create a particular system of notation which is derived from the choreographic work of EG|PC; it is suitable for both archiving and helping to understand and learn from its specific vocabulary and way of working. In the first phase, while they were still in residence, a documentary film was made about the systematically developed DOUBLE SKIN/DOUBLE MIND workshop, which already contained significant elements of the later idea to create a complex digital resource in the form of an interactive installation, such as filmed dance movements, discursive descriptions of basic methodology (by dancers, choreographers and students, gathered in a *glossary*), as well as the edited and compiled presentation of years of teaching.[12]

The interdisciplinary project team proceeds on the assumption that

---

10 | Ingrid van Schijndel: »Dance and Discourse, Reflections from the Practice: the Salon series of Emio Greco | PC«, in: *Company in School, Between Experiment and Heritage*, Amsterdam 2007, p. 8.

11 | Igor Dobricic/Bojana Cvejic: *Before and After the Show: Unfolding the Working Process*, part of the cultural programme »Almost Real« of the Alkantara Festival, Lisbon, June 2006. Cf. *www.almostreal.org* from 25 March 2007.

12 | DOUBLESKIN/DOUBLE MIND, a documentary film by Maite Bermudez, premiered at the Cinedans Festival in Amsterdam, July 2006.

the complex nature of dance cannot be adequately represented by a single technology. On the contrary: all participants are acutely aware that no single means of recording can do justice to what dance actually is.

The project therefore uses a variety of media and methods: Bertha Bermudez and Emio Greco have internalised the dance of the company and are the driving forces behind the project; Scott deLahunta, author and dance theorist, is comparing four current choreographic experiments with the aim of producing a choreographic resource;[13] Frederic Bevilacqua is developing the GESTURE ANALYSIS PROGRAM at the Paris IRCAM Institute. Marion Bastien and Elian Mirzabekiantz are contributing the well-known dance notation systems of Laban and Benesh; and finally Chris Ziegler, who was already involved in the production of Forsythe's CD-ROM IMPROVISATION TECHNOLOGIES ten years ago, is responsible for bringing together all these different approaches.

In joint working sessions, the various sources of information not only supplement each other, they also establish their respective limits and needs for development.

Despite this wealth of subject-specific research, it is still worth questioning the extent to which *what one does*, the physical sensations of the dancer, the mental note-taking or even the intention can actually be conveyed. William Forsythe, for his part, has limited its scope of representation:

We are not trying to recreate the experience of the piece, or the genesis of the piece, it's not etymological, it's not archaeological, it's not historical, it's not any of that. It's simply about saying watch space become occupied with complexity.[14]

Particularly in dance we might assume some contradiction if artistic processes and the immediacy of performance are externalised through mechanical means of documentation.

---

13 | Alongside EG|PC deLahunta is also working on comparable projects with Wayne McGregor, Siobhan Davies and William Forsythe. Cf. Scott deLahunta/Norah Zuniga Shaw: »Constructing Memory: Creation of the Choreographic Resource«, in: Ric Allsopp/Scott deLahunta (eds.): *Performance Research: Digital Resources* 11, 4 (forthcoming in fall 2007).

14 | Ibid., no page designation.

Screenshot from Chris Ziegler's preliminary design for a menu structure for the interactive installation of the NOTATION-Project, featuring Emio Greco, February 2007

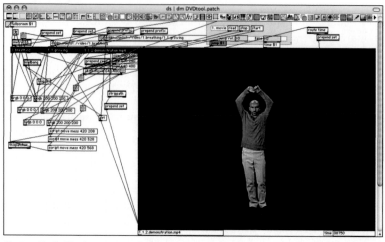

Photo: Chris Ziegler

On this point, the theorist Susan Melrose put forward an interesting proposal for a performative archive. The kind of archive Melrose is proposing is not an archive that conserves something that would otherwise be lost. It is not an archive that comes *after* the artwork itself has been completed. Melrose claims that all works, simply because they are compositions, choreographies or performances, already contain their own archives. »Because it is a spatio-temporal-organization, blocked in some sense, to permit repetition and transmission.«[15] »The time of the archive«[16] is present at all stages of the artistic process, and, in the interpretation of Melrose, is also the medium that completes the circle and generates new artworks and new creative processes.

There is the time before making the work (when it is thought about, in some manner or another); the times of making itself; the time of finishing, and the time of the finished work, when it has emerged, and been identified as such, and – so to speak – put out there. And then comes the time of the

---

15 | Susan Melrose, Transcription of a paper given at the conference »Performance as Knowledge«, ResCen, Middlesex University, May 2006. Cf. *www.mdx.ac.uk/rescen/archive/PaK_may06/PaK06_transcripts4_1.html* from 25 March 2007.

16 | Ibid.

archive, which tends, explicitly or implicitly, formally to thematise and allow reflection on time past and allow that effect of breaking and picking up again.[17]

The second phase of NEW WAYS OF NOTATING, DOCUMENTING AND RE-CREATING DANCE is completed with the documentary film and the publication of the prototype of Chris Ziegler's interactive installation.[18] In the third phase, which has already begun with new additions to the team and new institutional partners, the project will devote itself to debating the difficult question of how means of recording not only serve to analyse and document works of art, but can also function as a type of »real-time feedback« (Scott deLahunta) and flow directly into the creative process again.

This is a big step to take and it will undoubtedly present a great challenge to the ensemble and the organisational format of our project. Artistic research is obviously not a soliloquy. If we want to take the potential of such ventures seriously, we have to continue expanding interdisciplinary and cross-institutional cooperation between teaching, science and artistic practice. Here at the Amsterdam School for the Arts – at least in the context of the given possibilities, that is the conclusion we have come to.

Translation from German

---

17 | Ibid.

18 | Cinedans Festival 2007, cf. *www.cinedans.nl* from 25 March 2007.

References

Bauer, Ute Meta (ed.): *Education, Information, Entertainment. Neue Ansätze künstlerischer Hochschulbildung*, Vienna: edition selene 2000.

deLahunta, Scott/Zuniga Shaw, Norah: »Constructing Memory: Creation of the Choreographic Resource«, in: Ric Allsopp/Scott deLahunta (eds.): *Performance Research: Digital Resources* 11, 4 (forthcoming in fall 2007).

Dobricic, Igor/Cvejic, Bojana: *Before and After the Show: Unfolding the Working Process*, part of the cultural programme »Almost Real« of the Alkantara Festival, Lisbon, June 2006, *www.almostreal.org*.

Lycouris, Sophie: *Destabilising Dancing: Tensions between the Theory and Practice of Improvisational Performance*, dissertation, University of Surrey, September 1996.

Maharaj, Sarat: »Unfinishable Sketch of ›An Unknown Object in 4D‹: scenes of artistic research«, in: Annette W. Balkema/Henk Slager (eds.): *Artistic Research*, Amsterdam/New York: Lier & Boog 2004, pp. 39–58.

Melrose, Susan: Transcription of a paper given at the conference »Performance as Knowledge«, ResCen, Middlesex University, May 2006, *www.mdx.ac.uk/rescen/archive/PaK_may06/PaK06_transcripts4_1.html*.

Schijndel, Ingrid van: »Dance and Discourse, Reflections from the Practice: the Salon series of Emio Greco | PC«, in: *Company in School, Between Experiment and Heritage*, Amsterdam 2007, p. 8.

Online References

http://associatie.kuleuven.be/eng/ivok/index.htm.
www.ahk.nl/lectoraten/onderzoek/debate.pdf.
www.cinedans.nl.
www.edge.org/questioncenter.html.
www.emiogrecopc.nl.
www.lectoraten.ahk.nl.
www.lectoren.nl.
www.vub.ac.be/english/infoabout/associatie/platform.html.

Talking about Scores:
William Forsythe's Vision
for a New Form of »Dance Literature«

Rebecca Groves, Norah Zuniga Shaw und Scott deLahunta

In the following three-part essay, Rebecca Groves introduces the vision of William Forsythe and the Forsythe Foundation for creating a new kind of »dance literature« for a wide, interactive readership. Norah Zuniga Shaw elaborates on the project, describing procedures involved in developing an on-line interactive score for the piece ONE FLAT THING, REPRODUCED; how a team of individuals (designers, dancers, specialists from other disciplines etc.) is working in dialogue with Forsythe and other advisors in an iterative design process.[1] Building on some of Zuniga Shaw's closing questions, Scott deLahunta concludes the essay with observations drawn from earlier and similar initiatives.

MOTION BANK:
Investing in Dance Knowledge

By Rebecca Groves

The knowledge inherent in dance is notoriously difficult to capture and to document. In spite of the obstacles, choreographer William Forsythe insists that dance practitioners today need to develop a new kind of »dance literature« – or a set of core visual references – to stimulate the exchange of ideas and innovation in the discipline. In order for the art of dance to advance beyond its present state, Forsythe argues, an active

---

1 | »Iterative Design« is a well-known methodology utilized in the creation of interactive multi-media projects based on a cyclic process of prototyping, testing, analyzing and refining a work-in-progress.

archive of vivid representations of the ideas and structures that make certain kinds of choreography work should be made accessible to students and professionals in a wide range of practices. A large part of Forsythe's vision for amassing a body of dance research references also entails encouraging dancers to become better informed about recent research in fields such as cognitive science, architecture, aesthetic theory and phenomenology; to learn more about how moving bodies are perceived. More importantly, however, he constantly encourages dance artists to look for new ways to question their own practices and received ideologies from their own training and work environments. Forsythe says, »Perhaps our practices are outdated or can be improved. How can we doubt our own processes and question our own methods?«²

Forsythe conceives of his own choreographic work as a rigorous process of movement research. His current 18-member performance ensemble, The Forsythe Company, operates as much like a think tank as it does as a dance company. For years, he has been developing methods for training dancers and empowering them to become the kind of innovative collaborators with whom he enjoys working. In the mid-1990s, Forsythe began developing a multimedia dancer training program to codify and teach principles of improvisation he had created. In a series of over 100 short video segments, Forsythe performed demonstrations for the camera that were then marked with animated graphics tracing his movement paths and mapping spatial relationships in and around his body. IMPROVISATION TECHNOLOGIES: A TOOL FOR THE ANALYTICAL DANCE EYE emerged over the course of several prototypes for use in the rehearsal studio before being refined and released as a commercial CD-ROM in 1999. By clearly visualising ways of perceiving and thinking about movement, IMPROVISATION TECHNOLOGIES offered a new pedagogical tool for professional and student dancers. It provided audiences with a set of analytical skills to become better readers of dance performances. Furthermore, it created a legible graphical language and an accessible conceptual framework through which architects and researchers in other non-dance fields could approach dance as an interdisciplinary resource for ideas about space, structure and movement.

Forsythe's latest educational multimedia project, MOTION BANK, begins where IMPROVISATION TECHNOLOGIES left off by analysing how movement can be created and organised over time to create visually compelling choreography. MOTION BANK features a high definition video-based choreographic score and online interdisciplinary learning environment for Forsythe's 18-minute piece, ONE FLAT THING, REPRODUCED. Inspired by the conceptual metaphor of »baroque machinery«, ONE

2 | William Forsythe in conversation with Rebecca Groves, Berkeley, California, 22 February 2007.

FLAT THING, REPRODUCED investigates the formal principle of choreographic counterpoint developed in the ballet tradition of Marius Petipa and George Balanchine and reconceived in the post-modern idiom of such contemporary choreographers as Trisha Brown and Jonathan Burrows. The choreography of ONE FLAT THING, REPRODUCED is particularly exciting to translate into a multimedia choreographic score, due to the challenges it poses for visualising and elaborating a high density of interdependent themes and variations distributed across a network of 17 dancers navigating a landscape of a 20-table grid. However, as will be explored further on in this essay and in keeping with Forsythe's vision, the aim of the interactive score is to enable connections to be made that go far beyond the formal relations between movement phrases and material.

ONE FLAT THING, REPRODUCED by The Forsythe Company

Photo: Dieter Schwer

Literary, political and music critic Edward Said theorised and practiced a mode of »contrapuntal criticism« in which he analysed cultural texts, such as novels and operas, by making poly-vocal connections across cultures, genres and historical periods.[3] Said's aim was to reveal structures within these cultural artefacts that, when considered in relation to one another, destabilised culturally dominant categories of knowledge and furthered alternative strategies for reading these texts anew. Forsythe's vision for a new kind of dance literature seeks to harness the same quality of critical reflection by bringing a far wider range of perspectives and

---

3 | Cf. Edward Said: *Culture and Imperialism*, New York: Vintage Books 1993.

interrelations to bear on choreographic practice than has been done pre-viously. Through the development of new research tools and methods to enable these multiple connections to be made, the Motion Bank project aims to exploit the vital potential for contrapuntal readings to transport the art of dance into a renewed state of socio-cultural relevance.[4]

Researching Dancing

By Norah Zuniga Shaw

»Watch space become occupied with complexity.«[5]

Seventeen dancers fly, slide, reach and twist their bodies within a grid of twenty steel tables. Seemingly on the edge of chaos their actions are controlled by a complex array of interdependencies that challenge and excite your sense of order as you watch. Time slips and slides between constant acceleration and sudden moments of active stillness, elements align and dissolve, dancers come and go, your eyes flicker in search of pattern, seeing and not-seeing the changes that occur.[6] This is One Flat Thing, reproduced.

»This just happens to be dance.«

It could be mathematics or architecture. It is in-formation. It's about attention. It's about autonomy in a system. It is form and flow. It is an expression of a way of thinking that is shared among many forms of knowledge. And in this way, of course, this must be dance. It is a specific expression from within choreographic knowledge and enacted in the thinking dancers' actions. It is complexity theory in motion and it can teach us about human event perception. It is an interdependent system wherein each individual's actions rely on and influence the actions of

---

4 | Motion Bank is currently in development at the Advanced Computing Center for Art and Design (ACCAD) at Ohio State University and due for release online in the summer of 2008. Executive producer: Forsythe Foundation. Co-producers: Ohio State University, the Rotterdam Dance Academy, »Tanzplan Deutschland« and The Forsythe Company.

5 | Quotations excerpted from project meeting and conversation between Norah Zuniga Shaw and William Forsythe, New York City, May 2006.

6 | Working with philosopher and scientist Alva Noë we discovered a shared interest in the phenomena of change blindness in human perception articu-lated by the research of Kevin O'Regan and others cited in Alva Noë: *Action in Perception*, Cambridge: MIT Press 2004.

those around her allowing for a flow between control and randomness. It is a site of knowledge like any other and unlike any other. This is the research space of the project, to define what we know from within dance and in relation to other ways of knowing.

»Revealing the next level of imaginary trace.«

This then is the challenge set out for us by William Forsythe; use ONE FLAT THING, REPRODUCED to create the next level of imaginary trace. This is not a preservation project. It is not for reconstruction or repertory. It is not to help others make their own table dances. Instead it is to create a living artefact that leaves something behind and also elicits new information, new creativity. To do so we must treat the dance as a richly specific research resource. We are striving to locate and define its component parts or what we understand as the data of the piece. Not the choreography but the choreographic and performance structures. There are no existing methods by which to conduct this kind of dance analysis. We are approaching this from within dance and without.

The core of our research involves extensive work with William Forsythe and The Forsythe Company to systematically analyse the material and systems of exchange that make up ONE FLAT THING, REPRODUCED.[7] The research has become a process of developing new methodologies in order to progress. As we parse the dance into its hundreds of component parts we are challenged to determine fluid means of inputting and managing this new data and then using it to draw conclusions. We have used written and drawn notes, personal scoring strategies, copious video documents, spreadsheets (see screenshot), video annotations, and now a database. For dancers it can sometimes be uncomfortable to reduce the lived and performed essence of dancing to data sets that necessarily occlude certain aspects in order to reveal others. The hypothesis driving this process is that there are powerful, less known aspects of choreographic thinking and doing that can be articulated this way and included alongside the less quantifiable ephemera.

---

7 | The core group of Forsythe dancers working on the project are Elizabeth Waterhouse, Chris Roman and Jill Johnson.

Screenshot of evolving tools used for analysis of the dance and managing the information input from The Forsythe Company

Photo: Norah Zuniga Shaw

While working always from within dance, the project also reaches out to invite scholars from multiple disciplines (in what we call our Interdisciplinary Working Group, IWG) to view the piece on video and respond to it from their areas of expertise. After a first viewing, we bring them together in small groups to respond to key principles identified in the piece, pattern, spatial relationships, and so on. This information is chronicled in the form of a Wiki with written transcripts and relevant links. Our IWG feeds and influences the data gathering process and the design of the interactivity (how the users will be able to play with and learn from the piece through media tools) as well as the conceptual basis of the project.

»So show me, show and tell is one of the first things that we do.«

With this growing data set in hand, nothing is off-limits as Forsythe is open to radical reductions as well as elaborate visual embellishment. The team has been viewing and dissecting the complex intertwining pieces of the dance, learning its history and origins, learning with the interdisciplinary working group what it reveals about human perception in complex environments and considering its relationship to complexity science, information aesthetics, and current issues of surface and event in architecture.

The iterative design process continues, as does the pursuit of deeper and more complete data, as the team works to construct visualisations of the dance that stand apart from the dancers. What if everything was reduced to sound and we just listened to the patterns in the dance take place? What if all the interlocking movement themes in this poly-thematic piece were assigned a shape or colour, and then they were placed in space according to their duration and repetition, and finally the cues for each moment were indicated with a burst of light? What animated cloud of shapes and colour would emerge? What would this reveal about the complex system of relationships in the piece? How does this relate to the data visualisation strategies in neuroscience, statistics and bioinformatics? What if we traced each of the dancers' pathways, varying the qualities of the lines according to when they are under, over, or between the tables and then removed the dancers from the picture and let the pathways play out their own? What would we see then? How can we allow the eventual users of this score to change the principles and characteristics of the animations to create their own aesthetic universes from the richly specific data housed in the piece? And what kinds of objects or traces will this leave behind? These are the questions that are central to the project at present.

Working without an Overview

By Scott deLahunta

The concept of dance as a ›site of knowledge‹ begs a number of questions such as what is known, how it is acquired, when expertise is recognised etc. As already described by Groves and Zuniga Shaw, what is important is the possibility of dance knowledge being shareable with other knowledge domains or communities. The idea of expertise is critical here. Forsythe talks about »leading the non-dance expert in and the dance expert out«[8] through exploring the interactive score of One Flat Thing, reproduced, and, as Zuniga Shaw points out, experts from other disciplines (architects, cognitive and neuroscientists, engineers, philosophers) are being consulted during its creation. Still, the status of the knowledge contained in dancing and dance-making is not always seen to be equivalent to that of other domains, and this is implied by the vision that motivates this project in the first place.

Of course, it is apparent that dance is a site of knowledge; based on the existence of a community that has agreed to learn about it and advance this knowledge largely through the production of art-making processes and performances.[9] But its status as a form of knowledge is

8 | Quotation excerpted from project meeting and conversation between Norah Zuniga Shaw and William Forsythe, NYC, May 2006.

9 | There is a useful concept in the social sciences referred to as »communities of practice« in which the concept of knowledge is disassembled into its

largely evaluated on the strength of its contribution as ›art‹ to the public sphere. This evaluation is not always useful for understanding the full nature of what dancing contains; and here is where exchanges with other non-art disciplines and practices can be productive. Other contemporary choreographers, for example, Wayne McGregor (London) and Emio Greco|PC (Amsterdam), are also seeking clarification of the relation of dance as knowledge to other domains.[10] As with Forsythe's Motion Bank project, they do this not only through making dances for an audience, events conforming to the conventions of the field; but through innovating new and sometimes ›unconventional‹ types of traces and artefacts of the dance creation process. Through exploring fresh approaches to documenting, analysing and an/notating their creative work; they deepen their own understanding while simultaneously stimulating the attention of others who may utilise these traces as resources in their own research. All three choreographers are working with interdisciplinary teams from both art and non-art disciplines to investigate these possibilities.

This is not simply abstract thinking, for an important precedent exists in the interactive multimedia CD-ROM Improvisation Technologies. As Groves has already described, enthusiastically received by the dance community, the Improvisation Technologies CD-ROM also attracted the attention of non-dance disciplines. The innovative visualisations and systematic organisation of the materials presents in Forsythe's own words, »just some of the ways of thinking about analysing motion«[11], but it is done in such a way that it enables researchers in other fields to apply this thinking to their own areas. In a term drawn from anthropological practice, the CD-ROM provides one of the first clear »boundary objects« produced within the dance field to invigorate exchanges with other communities of practice.[12]

Whether through graphic visualisation of lectures about danced

---

function in the creation and sustaining of the practice-based relations of a particular community or field. One of the foremost theorists of »Communities of Practice« is Etienne Wenger. Cf. *www.ewenger.com* from 10 April 2007.

10 | Cf. Scott deLahunta/Norah Zuniga Shaw: »Constructing Memory: Creation of the Choreographic Resource«, in: Ric Allsopp/Scott deLahunta (eds.): *Performance Research, Digital Resources Issue* 11, 4 (2007).

11 | William Forsythe in an interview with Nik Haffner. »Observing Motion: an interview with William Forsythe«, in: ZKM Karlsruhe (ed.): *William Forsythe Improvisation Technologies: A Tool for the Analytical Dance Eye* (booklet to accompany CD-ROM), special issue, Ostfildern: Hatje Cantz 2003, p. 20.

12 | The notion of the »boundary object« in anthropological and science studies is seen to be a construct that can foster cooperation and communication among the diverse members of heterogeneous working groups.

movement, gesture tracking and analysis or the annotated segmentation of dance phrases (as in the projects of EG|PC and Wayne McGregor), what these traces and artefacts of dance and dance-making make possible through the setting of certain standards and related measurements is somewhat akin to when maps were created before aerial views. In an essay on music visualisation, long-time Forsythe collaborator, composer and programmer Joel Ryan calls this »working without an overview«[13] when the map had to be built up from what was known on the ground. After enough real measurements from the available information were made, the mapmaker would eventually start to infer new connections from what had been visualised on the page. The IMPROVISATION TECHNOLOGIES CD-ROM provides us with an example of just such a map – a map that reveals dance to be a site of shareable knowledge. It makes a new layer of information, about thinking, about moving, about space and time, explicit; and importantly someone does not have to be a dancer, dance maker or even a dance spectator to find the material on the CD-ROM stimulating and meaningful.

There are many signs that contemporary creative arts, including choreography and dance, has the potential for impact on a wider set of cultural practices (educational, scientific, enterprising, etc).[14] The shift is increasingly marked by discourses and debates regarding knowledge creation and production, sometimes with a lack of criticality. However, there is clearly new territory opening up and new connections to be made in exploring it. To ignore these cultural developments – i.e. the increasing emphasis on arts research – risks losing the opportunity to take part in change that is, inevitably, taking place. One of the difficulties for choreography and dance will be charting this volatile terrain, while sustaining a commitment to what is unique to dance. The researchers and designers working on the interactive score for ONE FLAT THING, REPRODUCED are attempting to do just that. In so doing, they – along with a growing number of other dance tracing and mapping research projects – are providing a form of leadership by example into the 21st century of choreographic and dance practice.

---

13 | Cf. Joel Ryan: »Master Class: Music Visualization«, in: *Making Art of Databases*, Rotterdam: V2/Nai Publishers 2003, p. 62 (accessible at *www.xs4all. nl/˜jr/MuViz.htm* from 10 April 2007).

14 | Cf. conference website: SUMMIT: Non-Aligned Initiatives in Education Culture, Berlin, 24–28 May 2007 – *http://summit.kein.org* from 10 April 2007, and Irit Rogoff's Blog: »Academy as Potentiality«, *http://summit.kein. org/node/191* from 10 April 2007.

References

deLahunta, Scott/Zuniga Shaw, Norah: »Constructing Memory: Creation of the Choreographic Resource«, in: Ric Allsopp/Scott deLahunta (eds.): *Performance Research, Digital Resources Issue* 11, 4 (2007).

Haffner, Nik: »Observing Motion: an interview with William Forsythe«, in: ZKM Karlsruhe (ed.): *William Forsythe Improvisation Technologies: A Tool for the Analytical Dance Eye* (booklet to accompany CD-ROM), special issue, Ostfildern: Hatje Cantz 2003, p. 16–27.

Noë, Alva: *Action in Perception*, Cambridge: MIT Press 2004.

Rogoff, Irit: »Academy as Potentiality«, *http://summit.kein.org/node/191*.

Ryan, Joel: »Master Class: Music Visualization«, in: *Making Art of Databases*, Rotterdam: V2/Nai Publishers 2003, p. 62 (accessible at *www.xs4all.nl/˜jr/MuViz.htm*).

Said, Edward: *Culture and Imperialism*, New York: Vintage Books 1993.

Online References

http://summit.kein.org.

www.ewenger.com.

If you don't know, why do you ask?[1]

An Introduction to the Method

of REAL-TIME COMPOSITION

João Fiadeiro

Preliminary Remarks

This essay examines the method of REAL-TIME COMPOSITION, a system with which I aim to answer many of the questions I ask myself in my capacity as an artist, researcher and teacher. This method forms the basis for my work, and provides me with an important point of reference in a wide-ranging debate about the process of creation, representation and perception in the arts.[2]

---

1 | »One day at Black Mountain College, David Tudor was eating his lunch. A student came over to his table and began asking him questions. David Tudor went on eating his lunch. The student kept on asking questions. Finally, David Tudor looked at him and said, ›If you don't know, why do you ask?‹« John Cage: *Silence*, Middletown: Wesleyan University Press 1961, without page designation.

2 | Being a practical sort of person, I work better if specific questions are directed at me. I waste hours and hours, and get my hands and feet tangled up if I try to put down in words something that I have to draw from the ›nothingness‹ of my mind. When I was confronted with the questions and observations of writer and dance theorist Paula Caspão, a dear friend and close associate, whom I had asked for feedback on the first draft of this text, I was very relieved to finally be dealing with real questions, doubts and fears. This text owes a lot to our correspondence.

Introduction

»Dance doesn't go through the body« is an assertion I made in a tel-
evised debate[3] in Portugal in 1999 on the occasion of the screening of
a documentary film about a Russian school for classical dance[4], which
inspired some dance ›experts‹[5] to meditate on whether the ›suffering‹ of
the students, the ›strictness‹ of the teacher or the training shown ›was a
form of slavery or not‹. What I meant to say was »dance is not just body«.
My assertion essentially gave vent to my impatience at the fact that the
body is invariably treated as the single focus of discussions related to
dance. I am not sure if it was because I was not clear in my formulation
or because of what I really meant, but my comment provoked a general
uproar on the show.

Some months later, RE.AL[6] organised a meeting of choreographers
and philosophers under the title »Does what I do mean anything to
you? The program included the dialogues between the choreographer
Vera Mantero and the philosopher José Gil, the choreographer Francisco
Camacho and the essayist Eduardo Prado Coelho and the philosopher
Nuno Nabais and myself.[7] Our initiative attempted to »remove the body
from dance« and, if only for a day, compare its practice with the process
of thinking and discuss the two disciplines on the same level. In my
contribution, I referred to the above-mentioned TV debate and repeated
my assertion, still with the same erroneous formulation and naively
assuming that this supposedly ›provocative‹ statement would come as
no surprise to a philosopher, who would see its ›obvious contradiction‹.
I remember the casual way I made this statement, again, with no idea of
the controversy it would unleash. Looking back, I realise what feelings
of perplexity were triggered. In both discussion panels, my statement
was interpreted as meaning that I denied that the body was the ›raw

---

3 | Noites Brancas (White Nights) by Pedro Rolo Duarte on RTP2.

4 | Terpsichore's Captives I, 1995, directed by Efim Reznikov, Granat Film
Studio. A film about daily life at the Perm City Ballet School in Perm,
Russia.

5 | Apart from myself, the participants included Maria José Fazenda, dance theo-
retician and, at the time, dance critic; Luísa Taveira, former classical dancer
and the actual dance programmer at the Belém Cultural Center in Lisbon;
as well as Ana Pereira Caldas, director of the Lisbon Dance Conservatory at
the time and the current artistic director of the National Ballet.

6 | RE.AL is a production structure for research and creation in contemporary
dance that I founded in 1990. Cf. *www.re-al.org* from 21 May 2007.

7 | Paula Caspão also took part in the debate and coordinated the edition of the
key contributions to this experience which was published. Cf. RE.AL (ed.):
DOC.LAB, Lisbon: RE.AL 2000.

material‹ of dance. What I meant and mean is that the body is no more fundamental to dance than it is, say, to literature, to photography, the visual arts or any other art form. I merely wanted to draw attention to the urgency of the community that lives and breathes and thinks dance to demand this space, to take dance once and for all ›out of its shell‹, to ›disembody‹ it, so to speak, and thus contribute to a genuinely searching debate – a debate not solely concerned with marking off territory.[8]

Today, I know that the ›body‹ I work with is ›the body that observes what it is doing while doing it‹ and that is why my focus, both as an artist and as a researcher, is not on body ›experience‹ but on its ›representation‹. And this is the body of REAL-TIME COMPOSITION, a method I have been working on since 1997 that struggles with the trained body of the dancer, and with the linguistic conventions of dance. The system I developed over these past ten years is thus not a ›style‹, but rather no more than a tool, a reference map for my collaborators and myself. The method functions rather as a sort of work ethic, a way of looking for different ways of representing things, an openness to the various possibilities of art making.

It is a method which is still very much a work in progress. Many people, among dancers, theoreticians or students, have been and are still actively involved with me in consolidating this system in workshops, laboratories, coaching and above all theoretical discussions. The system aims to provide an answer, as far as possible, to the paradox that the dancer is both the subject and the object of his practice.[9]

---

8 | Regarding this question, Paula Caspão made, in my perspective, a remarkable comment: »Your statement was simply an attempt to say that this body is something more than a body that dances, and more complex than a dance that is a body [...]. Many philosophers, poets and thinkers still make the mistake [...] of seeking the body through dance, departing from an erroneous assumption about the body and about dance, which they believe to reveal the wonderful ›otherness‹ of thinking, and end up finding something that can serve as the basis of all art or even thinking. Dance, for them, is not an art like any other, with a canon of specific works, but the anthropological basis of all the arts and a metaphor for thought itself, but only a metaphor, because dance, despite its movement, remains mute and without words [...].«

9 | In 2001, in on one of the research ateliers I organised in order to practice and think REAL-TIME COMPOSITION, Paula Caspão made this ›premonitory‹ reflection: »The meeting of the body of the reading with the object of the same reading that occurs in this work means, for the composition (in realtime), that the performer must forge this crossover point in him/herself: not as a reader/spectator on the outside (as this would be the location of the spectator) but as a reader/observer of him/herself, seeing his/her own inner and outer self at the same time«.

Real-Time Composition[10]

The method of REAL-TIME COMPOSITION is a system of principles and rules designed to »protect me from what I want«.[11] »›What I want« is exactly what prevents me from ›listening‹ to myself, to the others and the space that surrounds me. ›Listening‹ (with all of my body) is a basic condition for the correct application of the method and, as a consequence, the only way I am sure that each play or each object that I create comes as a revelation, a discovery and not just as a virtuous exercise or a mere confirmation of what I already know.

The core of the REAL-TIME COMPOSITION method, and the focus of this essay, is the moment when the interpreter-improviser[12] is ›caught‹, during the course of an action or thought, by the possibility of a change. This is the moment the ›body-that-sees-what-it-does-while-it-is-doing-it‹ is activated – when confronted with a situation in which a choice has to be made. We refer to this turbulent zone of doubt as the CRITICAL ZONE. When the new coordinates have been fixed, the interpreter-improviser is asked to come back to its previous state (not to be confused with its previous place) and let go of the extreme consciousness associated with the CRITICAL ZONE. We refer to this intermediate phase as the DIG IN. This ›in-out‹ movement (between inside and outside and doing and thinking) is crucial to this method. Just as important as knowing *what* to do during an action is knowing *when* we are ›in‹ and *when* we are ›out‹. This principle, that provides the basis which all the other principles of the method is comprised of rest on, is simple and based on common sense: I can only ›get lost‹ (the condition to protect myself from what I want) if I know where I am.[13] Once the difference between the CRITICAL ZONE and

---

10 | The »real-time« I am talking of here does not, as one might at first suppose, refer to »live« or »instant« compositions as used by improvisers that presumably refer to the »direct« instant the spectator witnesses the composition unfolding before his eyes. The »real-time« I am talking about here is exclusively played out in the mind of the dancer. It is about a temporal interval comprised of the following stages: 1.) a pictorial event, i.e. the result of an external or internal ›accident‹, 2.) its identification (as this or that) as well as the creation of hypotheses of reaction (I could react in this way or that), and finally 3.) the answer that is actually given.

11 | Jenny Holzer, The Survival Series: PROTECT ME FROM WHAT I WANT, New York 1985–86.

12 | The term interpreter-improviser emphasises the fact that an improviser is always already an interpreter of his own actions or of the things he finds during an improvisation.

13 | My first choreography, back in 1989, had the title PLAN(E) TO IDENTIFY THE CENTRE, which reveals the length of time I have been dealing with this ›problem‹.

the DIG IN phase has been established, the performer will be in a position to let go of wanting to ›produce meaning‹ without losing his ability to differentiate between what he does and how he does it. By working on the recognition of the problem and actively waiting, the performer acquires complete freedom[14] to act within a referential cartography.

Sketches of REAL-TIME COMPOSITION by João Fiadeiro

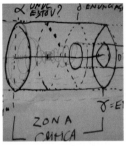 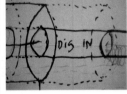 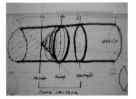

Photos: João Fiadeiro

The challenge and the paradox for the performer that uses and applies the REAL-TIME COMPOSITION method is to develop the ability to 1) distinguish between the CRITICAL ZONE and DIG IN PHASE and 2) be able to live a kind of parallel life during the CRITICAL ZONE by becoming acutely aware of his relationship to his counterpart on the one hand, and the workings of his inner body on the other. This parallel life functions like an »antechamber« for the outside world and prevents contradictory signals and reflected actions permeating ›to the outside‹ at a premature stage. It allows the interpreter-improviser to develop his ability to differentiate as well as his critical sense, and it activates his intuition[15], a key faculty in this method.

---

14 | I use the term »freedom« here in the sense defined by the philosopher Benedictus de Spinoza. I mean »a radical freedom, in which the object-related emotional needs that enslave us are reduced to a minimum« as opposed to the freedom that is »generally meant in discussions about free will.« (António Damásio: *Der Spinoza-Effekt*, Berlin: List 2006, p. 317)

15 | »[...] an acrobatic ability to think things through right up close, as if you were immersed in it, even up to the point that you get so deep into it that it is no longer possible to think it.« (Vladimir Jankélévitch, excerpt from an hommage to Henri Bergson, in: »Anthologie sonore de la pensée française«, Vincennes: Ina/Frémeaux & Associés 2003)

A Brief Introduction to the Principles of the Method

The interpreter-improviser, before anything else, must not confuse ›sense‹ as in meaning with ›sense‹ as in orientation. He must realise that his ›function‹ does not consist of knowing what he represents or what the meaning of his actions is. Instead he has to orient himself, find a direction that arouses and sustains the attention of the ›self that watches the self act‹.

Having said that, there are three structuring principles which the interpreter-improviser must embody. The first and the third principles refer to the CRITICAL ZONE and the second ›supports‹ the action, the DIG IN phase.

The first principle: the above-mentioned ›direction‹ is not a matter of searching, but a matter of finding. What sustains this principle is the idea that things can be found because they already exist in the periphery of our attention. They are just waiting to be ›discovered‹[16] and the work of the interpreter-improviser thus consists of revealing this latent option.

The second principle: Once he has found this orientation or direction for his action, the interpreter-improviser must sustain it to the end (an end which is much further away than one imagines) – with the same conviction and commitment he would have were he to know the purpose it served and where it would take him.[17]

The third principle: a change of direction can only happen if the end of the action really is imminent or has already occurred.[18] The end cannot be brought about prematurely by a feeling of ›boredom‹, excitement or any other reason to want to finish a particular action. The ›end of an action‹ can be ›objective‹ because it results directly from the ›material‹ one is working with (I cannot continue to walk because there is a wall in front of me or someone is holding my arm), or it can be ›subjective‹, resulting, for example, from a feeling that the tension and attention produced by the action has gone.

---

16 | For example: while I am typing this text into the computer, a whole range of subsidiary actions contribute to making the main action possible: ›looking at the screen‹, ›sitting on a chair‹, ›tapping into the keyboard with my fingers‹, ›getting a neck and shoulder massage while I write‹ etc. If I were in the studio now and applied the method, those would be the only places ›to discover‹ and change for.

17 | As in everyday life, where, because we know where and how and why we do what we do, we emanate a ›natural‹ conviction and commitment with our presence. REAL-TIME COMPOSITION aims for the same conviction and commitment, not necessarily natural, but without the pressure of the ›why‹, a responsibility we leave for the spectator.

18 | In this case, the change can only be to accept the end (which is a very difficult choice and not as evident as it sounds).

Those principles are constantly shifting from one to the other. Needless to say, the aim is to ›stay‹ as much as possible in the second principle (the ›till the end‹ principle). It would mean that a state of balance had been found. But, as we all know, that is just impossible. By definition, physical systems lean towards chaos[19] and that is their ›natural‹ state. My main concern as an artist is not to avoid chaos but to survive it, so I can talk about it. And one of the ways to do this is by accepting the inevitability of change and integrating the concept that ›entropy is just another form of order«.[20] My main concern as a researcher is to find a way in which this movement from order to disorder and vice-versa is done in a smooth way (otherwise I will never move from a place where I feel comfortable). That is why the notion of *raccord*[21] is central to this work. In connection to the method discussed here, it refers to the idea that there is a main axis in the action to which all subsidiary, peripheral actions are subordinate. That is the only way in which the coherence and logic of the preceding action can be maintained during a change of ›order‹ – a coherence that is preserved despite the fact that there is no script and no pre-established future.[22]

Of course, there is a plethora of rules and practical examples that support these three principles, but which – for brevity's sake – cannot be discussed or put into a meaningful context here.

---

19 | »Self-abandonment – a physical system that tends to maximise its entropy; a process linked to the disbandment and retreat of and increasing disarray in the system.« (David Bohm/F. David Peat (eds.): *Ciência, Ordem e Criatividade*, Lisbon: Gradiva 1989, p. 183)

20 | Cf. Ibid.

21 | It's a cinematographic expression that refers to the way in which two consecutive camera settings are blended to give the impression of continuity, despite the cut between them.

22 | This principle is reminiscent of Jacques Derrida's distinction between *futur* and *avenir*. According to him, there is the foreseeable future (*futur*), that happens the way we plan it, and the unforeseeable future (*avenir*) that simply surprises us. Cf. DERRIDA, a film by Kirby Dick and Amy Ziering, 2006: Jane Doe Films.

NOTEBOOK *of João Fiadeiro*

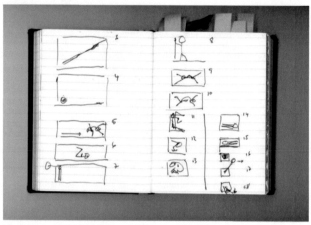

Photo: José Tomás Féria

Epilogue

I like to think that my work requires an attention and a tension similar to that of a chess game, in which there are, for example, at least three moves (usually many more), until you reach the King, the final objective. The containment limit imposed by the very nature of the game is an image that seems quite suitable for the work we develop, as with another strong idea that refers to the need to zero out each time the adversary makes a move. We can tell a player's expertise by the way each of his moves opens possibilities and creates room to ›kill‹ the game all in one go, at a precise moment (unexpected for the opponent, but minutely controlled by the player). We have to let go of all the possibilities from the moment we are confronted with the evidence of an unexpected fact. Although the ›unexpected‹ is extremely rare to an experienced player, it is precisely for that moment that I work – to see a good player in suspense before an ›unexpected‹, ›intriguing‹ and ›enigmatic‹ move from his opponent. I truly believe that it is exactly in that void, the time parentheses where life stays on hold for a brief moment, that art (like the game) becomes sublime.

But there is a very fundamental difference between REAL-TIME COMPOSITION and any other game: the opponent in real-time composition is not ›the other‹ but ›ourselves‹. We mostly win when we ›get lost‹ (because this is when we revel in ourselves) and, last but not the least, because the rules of the game only manifest themselves in the course of playing. Any shift in the level of difficulty changes the rules – even if ever so slightly – and the game has to adapt to new conditions (not vice versa). And to make everything even more complicated, this adaptation must be valid ›in retrospect‹ from the very beginning of the ›game‹.

NOTEBOOK *of João Fiadeiro*

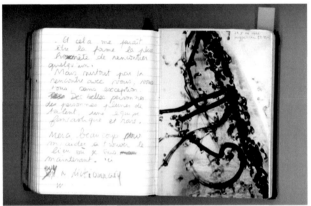

Photo: José Tomás Féria

Translation from Portuguese

References

Bohm, David/Peat, F. David (eds.): *Ciência, Ordem e Criatividade*, Lisbon: Gradiva 1989.
Cage, John: *Silence*, Middletown: Wesleyan University Press 1961.
Damásio, António: *Der Spinoza-Effekt*, Berlin: List 2006.
Jankélévitch, Vladimir: Excerpt from an hommage to Henri Bergson, in: »Anthologie sonore de la pensée française«, Vincennes: Ina/Frémeaux & Associés 2003.
RE.AL (ed.): *DOC.LAB*, Lisbon: RE.AL 2000.

Online References

www.re-al.org.

How Do You Want to Work Today?

Notes on an Alternative Choreographic Mode for

the Production of Speech

Jeroen Peeters

How do you want to work today? Simple as it may sound, addressed to choreographers, performers and other workers in the field of dance and performance, this question yields myriad answers. Asked moreover within a DANCE CONGRESS that operated under the lofty banner KNOW-LEDGE IN MOTION[1], the performativity of the question uncovers ambiguous and conflicting discursive streams and ideologies that nurture today's debate on artistic research. Even if critical in nature, does not the aim to mobilise dance as a field of knowledge risk to adopt the vocabulary of the ›knowledge society‹?[2] When artists are expected to be developers, researchers, even managers of ›creative knowledge‹, is not their experience all too easily labelled and instrumentalised? Aiming to standardise higher education in Europe and introduce a PhD in the arts, Bologna has stirred the question whether artistic and scientific research have a comparable status. If artistic research and production are not only to be discussed in frameworks that are foreign to them, but have to meet their standards and discourses, then aren't we far from home? Even when artistic research is recognised to be intertwined with people's experience

---

1 | This essay departs from the salon CHOREOGRAPHIC MODES OF WORK, which was curated and hosted by performance theorist André Lepecki and dramaturge Myriam Van Imschoot, and took place in the context of the DANCE CONGRESS. I'd like to thank them and Pirkko Husemann for their suggestions and comments on this essay.

2 | For a recent critical analysis of the ›knowledge society‹ and its vocabulary in relation to humanism and education cf. Konrad Paul Liessmann: *Theorie der Unbildung. Die Irrtümer der Wissensgesellschaft*, Vienna: Paul Zsolnay 2006.

– the knowledge it produces being specific, practical and often implicit of nature – what does all this neo-humanist speech about ›knowledge‹ actually bring?

What kind of art do you want to make? What does this mean in the context of a congress that emphasises knowledge so strongly? How can knowledge, theory and politics be transformed into choreographic modes of work? What could be the possibility of creating art today? What are the performative implications of naming? How do labels relate to different waves in art history? What structure or form do you need to be able to address certain questions through choreographic means? How can the intersection of questions clarify the politics of different areas or produce something else?[3]

At the DANCE CONGRESS in April 2006, André Lepecki and Myriam Van Imschoot, both dance theoreticians and dramaturges, curated and hosted a salon during two afternoons on the topic CHOREOGRAPHIC MODES OF WORK. A core group of guests, including choreographers Amos Hetz, Thomas Lehmen and Lisa Nelson, researcher Scott DeLahunta, and producer Eva-Maria Hoerster, and many visitors participated in a series of conversations around a large table. Issues of artistic research, knowledge and productivity were addressed in an oblique way through the question: »How do you want to work today?« Indeed, without mapping the field of options and practices first, giving substance to the question, discussions about epistemology and politics may become futile. To deal with all those issues, avoiding at the same time the obtrusive vocabulary of the society of knowledge, the unambiguous romanticisation of artistic practice, as well as the inclination to rehearse the commonplaces of critical theory, the salon's option was an awry choreographic mode of discussion.

Throughout the conversations, Van Imschoot proposed a shift of focus from the ›choreographer‹ as a function to the ›choreographic‹, opening up the link with a certain person to a variety of choreographic activities, stances, questions, modes, processes and products: »There are activities that have certain features, tasks, responsibilities and modes that do not necessarily solidify in a function.« Considered even more broadly, choreographic modes of work concern creation as much as creativity, production, teaching, training, dramaturgy etc. Lepecki related this issue also with performance studies, which are interested not in the accumulation of knowledge, but the creation of possibilities, the transformation of reality through the discourses, representations and imaginations that shape it. And to unravel the salon's title a little further, a ›mode‹ allows for a specific kind of expression: it ties subject matter to its expression

---

3 | All questions in italics are integrally based on interventions by participants in the salon CHOREOGRAPHIC MODES OF WORK.

and modification in a particular form, which is also expressive of expression itself.[4] Thus, a different way of thinking or speaking is not only a matter of content, but also requires a different mode of work, body, form or process. In that respect the salon CHOREOGRAPHIC MODES OF WORK cannot be reduced to its content, the experimentation with an alternative conversational mode reveals as much its aboutness and gravity.

How do you want to work today? It is impossible to give an encompassing account of the salon here, or to trace the genealogy of all the thoughts that were uttered or developed in the conversations. I will simply suggest some of them in the form of questions extracted from my notebook, hoping that they will keep their openness and resistance towards compression. At the risk of generalisation, I will draw from there some observations about the ›incompressibility‹ of artistic research and the knowledge it proffers.

What is choreography? What is its meaning? What is its (ir)relevance for your work? Are the processes visible in the result? How can the product be kept open? How do you perceive or read the ways of working? What do you see? What do you project? How can you choreograph this? What material do you gain when you observe the world through the lens of an artist? What is your responsibility when you claim to make art? What do you offer to people? How do you expect them to react? What if you do not keep the distinction between life and art clear? Would you be lost?

Salon *CHOREOGRAPHIC MODES OF WORK,*
DANCE CONGRESS GERMANY 2006

Photo: Thomas Aurin

---

4 | Cf. Gilles Deleuze: *Expressionism in Philosophy: Spinoza,* New York: Zone Books 1990, pp. 13f.

These questions not only point in many directions, they also represent a multitude of voices and are in that reminiscent of a fundamental gesture: taking the floor. Throughout the salon, people's eagerness to speak up, make themselves heard and participate in the conversation was striking. It was perhaps symptomatic of the institutionalised German dance field, in which many artists are invisible, and of a congress that left little space for audience participation and artists' voices. What else does it speak of?

In the aftermath of May 1968, the French sociologist and philosopher Michel De Certeau wrote about the »capture of speech«[5] as a new right that equals the right of being human and affirms existence. It is a gesture of refusal and contestation that rejects all identification, but in that specific context also

[...] a ›detained‹ knowledge whose apprenticeship would turn those acquiring it into the instruments of a system; institutions enrolling each of its ›employees‹ in causes that are not its own; an authority devoted to imposing its language and in censuring nonconformity, and so on.[6]

It requires little imagination to realise the topicality of De Certeau's words and link them to today's »knowledge society«, whose language permeates many areas and has been interiorised to a serious extent. The capture of speech needs to be repeated time and again in order to keep its question alive, to unhinge the power of legitimised knowledge and allow for new languages and forms of expression to emerge.

The capture of speech gave everyone access to debates about important matters such as society, knowledge, art and politics. But for De Certeau it is foremost the deep ambiguity of the gesture that has political value and contains the possibility to underpin a new society. The capture of speech creates difference through many (unheard) voices. Yet it also *symbolises* difference, as it precedes a new, different language to come. Fundamentally provisional, confused and irreducible, the capture of speech challenges us: »life in the future can be lived only by alienating one's speech, just as existence will end when we begin to renounce the temptation to create.«[7]

How do you want to work today? With each answer, this question entails another one: *How* can one speak about choreographic modes of work and productivity? Or also: how does one speak about artistic research in a different language than that of neo-humanism or the society of know-

---

5 | Cf. Michel De Certeau: *The Capture of Speech and Other Political Writings*, ed. by Luce Giard, Minneapolis/London: University of Minnesota Press 1997.
6 | Ibid., pp. 12f.
7 | Ibid., p. 24.

ledge? It's worthwhile to remark that within the European field of dance, the modernist hierarchy of knowledge production was overturned when Pina Bausch began to address questions to her dancers and listened to their answers, thus redistributing with speech the position of those who know. André Lepecki observes an epistemological break in Bausch's gesture that undermined existing authorities and turned the field< of dance definitively into a domain of knowledge[8], but one in which all the parties involved in the creative process share the premise – and the promise – of ›not-know-ing‹ as a point of departure. The enthusiasm of many people speaking up also made the salon CHOREOGRAPHIC MODES OF WORK ramble a little, propelled by the difficult task of departing from confusion and not-know-ing, and embracing the potentiality of all this as a mode of conversation.

How can you exhaust your habits? Can you actually make dance without habits? What about the habit of making dance or performing? With the expansion of modes of work, how do you choose? Are we facing a disappear-ance of clear expectations? How do culture and the formation of attention relate? How can you transform culture through managing attention? How can you make new sensorial systems to create attention? How do we read intention and attention in each other in order to survive in a social context? How do you craft the inner attention of the performer? How can you be aware of holes that you will never be able to cover?

»Can we be more clear about what it is exactly that we are talking about, these choreographic modes of work?« Lost in the salon's meandering con-versation, this participant's request for clarity speaks about yet another ambiguity. The vagueness that lingers around ›choreographic modes of work‹, ›artistic research‹ and related issues is intrinsically part of the terms, as they are so-called »Essentially Contested Concepts«.[9] The latter were defined by William Gallie as appraising, internally complex and *initially* describable in various ways, but also liable to circumstances and therefore highly malleable.[10] A strong ambiguity is at work in these con-cepts, which links a shared, generalised intuition with the development of specific views, ideologies and agencies. The openness and performativity of these concepts allow for a different exploration of reality that is not striving for an objective, general account, but leaves space to include the singular, contingent and arbitrary. At stake are not universalist claims and certainties, but a continuous critical reflection on the ›present‹.

---

8 | Cf. André Lepecki: »Dance without Distance«, in: *ballettanz* 2 (2001), p. 30.

9 | Walter Bryce Gallie: »Essentially contested concept«, in: *Proceedings of the Aristotelian Society* 56 (1965), pp. 167–198.

10 | Ibid., pp. 171f.

In the essay »What is Enlightenment?«[11], Michel Foucault proposes to approach modernity and Enlightenment as a critical attitude, a reflexive mode of relating to the present.[12] He sketches the contours of a »historical ontology of ourselves« as philosophical project. It is a liminal, experimental and incessant attitude that enquires into the contingencies that made us who we are and enable us to be different. A particular body of practices and discourses serves as field of reference: what do people do, think and say, and how do they do it? And with what kind of liberty do they act within systems and modify the rules of the game? Against a backdrop of existing habits and beliefs, the present reality is the touchstone for working on our own limits and sense of possibility. The ontology of the present provides only temporary, partial and local answers; it has a process-like character and is necessarily vague as it strokes our limits of understanding. With choreographic modes of work as an ensemble of practices, to make a start with the ontology of the present was perhaps the actual endeavour of the salon. How do you want to work today?

Is making art about launching into the unknown? Which intuitions, moments, choices travel with you and make up a mode that prepares for creativity? What are the conditions to enter a state of not-knowing? How do you listen to the melody of words, the gestures, the breaks, the hesitation, and feel less threatened by the unknown? How can you deal with your own history, desires, secrets and invisibilities? How do you find the mind of a piece rather than project your own mind? How do you reflect the world without knowing how to do that? What about the authorial power of the choreographer? What about improvisation? How can you relate life outside the theatre in choreographic structures? How do you get to the outside? How do you understand that there are other perspectives?

Choreographic modes of work and the knowledge they yield are linked with the practices and experience of people. A recurring topic in the salon concerned the limits of our understanding and agency, formulated as a desire to relate to the unknown or to enter a state of not-knowing in one's work. Rather than celebrating dance as the other within culture, this asks for an observation on the subject notion acknowledged in artistic research – adopting a modest stance towards both knowledge and not-knowing.

Roughly speaking, two kinds of heteronomy were discussed: first, production conditions, canonical legitimacy, economics, politics of visibility, and other external circumstances that thwart the artist's autonomy.

---

11 | Michel Foucault: »What is Enlightenment?«, in: Paul Rabinow (ed.): *The Foucault Reader*, New York: Pantheon Books 1984, pp. 32–50.

12 | Cf. René Boomkens: *De nieuwe wanorde. Globalisering en het einde van de maakbare samenleving*, Amsterdam: Van Gennep 2006, pp. 24–27.

And second, technical skill and lack of control, authorship and the difficulty to grasp a piece's mind, the quasi-autonomous logic of a method, etc: they remind one of the limitations and insecure position of the knowing subject, which is not self-transparent, but vulnerable. No need to stress that both categories challenge the modern, enlightened notion of the subject as well as the self-assured voluntarism of the knowledge society, in which we are all managers of our own reality – shopping and googling knowledge rather than collecting experience, that is to say »personally integrated, narratively and conceptually structured aggregates of knowledge«.[13]

How do you want to work today? How can one think, speak and act *through* heteronomy? It is a fundamental question on subjectivity that surfaces in artistic research enquiring into the ontology of the present. Foucault insists on the present as a touchstone to avoid the grand narratives and projects of modernity, and to simply sculpt and shape what is around with critical awareness. A similar dissent permeated a discussion in the salon that revolved around Thomas Lehmen's proposal to regard art and other human activity as »making a piece of world«. Are you then adding, transforming, or creating a parallel universe? Who has access to the creation of reality, of the imagination and representations that shape it? What is the artist's role? What is the ideology behind it? Are we actually the producers of our own life and its conditions? The weightier the subject matter taken on, the more delicate, contested and disparate the discussion on choreographic modes of work grew.

Unresolved as the discussion content was, heteronomy was also explicitly addressed in the salon's alternative mode for the production of speech: a choreographed conversation. Starting as an »open improvisation«, it moved to working with playful scores and game structures. The second afternoon, Van Imschoot proposed a score, in which people passed on the word to someone else through addressing a question, while others could intervene through »calls« for clarification, expansion or emergency. It redistributed speech and left space for modification: the knowing resided in the doing, resistant and incompressible. Rather than conclude the salon with a final word, Van Imschoot lingered in the thickness of the conversational mode, took up a suggestion by Lisa Nelson and invited all the participants to close their eyes and wander off groping.

---

13 | Peter Sloterdijk: *Im Weltinnenraum des Kapitals. Für eine philosophische Theorie der Globalisierung*, Frankfurt a.M.: Suhrkamp 2006, p. 344. Cf. also pp. 93–96.

References

Boomkens, René: *De nieuwe wanorde. Globalisering en het einde van de maakbare samenleving*, Amsterdam: Van Gennep 2006.

De Certeau, Michel: *The Capture of Speech and Other Political Writings*, ed. by Luce Giard, Minneapolis/London: University of Minnesota Press 1997.

Deleuze, Gilles: *Expressionism in Philosophy: Spinoza*, New York: Zone Books 1990.

Foucault, Michel: »What is Enlightenment?«, in: Paul Rabinow (ed.): *The Foucault Reader*, New York: Pantheon Books 1984, pp. 32–50.

Gallie, Walter Bryce: »Essentially contested concept«, in: *Proceedings of the Aristotelian Society* 56 (1965), pp. 167–198.

Lepecki, André: »Dance without Distance«, in: *ballettanz* 2 (2001), pp. 29–31.

Liessmann, Konrad Paul: *Theorie der Unbildung. Die Irrtümer der Wissensgesellschaft*, Vienna: Paul Zsolnay 2006.

Sloterdijk, Peter: *Im Weltinnenraum des Kapitals. Für eine philosophische Theorie der Globalisierung*, Frankfurt a.M.: Suhrkamp 2006.

Body Knowledge and Body Memory

HautSache Bewegung – Moving From the Skin by Dieter Heitkamp,
Dance Congress Germany 2006, *Photo: Thomas Aurin*

Making Worlds Available

Alva Noë

Understanding Experience

You go to an art gallery and you look at a work of art in an unfamiliar style by an artist you do not know. It happens, sometimes, in a situation like this, that the work of art strikes you as flat or opaque. You do not get it. But you do not give up. You look harder. Maybe you discuss the piece with your companion. Or you read the title of the piece and that gives you an idea. Something remarkable can now occur. The piece opens up to you; you can see into it now and appreciate its structure.

There are two points to be made about this phenomenon. First, although your experience of the art work has been transformed, there is no change in the work itself. It has no more structure or meaning now than it did at the outset. So if there is a change, a transformation, it is a transformation in you. Second, whatever change it is that is brought about in you, it is not a merely subjective change. It is not as if what has happened is that you now feel different about what you see, or have different beliefs about it. Whatever change has occurred, it enables you now to perceive, in the work, what you could not perceive before.

There is a name for the transformation in you that makes it possible for you first to perceive the thing you are confronting; it is called understanding. The work of art becomes visible through the understanding. Understanding enables us to perceive, factively, in the work, what we could not perceive before.

I have argued (elsewhere) that what is true of the experience of the work of art is true of human experience quite generally. The world shows up for us in experience only in so far as we understand, that is, know or anticipate it. One reason why art is so important to us, and, in particular, why we place, or ought to place, importance on art (and on dance) in education, is that it recapitulates this fundamental fact about our relation to the world around us: the world shows up as blank and flat until we understand it.

All this raises a puzzle. How can we perceive anything at all if we must already know it in order to perceive it? How can we ever perceive anything new? This is not a new puzzle. Plato articulates a version of it in »Meno«[1] and we find it in the writings of Augustine as well. For philosophers or scientists interested in the nature of perception, the puzzle has a special importance today.

Alva Noë, DANCE CONGRESS GERMANY 2006

Photo: Thomas Aurin

Learning Your Way About

My objective in this essay is to shed light on the puzzle by turning attention to the dance work of Lisa Nelson. Nelson has devised what she describes as »an approach to spontaneous ensemble composition«; she refers to this approach as TUNING SCORES.

A TUNING SCORE, as I understand the idea, is a simplified dance situation. It is a structure, or rubric, within which dancers are free to compose (to compose themselves). A TUNING SCORE has several elements: the dancers or players, the stage or, as Nelson calls it, the »image space«, and rules that organise and constrain the play. Dancers enter the »image space« with their eyes closed. They attend and aim to begin acting at the same time as the other dancers. They seek to attune themselves to the situation. The players use calls such as »Repeat!«, »Undo!«, »Enhance!« and »End!«. In this way, the image develops.

---

1 | Cf. Plato: Meno, Indianapolis: Hackett 1976.

I have said that a TUNING SCORE is a simplified dance situation. No TUNING SCORE is so simple, however, that it is anything less than a *complete* dance situation. A TUNING SCORE requires an »image space«, more than one person, and at least one call (i.e. »End!«) to govern communication among the players.

To participate in the score you must be a dancer, and you must also be an observer of dancers. You must be performer and member of the audience. You must play, and watch. And you must understand. In this way, the TUNING SCORE models life.

Philosophers can usefully compare Nelson's TUNING SCORES to Wittgenstein's language games. Wittgenstein believed that language is a medium for thought; that getting clear about the structure of language can be a way of getting clear about our concepts, intellectual values and commitments. He introduced the idea of language games in order to elucidate the nature of language. To appreciate what he had in mind, consider an important example from »Philosophical Investigations«. Close to the beginning of this book Wittgenstein asks us to imagine a language

[...] meant to serve for communication between a builder A and an assistant B. A is building with building-stones: there are blocks, pillars, slabs and beams. B has to pass the stones, one after the other, in the order in which A needs them. For this purpose they use a language consisting of the words »block, »pillar«, »slab«, »beam«. A calls them out; – B brings the stone he has learnt to bring at such-and-such a call. – Conceive this as a complete primitive language.[2]

Wittgenstein tells us to think of the language game of the builders as a complete, primitive language. What he seems to have had in mind is the thought that although language games – which he might just as well have called *job games* or *society games* – are *simplified*, they nevertheless exhibit the elements essential to more complicated forms of linguistic exchange. Importantly, language games have a *point*, that is, a purpose (in Wittgenstein's example, to facilitate building); they have *players* (the builders); they take place in a *context* (the building context, the aims and interests of the players etc.). They are linguistic in that they involve words. But the words are displayed as tools or instruments of the whole practice of the game. (The words play a role in the game comparable to the role played by the stones themselves.) It is in this setting that Wittgenstein could argue, famously, that the meaning of a word is its use. What Wittgenstein illustrates by this example is that use is not, as it were, an isolated property of the word itself. It depends on the larger context of the players and the game. To specify a language game, and so

2 | Ludwig Wittgenstein: *Philosophical Investigations*, Oxford: Blackwell 1953, PI §2.

to explain the meaning of words, you need to describe all this – context, point, players, activity. You have to describe a way of living – what Wittgenstein sometimes called a »*Lebensform*« (form of life).

Now, as I have already mentioned, Wittgenstein thought that language games can teach us about language. What Wittgenstein saw is that language games exhibit *on a small scale* the essential features of language *on the large*. For example, reflection on the simplified language of the builders can help us appreciate that the meaning of a word can only be grasped by appreciating the way the word gets used in a specific context, i.e. in relation to the needs, goals, interests and problems of people. Since language is the medium of thought, Wittgenstein believed that getting clear about language would enable us to get clear about thought and, indeed, about the sources of our own philosophical concern and confusion.

Why do we need language games to get to the basic features of language as a whole? What stands in the way of direct study of language itself? The problem with language is that it is complicated. Wittgenstein sometimes said that language is like a city.

Our language can be seen as an ancient city: a maze of little streets and squares, of old and new houses, and of houses with additions from various periods; and this surrounded by a multitude of new boroughs with straight regular streets and uniform houses.[3]

Crucially, to be a competent speaker, or thinker, or *resident*, you need to know your way around. Wittgenstein recommended using language games to help us find our way around in language itself.

I have suggested that we compare Nelson's TUNING SCORES to Wittgenstein's language games. When we do so, we can begin to appreciate how Nelson's dance method can serve *also* as a practice for better getting to know our way around.

Consider that to be part of a TUNING SCORE ensemble with Nelson is to learn, as one member in the collective, one's way around jointly imagined spaces, spaces that are projected imaginatively in the *real* space of the studio and that are occupied, in reality, by the dancers. To learn your way around in the tuning score is to communicate skilfully and effectively with the others; this requires sensitivity to them.

Now, a striking feature of Nelson's own understanding of the TUNING SCORE is that she thinks of it as a *research* tool for the study of movement and performance and, also, for the study of perceptual consciousness itself. Let us ask: How can an improvisational dance activity of the sort Nelson constructs be a research tool?

The kinship with Wittgenstein's language games is helpful here. Lan-

---

3 | Ibid., PI §18.

guage games cast light on the nature of language by letting us appreciate, on a small scale, the workings of the sorts of embedded, contextualised practices that, on the large, make up our use of language and, as a result, our intellectual spaces. TUNING SCORES are like language games, I am suggesting. So let us ask: What is it that TUNING SCORES cast light on in the way that language games cast light on thinking?

A first answer that comes to mind is that TUNING SCORES cast light on dance itself. They inform us of dance possibilities. This may be so. But it is not the answer I am looking for. It does not satisfy. For one thing, it is not surprising to learn that the TUNING SCORE method will teach us about *dance*. The question is whether dance, explored by using TUNING SCORES, can teach us about *something else* (i.e. about the mind). Think of the Wittgenstein case again. We might say that it is not surprising that *language games* can teach us about language. What is surprising, and what interests us, is the fact that language games, by helping us understand the structure of language, can actually help us gain clarity about the intellectual worlds we inhabit. – *What* then?

To answer this let us pose a question that Nelson has posed: »What do we see when we are looking at dance?« Keeping the TUNING SCORE project in mind, we can venture an answer: when we look at dance, we look at *a situation into which we can, into which we are invited, into which we need to enter.*

Go, lecture-performance by Lisa Nelson and Scott Smith, DANCE CONGRESS GERMANY 2006

Photo: Thomas Aurin

That's a beginning. But can we say more? When we look at dance, we see *opportunities for movement,* we see *obstacles, limitations.* We *see* the world, but we see it as a world-for-movement, that is, the world as a domain for action. To put this in another way: what we see when we look at dance is the *environment*. I use this term in James J. Gibson's[4] sense. Gibson is the most important twentieth-century theorist of perception, outside of philosophy at least; he is also an important source for Nelson. Nelson reads Gibson. The environment, in Gibson's framework, is not the physical world. Two different species of animal, located beside one and the same tree, may occupy one place in the physical world, but they inhabit different environments. The environment, for Gibson, is the animal's *surroundings*. The German word captures the intuition. It is the *Umgebung*; that is, the world given around the animal. It is the world as it makes itself available to the animal as a domain for the animal's activity. Animals and environments are inseparable terms; animals and environments are co-determining.

What we experience, what we see, when we are looking at dance, in the setting of the TUNING SCORE at least, is the environment. *Our* environment. Not the physical world. Not mere *things*. We see, that is to say, we *encounter* the meaningful world of our possible action.

Gibson wrote that »Every animal is, in some degree at least, a perceiver and a behaver«.[5] Nelson might have written that every dancer is to some degree at least a behaver *and* a perceiver. What does a dancer see when she looks into the »image space«, or when she tries to find a path in it? She experiences the environment, the world as it correlates with our embodied perceptual orientation to it.

If language games are tools for laying out and making perspicuous *intellectual* spaces, or linguistic cityscapes, then TUNING SCORES lay out and make perspicuous our mode of perceptual being-in-the-world, our being perceptually attuned to the cities in which we find ourselves, to our environment, *and* to the ways – this is a new point – in which our environment is not merely affected by what we do, not merely transformed by it, but is actually *brought forth* by us. The point is not merely conceptual – that is, the point is not that without the person or animal there is no environment at all, only *a meaningless physical world*. The point is more textured than that, and *more realistic*. The point is that the environment in which we find ourselves, the space itself, is one whose meaning is always specified relative to us and the situation in which we find ourselves, to our relation to each other, to the environment. When we as dancers enter the »image space«, when we perform actions, when we issue calls and respond to calls, when we listen, and watch, we *make* the environment. We *enact* our environments thanks to our skilful engagement with them. We enact our perceptual world by attuning ourselves

---

4 | James Jerome Gibson: *The Ecological Approach to Visual Perception*, Hillsdale: Lawrence Erlbaum 1979.

5 | Ibid., p. 8.

to it. Nelson's TUNING SCORE recapitulates this fundamental fact about our lives – that our worlds are made by us through our dynamic coupling with our surroundings.

Skilful Access to the World

In perception, nothing is hidden. The world is there to be taken in. But in perception, in a sense, *everything* is hidden. For wherever you look there is unbounded complexity, there is too much to be taken in. Consider the case of listening to speech in an unfamiliar language. The sounds are all there for you, at least in a sense. But the words and what is being said are invisible to you. Because you can only perceive them – as with the art object at the outset – once you understand them. Knowing them makes them perceptible. But how do you achieve understanding? How can you learn a new language, which is to say, a new modality for taking in bits of the world? It would seem that you cannot perceive it until you are acquainted with what you perceive, but you cannot come to know anything before you perceive it. This is the puzzle we began with at the outset.

Nelson's TUNING SCORES, like Wittgenstein's language games, provide a method. A TUNING SCORE, like a grammatical exercise, is an occasion to begin to acquire the skills necessary for access to the world. Participation in a TUNING SCORE is like conversing about a work of art. It is an activity of bringing the world into focus for perceptual consciousness. It is an activity of attuning oneself to what is happening around one.

In this way Nelson, like Wittgenstein, provides an intellectual technology or prosthesis for bringing the world into focus. Nelson and Wittgenstein offer, in effect, tools for achieving perceptual contact. Nelson enables us not only to see dance, but to understand seeing. And so this practical technology for modelling dance possibilities makes a theoretical contribution to our understanding of perceptual consciousness, just as Wittgenstein's linguistic miniatures enable us to rethink the nature of language and linguistic understanding. Theory depends on practice; Nelson's work, like that of Wittgenstein, illustrates the ways in which attention to practice provide the ground for new theory.

References

Gibson, James Jerome: *The Ecological Approach to Visual Perception*, Hillsdale: Lawrence Erlbaum 1979.

Plato: *Meno*, Indianapolis: Hackett 1976.

Wittgenstein, Ludwig: *Philosophical Investigations*, Oxford: Blackwell 1953.

Flickering and Change

MEG STUART IN DIALOGUE WITH SCOTT DELAHUNTA

Scott deLahunta: Let's start with the theme the editors have proposed for us to discuss: Body Knowledge/Body Memory. How would you like to approach these concepts?

I wouldn't refer only to the body. I have spent many hours in the dance studio doing movement research and exploring aspects of emotional states and particularly non-ordinary ones. I've done a lot of research into trance for example. So that would be a subject I would like to talk about. About memory, I would say I have mostly been concerned with issues of forgetting and how we forget, related to improvisation. And, as I understand it, the scientific approach may be to research what is perceived to be a lack or a problem. My own research is based on exploring and highlighting such problems without judgement with a very open and hopefully compassionate approach to malfunction or gaps. At some point when I am trying to fold or weave this research into something, then of course I think about *why* these problems did occur. Then I may think about the forgetting or disassociation, and explore why there is this inability to hold on and concentrate, why the mind may be fluttering.

I think in general you are right. Some areas of science advance through the study of dysfunction or malfunction, perhaps through an accident resulting in brain damage for example; or studying a mental condition like dissociation, which is seen as a problem for the one experiencing it. You are saying that these are things you explore creatively, as non-ordinary states. I wonder, how do you trigger a non-ordinary state of dissociation or mental gaps like forgetting, when you are in the research period? Do you just break your dancer's concentration somehow? And why do you find this interesting as material?

It's not as simple as that. I try to get people working on several different channels at the same time, which becomes a kind of virtuosity in itself in terms of being able to switch. There is an exercise I've proposed for 15 years, called »change«. So let's say a performer is doing an action, before they arrive at any one reality or awareness or state, I jar them or sort of push them to make another switch and then I try to compose out of that. I consider it similar to automatic writing but with movement. It is important that the performers don't think or prepare in advance, that they are open to enter into unfamiliar states and movements that are very different from one shift to the next. It is amazing that the dancers don't freak out, that they are able to change at such rapid speeds. It is kind of unnerving that that's possible for them.

REPLACEMENT *by Meg Stuart/Damaged Goods*

Photo: Chris Van der Burght

My next question relates to when you are watching the dancers perform some kind of action and then you trigger a change or switch. What informs you? How do you know when to do this?

Basically, I feel that I push them to spaces that are uncomfortable for them. Sometimes I trigger the change and sometimes they change on their own. I may talk them into an emotional state, or I may have them learn something ›verbatim‹ from video and work on it after. This may sound like most of the time I am seducing, suggesting, extracting etc., but I don't have a technique. It's always shifting per piece and per person. I do have this sense that I can walk them into a state I am searching for, and they kind of yield to my proposals and suggestions. But when it is working, this brings up material for me to compose with. And I always have this distance, because I am constructing, I am making work.

So you are being intuitive, but somehow know, when to perturb them at a certain point in order to coax something, or them, into another kind of space. And this can be fast, so they are processing many things at the same time.

Yes. Interestingly, last year in Brussels, I tried a new approach with the »change« exercise during a research project with P.A.R.T.S. students and dancers and others who are interested in the work. It was the first time I had worked specifically on the exercise. I had met Catherine Sullivan, a video artist who works with performers, and she had this chart she uses to create her material; which is not how I work at all so it was fascinating. It is derived from minimal music, and you can take any slice of performance and divide it into three different lines; so one could be the physicality, one is the drama and one is the time. On the chart each of these separate lines can be scaled from zero to one hundred. So, you can have somebody doing a movement and you can say it is 70 percent physicality and 70 percent drama, or you can have 0 percent drama and 70 percent physicality. This way you can separate these types of materials and you have a language so you can tweak them.

So it's a creative tool?

Yes, but it's most useful for providing a language you can use to pull things out. In a way, I was doing this instinctively before. For example, when somebody would have very physical movement, I might ask them to »take the power out«. Then it's like they are ghosting themselves. What is great about the chart, and I think it's clear for an actor or a dancer working with it, is that you can tweak abstract movement in order to see its inherent drama. Maybe it is something like a picture that has just been scratched out and you only get these traces or just like a little corner of the drama or of the movement. Because I am interested in theatre and drama, working with the chart helped to connect these with more abstract dance.

How did it change or support the »change« exercise?

Only in the sense of modulating the state. I would say »Change!« repeatedly; then with material that intrigues me »Okay, stay with that state«. Then I ask them »Increase physicality!«, »Increase drama!«, »Lower drama!« etc. So, they would fully explore all aspects of that state using this chart. Sometimes we put on a metronome and they changed a series of six states increasing the tempo by degrees. Basically at a fast speed you get very disturbed people, almost schizophrenic states of performing. At the end of the workshop I confronted these states with another question. Would it be possible to conduct a group improvisation? So there we were, all standing with our material and the chart finding the signs and the language in which this could be conducted improvisationally. Sometimes the dancers conducted for each other. It was great to be able to have the distance the chart provided, and at the same time strange that it seemed to be something measurable.

So it's kind of a device for orchestration. This chart introduced a new vocabulary, some new structured thinking, something that you could borrow from and then use to apply to something you had been doing before. It added a new stimulus.

Yes, I don't work on scores or structures so much. That is not my first attraction. I think I am much more generally interested in movement vocabulary, a radical vocabulary. And each situation requires another vocabulary that has a certain way of presenting itself. I realise now that that is my main concern – the language comes first.

Just to stay with the »change« exercise for a moment more. It reminds me that cognitive neuropsychologists use something like »change« or perturbations as a diagnostic tool to identify how the mind or brain may be malfunctioning. Using interference to determine if someone's sensing has a conflict that would indicate a specific problem as you were saying earlier. When you were talking about the »change« exercise it made me think about this. So, clearly you are interested in mental states, in minds. Do you think of this in terms of their psychology when you are working with people?

I think about how I connect to that person. I have been using contact improvisation as a model, finding the information about the person through contact, trying to find the deepest point of connection. Like through the bones. Out of that approach or model is how I try to interact with people I am working with. I can only say that now, because I understand the model better. Before it was intuitive, more about finding a language that dealt with the doubt of the body, or the body questioning itself and struggling with itself. And in the last four years it has been more about perception, looking for these non-ordinary states of mind.

Contact Improvisation seems to me a quite specific approach to the body and its knowledge. Do you have approaches you use that might constitute other types of knowing through the body? You mentioned trance and that you have been in contact with hypnotists. This seems to be about putting people in non-ordinary states or altered states.

I am interested in the desire to be possessed or to be a channel or to be a container. When the body is this container, one that filters and connects. We have tried different approaches to this like »holotropic breathing«, invented by Stanislav Grof, a scientist who did LSD research. He developed this technique with breathing that basically means without drugs you can achieve the equivalent of an altered state, with the potential to somehow heal your psyche. We did it once with someone who is a regular practitioner of the technique. You lie on a mattress and have a witness as you do the breathing practice, which combines relaxation and hyperventilation. The practice goes on for two hours and produces first a tingling and then quite a different sensation.

I wonder if it is possible to consider holotropic breathing as a form of knowledge. As a psychotherapeutic technique, even if the aim is to access non-ordinary states of consciousness, it presupposes certain things about the relationship between body and mind. How do other body knowledge techniques, for example contemporary dance or classical ballet get used in your creative work?

Well, these techniques, like the breathing or trance, are not really my main subject; they are more like an exploration sideline. However, in general, the approaches to working with the body I use do not come from contemporary dance. These techniques I am interested in are useful if one is trying to think about how we move without our bodies, in what ways our ideas are moving, how I have experiences that I can't explain. What is interesting, for example, is this moment when someone comes down from a trance. They are trying to be in this state, and in the moment of coming out of that state they are very vulnerable. For me, this is material. But it's also tricky because a trance is any kind of formed awareness, a cognitive awareness. I mean, to be honest, any performer whose concentration is very focussed is in a kind of state of trance.

Given recent claims about neuroscience bringing interesting information to the dance field, for example this theory of mirror neurons that suggests the brain simulates actions that we observe, I wonder if neuroscience is another form of body knowledge that might be interesting for you?

We once had a lecture from someone who showed a diagram about people having injuries to their brain and talked about the history of neuroscience. But the approach is one I may be a bit allergic to, because while I am making work I don't want to read about it or try to analyse it in that way. Of course, when I read about developments in neuroscience I'm very interested, but I can never go and use it in the studio in doing practical research or work. I don't have the access to this knowledge in that sense, but the moment of reading about it is thrilling. But my main interest is in what works in the creative research process.

As you said earlier, you tend to look for disconnections or how to trigger »change«.

I'd say with my process I let the performers know that with every move they could be another person. So there is never the idea that ›I am going to move and I am going to stay in this mode‹. Fast, slow, broken, virtuosic, whatever it is. If they do stay with a particular experience or vehicle, it's more like that vehicle is a runaway truck or it's a car, it's a bicycle or it's limping. I don't know what, but the experience is constantly on the move, changing. Somehow for me the person, whoever that is, is then in question; and the body is sort of transparent and flickering, it's not fixed.

I like this idea of flickering, and the instability of the subject – this person, this identity is not stable.

And I am very obsessed about the same state of instability in the audience, and the sense of consciousness awareness the audience creates in relation to the performance. I always have this feeling of something on the night of a performance and wonder where the feeling comes from. I tend to be a little superstitious about this also, but I am very much interested in what creates this feeling, this sense. So the actual performance is going out and around in a circle through the audience and then it's coming back; they are co-creating it.

HIGHWAY 101 by Meg Stuart/Damaged Goods

Photo: Chris Van der Burght

We have gone from discussing the performer's state of mind to that of the audience. I'm wondering about you as the maker working on the research and collecting materials; working with your performers, doing exercises like »change« and morphing. How do you change yourself, how do you switch in your own process?

In my piece REPLACEMENT the proposal for the research process was to create a lab in which we spent a lot of time purposely trying not to make anything. So everyone had to explore and experiment with this idea. I think my making process is very goal oriented, or opportunistic, because I am always thinking when I am watching ›what can I pull out of that?‹ So in this lab the goal was only the research itself, and everyone just did small experiments. One of the most interesting experiments was when they went out in Berlin and looked for someone who looked like them, documenting this with a video camera. Some of them became flirtatious if they found somebody looking like them. It was often very funny.

This is really a departure then. You set up the conditions so that you didn't have to be making something during the lab. And you mentioned being normally goal-oriented, so it seems that usually your relation to the process is one of always looking for something. For this recent research process you were trying to not pay attention to things in a way that you might normally do.

Exactly. And ultimately the situation also meant that I could be replaced as the choreographer. But I have to say that not knowing what will happen, but knowing something will happen is a condition that I am used to from being the host of improvisation projects. Otherwise, if you stay with known models or types of body knowledge, you often enter into the same relationships as before. In the not knowing there seems to be a greater possibility for igniting a creative spark.

Expeditions to the Inner Teacher

How the Pioneers

of Movement Studies Inspire Dance

IRENE SIEBEN

When a roe deer sniffs the air, it stands motionless. Its head slightly facing the wind; its posture seems effortlessly erected with a mini-mum of muscular strength. »We sense its body endowed with life from inside, in perfect balance and ready to move«.[1] The Czech dancer Jarmila Kröschlová compares this state of vital motionlessness with the psycho-physical presence of a dancer before going on stage, when the body »glows with enlivened grace«.[2] This is how she describes the kinaesthetic process of awareness as the key to expression and creativity.

Though Kröschlová left a highly inspiring book, she did not deliver a technique. In search of a »general physical education« that would fortify any kind of specialisation in dance technique, she belongs to the forerunners of the following methods: »Alexander Technique«, »Gindler-Bodywork«, »Eutony«, »Ideokinesis«, »Feldenkrais Method« and »Body-Mind Centering«. Increased body sensitivity as a basis for meaningful behaviour and conduct links the philosophies that these founders of movement and body-oriented learning methods were concerned with in the 20th century, and which were brought to an abrupt end with the onset of National Socialism. They influenced the development of the arts and education as well as bodywork and psycho-therapy. Every discovery in the field of body research led to an ideology or school whose contents had an aesthetic, anthropological or thera-peutic alignment. These realisations did not emerge in vacuo. But who launched the expedition which led to the redefinition of body images,

1 | Jarmila Kröschlová: *Movement Theory and Practice*, Sydney: Current Press 2000, p. 11.

2 | Ibid.

to the liberation of dance, to attempts to emancipate gender roles and social behaviour patterns?

Apart from François Delsartes' ideas regarding the value of information in a movement, which lent wings to Isadora Duncan's dances and inspired Rudolf von Laban's »motile knowledge«, it was a scientific discovery that hit the nerve of the time with the Gymnastic revivalists and the elite obsessed with rhythm in Emile Jaques-Dalcroze's Hellerauer »educational establishment«: the physiologist Charles Scott Sherrington assigned a sixth sense to the five traditional ones: the motion sense. To distinguish it from exteroception (sensory perception of external stimuli) and interoception (sensory perception of inner stimuli), he named it proprioception (stimuli from within the body itself). This kinaesthetic sense is distributed over the body's tendons, muscles, ligaments, joints, organs, glands and vessels. By giving feedback, it gives human beings a feeling for themselves. This sense is neglected even today, which makes movement appear to be a result of sensing. The opposite is the case. In all senses, movement gets the sensing of dynamism going, is the key to experience, learning, feeling, thinking and remembering.

The forefathers of holistic methods continued tracking down »moment awareness« independently of each other. In self-experiments they observed their physical functions with curiosity, mostly in search of solutions for their own problems. In the process they were simultaneously subject and object, seeker and expert: through participation and experience. Using test methods, their critical reflection regarding the division of body and mind revealed facts that are today being confirmed by knowledge theorists, psychologists, philosophers, neuroscientists and sports scientists. However, since the sciences did not display much interest in the practitioners of phenomenological research, their findings regarding the plasticity of the brain or the effect of thought on the sensory-motor functions appear to be totally new from today's point of view. There are no references to the progressive thinkers, for example the movement scientists Moshe Feldenkrais, Mabel Todd or Bonnie Bainbridge Cohen. They only made tentative efforts to approach the world of science because they placed the emphasis of their experiential research on the creative aspect. This only changed in the past decade, which also led to a convergence of the approaches and to ideas of founding an all-embracing somatic movement discipline.

Frederick Matthias Alexander (1869–1955) was the first person to define the kinaesthetic sense. He discovered that practically every influence – physical, mental and emotional – is translated into muscular tension. This often results in too much tension, which habitually shortens the body. This finding was based on his own experiences giving recitals. Alexander lost his voice on stage time and again. He discovered the key to the cure in the »primary control« which employs the dynamic relationship between head, neck and spine. With mental instructions and path-breaking contact he was able to check disturbing factors of the so-called use of self. He found out that the process between ›end-gaining‹ and action creates more tension than necessary. Correspondingly, his strategy consisted of learning to ›inhibit‹ (aware as a roe deer) and undoing in doing.

Elsa Gindler (1885–1961) urged us to trust in the senses. »Coming to our senses«, »Listening and getting ready for experience«, »Calming Down«.[3] Gindler was trained by Hedwig Kallmeyer, the advocate of »Harmonische Gymnastik« (harmonious gymnastics). However, as a co-designer of a cultural reform movement she followed her own exploratory path. Not exercises but rather simple actions such as standing, sitting, lying down and walking were »experimented« with in order to make daily tasks »thoughtful«. Gindler was in search of »human resourcing« in cooperation with the musician and talent researcher Heinrich Jacoby, who in turn taught for Dalcroze in Hellerau, and advocated the rejection of mechanical practice when dancing or playing an instrument because »regardless of the ›successes‹, as long as one exerts oneself, one is always deprived of the essence«.[4] Comparable with the methods of a Zen master, she threw her pupils back upon themselves with »purposeful« questions and stimulated »antenna« behaviour.

In Eutony, a method developed by Gerda Alexander (1908–1994) who stemmed from the Dalcroze tradition, »tonus transfer«[5] defines the phenomenon of presence, of »being present« and the transfer of one's own posture and movement organisation to another person. Tonus describes the basic tension in the striped and smooth muscles, but also the basic mood controlled by the neuro-vegetative system in human beings. In developing this method, she also disclosed one of the secrets of empathy and transfer that occurs between teacher and pupil, artist and audience, mother and child, and which today can be explained by means of the mirror neuron theory.[6] Alexander used the term »hyper-

---

3 | Sophie Ludwig: *Elsa Gindler – von ihrem Leben und Wirken, Wahrnehmen, was wir empfinden*, Hamburg: Christians 2002, p. 149.

4 | Heinrich Jacoby: *Jenseits von begabt und unbegabt. Zweckmäßige Fragestellung und zweckmäßiges Verhalten, Schlüssel für die Entfaltung des Menschen*, Hamburg: Christians [1983] 1994, p. 47.

5 | Gerda Alexander: *Eutonie*, Munich: Kösel 1976, p. 53.

6 | Cf. Christian Keysers/Valeria Gazzola: »Towards a Unifying Neural Theory of Social Cognition«, in: *Lernen in Bewegung*, publication of the 2. European Feldenkrais-Congress Berlin, Munich: Feldenkrais Society 2005, pp. 19–33.

tonia« to describe the faulty tensions as well as the good tension that have physical and mental effects. As with Gindler, Eutony experiments with balls, poles, stones, chestnuts, sandbags in order to make contact with the organs, the skeleton and the ground via the skin. One of the most important elements to obtain maximum effort with a minimum of energy is the reflexive »transport« (thrust) through the bones. This also regulates the muscular tonus.

The voice teacher Mabel Todd (1874–1956) developed an early form of mental training in the United States, which she named »structural hygiene«. Her pupils later described the learning system as »Ideokinesis«.[7] Todd found out that simply imagining inner images from anatomy and nature stimulated the synergy of the senses and by doing so improved the function of the organism. She concluded that thought and imagination created movement and »proprioceptive sensations«.[8] Her book »The Thinking Body« not only covers her kinaesthetic (re)thinking theories – doing without doing – but also combines physiological and kinesiological knowledge in order to reach a deeper understanding of movement relations that also serves in injury prevention.[9]

Moshe Feldenkrais (1904–1984), the Russian-Israeli physicist and judo expert, was the only ›proper‹ scientist among the movement researchers and discovered the secret of learning through movement in self-experiments. While examining developmental processes, he noticed that the motor vestibular nerve is the first of the twelve cranial nerves to develop in the inner ear, even before the sensory ability of hearing is obtained. This proved that the function of this »coordination switchboard« for balance in gravity, space and time is essential for movement and as such for the development of the species. Subsequently, he classified the kinaesthetic sense in his 1943 neuro-physiological lectures as the most important stimulant for upright motion in human beings.[10]

Feldenkrais put this knowledge to practice. His goal was to promote the ability of »learning how to learn«. He intended to waken dormant potential by using the *trial and error* strategies he had observed in young children. He spoke of learning as: »to understand the unknown [...] to

---

7 | Cf. André Bernard/Ursula Stricker/Wolfgang Steinmüller (eds.): *Ideokinese – Ein kreativer Weg zu Bewegung und Körperhaltung*, Bern: Huber 2003, pp. 11–13.

8 | Mabel E. Todd: *The Thinking Body. A Study of the Balancing Forces of Dynamic Man*, London: Dance Books [1937] 1997, p. 27.

9 | Cf. Eric Franklin: *Befreite Körper. Handbuch zur imaginativen Bewegungspädagogik*, Kirchzarten: VAK 1999.

10 | Cf. Moshe Feldenkrais: *Der Weg zum reifen Selbst*, Paderborn: Junfermann 1994, pp. 173ff.

learn you first have to know the trees and then the forest to which they belong«.[11] Starting with the assumption that movement patterns are also behaviour patterns that are affected by fears and repressive upbringing, Feldenkrais strived for the clarification of the self-image. The fact that he had a black belt in judo is also demonstrated in his learning experiments, which lead through the development with aspired lightness and in which highly complicated movements develop at all levels. Upright posture burgeons like fruit on a tree and not through a »primary control«. This »tonic« state (of the roe deer) gives the spine stability, also when rolling and falling.

Moshe Feldenkrais at a workshop in Freiburg in 1981 demonstrating the effortlessness of a backward roll on a pupil. This was the only seminar he ever ran in Germany.

Photo: Irene Sieben

In the United States, Bonnie Bainbridge Cohen (born 1942) the developer of »Body-Mind Centering« (BMC) exemplifies how knowledge begins to move beyond time and continents. Termed »experiential«, the explorations of the dancer and occupational therapist also root in the studies of anatomy, neuro-physiological learning concepts, yoga, Ideokinesis and Japanese martial arts. Apart from understanding how the mind is expressed through the body, Cohen works with the relearning of infant movement patterns. It is based on the knowledge that the sensory motor functions provide a basis for how people will handle experiences, how they perceive, move and express themselves. According to Cohen, it was Irmgard Bartenieff who combined the Laban space and effort theory with

---

11 | Moshe Feldenkrais: *Die Entdeckung des Selbstverständlichen*, Frankfurt a.M.: Insel 1985, p. 137.

physiotherapeutic know-how, who gave her the most important impulses for the development of her learning method.[12]

Like Feldenkrais, Cohen also emphasises that the motor spinal nerves in the foetus are the first to function. Movement is necessary to obtain sensory feedback. »Each experience sets a baseline for future experiences. Movement helps to establish the process of how we perceive«[13] In his theory Cohen differentiates between the terms »sensing« and »perceiving«:

Sensing is the more mechanical aspect, involving the stimulation of the sensory receptors and the sensory nerves. Perceiving is about one's personal relationship to the incoming information. We all have sense organs which are similar, but our perceptions are totally unique. Perception is about relationship – to ourselves, others, the earth and the universe. And it contains the interweaving of both sensory and motor components.[14]

Lisa Nelson and Nancy Stark Smith, two cofounders of contact improvisation, already interviewed Cohen for their magazine »Contact Quarterly« in the 1980s. The editors were looking for an interpretation of this ›dance revolution‹ phenomenon that was also linked to experiences in early childhood and abandoned the fixation of the vertical axis: yield to the pull of gravity in carrying/being carried, falling/floating, leading/following, lifting/flying. Sensing in contact improvisation also isn't a passive state but rather calls for movement. »In purposeful movement, nothing is ever passive. Being passive is an active choice«.[15]

The collective term »Release techniques« or »Somatics« describes various methods of learning movement in the dance departments of colleges and universities in the United States. On the other side of the ocean they also determined the aesthetic direction of the schools for new dance development in Holland and Belgium. The emphasis is mainly on methods that do not merely adopt the anatomy theoretically, but instead embody it with movement, touch, voice and image resources as for instance in BMC and ideokinesis. The clients transform their chests into ›breathing‹ umbrellas, stack vertebrae like building blocks, lengthen the coccyx like a dinosaur tail, let the head float like a balloon or imagine that the ›ball‹ of the femur rolls into the hip socket like a golf ball into

---

12 | Cf. Antja Kennedy: *Bewegtes Wissen – Laban/Bartenieff Bewegungsstudien*, unpublished manuscript forthcoming in 2008.

13 | Bonnie Bainbridge Cohen: *Sensing, Feeling and Action*, Northampton: Contact Editions 1993, p. 118.

14 | Ibid., pp. 114–117.

15 | Beth Goren: *Rapidas – Visions for Body-Mind Centering*, Northampton: Contact Editions [1986] 2006, p. 54.

the hole. The greatest gift working with these moving images can give a dancer is the ability to find balance, tension and relaxation, transparency and effortlessness aligned in a centre axis.

The aesthetic of post-modern dance has been significantly influenced by the »Release techniques«. They gave impulses for the disassociation from formative styles of dance techniques or purely athletic virtuosity to the appreciation of movements in normal everyday life. Furthermore, they provoked a trend in performers to move away from the black box of the stage into the public space. The effect of the Alexander technique is clearly visible for instance in Trisha Brown's characteristic swinging, swimming quality of movement in space. The strategy of mentally isolating the head from the atlas, simultaneously lengthening the spine up and down, giving the arms and legs full freedom in all their joints bestows optimal lightness to extreme changes of levels in the large group choreographies of the 1970s and 1980s. In the viewer this evokes the illusion of watching fish dive in an aquarium. The dancer's ability of double awareness – to be at the same time observer and observed while dancing – significantly improves the stage presence and their orientation amongst themselves.

Anna Huber and Fritz Hauser in HANDUNDFUSS

Photo: Bernd Uhlig

In contemporary dance the movement research methods are also applied in different ways. For instance, the Berlin-based Dance Company Rubato uses the understanding of the liquid body systems such as blood, lymph, synovial and brain fluids as a tool. This perfected art of BMC leads into the glandular world and allows conditions that provoke surges of adrenalin and lead to survival reactions in the dance. Overcoming one's own fear to be able to penetrate into regions of previously unknown experiences – movement by movement – requires the courage to metamorphose. This process also becomes visible in the experimental crossing of frontiers by dancer and choreographer Anna Huber, who works in Berlin and Bern. Her often humorous entanglement of the limbs seem to disclose the Feldenkrais inspiration, by repeatedly letting herself be dared into new movement constellations, by breaking individual functions down into small puzzle pieces, rearranging them and putting them back together again.

Back to Hellerau and the roe deer: With her anatomic research Jarmila Kröschlová (1893–1983), as mentioned above, carried out early preliminary work for the dance. Her pupil and later teaching colleague Rosalia Chladek developed her own system, which is still being used in the rhythmics department of music academies. For a long time it was the only thing in dance that was not based on demonstrating/copying but rather on the autonomous experimenting in accordance with elementary laws of movement in gravity. With the help of Kröschlová's findings, Chladek was able to find an approach in furtherance of the learner's competency that links all the previously mentioned methods: it is ultimately about finding the inner teacher.

Translation from German

References

Alexander, Gerda: *Eutonie*, Munich: Kösel 1976.
Bainbridge Cohen, Bonnie: *Sensing, Feeling and Action*, Northampton: Contact Editions 1993.
Bernard, André/Stricker, Ursula/Steinmüller, Wolfgang (eds.): *Ideokinese – Ein kreativer Weg zu Bewegung und Körperhaltung*, Bern: Huber 2003.
Brooks, Charles W. (1984): *Sensory Awareness*, German adaptation by Charlotte Selver, Paderborn: Junfermann.
Feldenkrais, Moshe: *Der Weg zum reifen Selbst*, Paderborn: Junfermann 1994.
Feldenkrais, Moshe: *Die Entdeckung des Selbstverständlichen*, Frankfurt a.M.: Insel 1985.
Franklin, Eric: *Befreite Körper. Handbuch zur imaginativen Bewegungspädagogik*, Kirchzarten: VAK 1999.
Goren, Beth: *Rapidas – Visions for Body-Mind Centering*, Northampton: Contact Editions [1986] 2006.
Jacoby, Heinrich: *Jenseits von begabt und unbegabt. Zweckmäßige Fragestellung und zweckmäßiges Verhalten, Schlüssel für die Entfaltung des Menschen*, Hamburg: Christians [1983] 1994.
Kennedy, Antja: *Bewegtes Wissen – Laban/Bartenieff Bewegungsstudien*, unpublished manuscript forthcoming in 2008.

Keysers, Christian/Gazzola, Valeria: »Towards a Unifying Neural Theory of Social Cognition«, in: *Lernen in Bewegung*, publication of the 2. European Feldenkrais-Congress Berlin, Munich: Feldenkrais Society 2005, pp. 19–33.

Kröschlová, Jarmila: *Movement Theory and Practice*, Sydney: Current Press 2000.

Ludwig, Sophie: *Elsa Gindler – von ihrem Leben und Wirken, Wahrnehmen, was wir empfinden*, Hamburg: Christians 2002.

Todd, Mabel E.: *The Thinking Body. A Study of the Balancing Forces of Dynamic Man*, London: Dance Books [1937] 1997.

Sharing with Others

DIETER HEITKAMP IN DIALOGUE WITH GABRIELE WITTMANN

Prof. Dieter Heitkamp heads the Department for Contemporary and Classical Dance at the Frankfurt University of Music and Performing Arts. During the DANCE CONGRESS, he presented a lecture performance entitled HAUTSACHE BEWEGUNG – MOVING FROM THE SKIN, which he had developed with the assistance of students and guests. Dance journalist Gabriele Wittmann talked to him about academic lecturing and alternative forms of presentation, about the significance of skin in contemporary dance and the social implications this carries.

Gabriele Wittmann: HAUTSACHE BEWEGUNG is not an ordinary lecture but a lecture performance for the stage. What made you choose this form?
Dieter Heitkamp: This had to do with my frustration at conferences and symposiums. A few years ago, I heard numerous lectures at the »Wissen schaffen über Tanz« (generating knowledge about dance) conference held at the Academy of Arts in Berlin. At the time, I noticed that a lecture ultimately is really something of a performance – so why is so little attention paid to this aspect of it? After all, we're dealing with body and dance here. Why is it that academics often only read from a manuscript? To me, that is non-sensuous and causes me to shut off.
In your opinion, is there a general communication problem between the academic and the practical world?
Quite simply, there is a very specific academic language involved here – one that academics understand among themselves. But when this language is lectured so dryly, I personally have a hard time to get involved in it. Now, reading on the other hand is a totally different story – because I can dictate my own pace and can put the text aside for a

while if necessary, too. But when I'm at a lecture, the text comes at me at a certain pace. And for me that means: ›swim or sink‹.

How did your lecture performance come about?

It all started with a text I wrote for the GTF yearbook on the subject of ›communication‹.[1] The thought crossed my mind that contact improvisation is in itself communication expressed through dance, just that the communication comes about through contact. And contact takes place via the skin. To help me, I then drew on experiences from »Body-Mind Centering«. And then there was this book I had read by a French psychoanalyst called Didier Anzieu: »Skin Ego«.[2] Anzieu offers an exciting angle on how this organ has developed from a psychological perspective, and I thought that it made a lot of sense to transfer his system to dance. He divides the function of skin into three areas: it is a vessel, a protective boundary and the place and tool for communication and for the creation of meaningful relationships. This last aspect is something I find particularly important: that, when engaging in contact improvisation, you don't just ›rub against someone‹ or pull out acrobatic movements from a box of tricks but that you hone your senses in order to realize that something spontaneous occurs between people – and allowing others to share this spontaneously evolving form of communication.

And how did a performance emerge from the text?

I thought about how to create a structure for a performance based on this text. I wanted to establish a framework that gave the dancers as much freedom as possible to venture into the subject and still allow them to ›let themselves go‹ and just be present without having to produce something. In the meantime, the script has moved on from being just a theoretical text to a kind of manual where the chapters have been arranged in such a way that they provide clear suggestions or ideas of movement on a variety of topics. It is then up to the dancers to decide, during the performance itself, which of these elements they wish to employ: They do not have to ›portray‹ anything but can simply ›explore‹[3] during the lecture. The audience is involved and is given information on a number of different levels: they hear the lecture and observe the

---

1 | Cf. Dieter Heitkamp: »Hautsache Bewegung. Moving from the skin«, in: Antje Klinge/Martina Leeker (eds.): *Tanz Kommunikation Praxis, Jahrbuch der Gesellschaft für Tanzforschung* Vol. 13, Münster: LIT 2003, pp. 125–146.

2 | Cf. Didier Anzieu: *The Skin Ego*, Yale: University Press 1989.

3 | ›Exploring‹ is a term commonly used in contemporary dance and denotes the general attempt at understanding but also the exploration of kinaesthetic ideas, tasks, imagery or exercises and how people make their own experiences through improvisation which – depending on the purpose of the exploration – raise awareness for their own sense of movement or changes it, or even gives rise to new types of movement (annotation G.W.).

dancers. What's more, they can make their own physical experiences to some extent, because there are also exercises for the audience. Experiencing these things first hand gives rise to a different perception of the spoken word – but also a different perception of what happens when dance is performed on stage.

HAUTSACHE BEWEGUNG involves one speaker, eight dancers and two live musicians. There were also stage lighting and video projections. How does this interaction of the senses work for the audience?

The subject of »skin as a surface structure«, for example, is transported on an audio and visual level. This involves someone generating an acoustic area, in this case by plucking cactus needles. This can be heard, but also seen on a large live video screen. Or someone rubs a cork mask which, because of the wrinkles on the bark, produces a haptic quality that is also transmitted visually via video. The result is a constant transmission of the sensory perception via the media.

HAUTSACHE BEWEGUNG – MOVING FROM THE SKIN by Dieter Heitkamp, DANCE CONGRESS GERMANY 2006

Photo: Thomas Aurin

This is evocative of the fundamental elements used in successful didactics: reaching all the senses; offering something for every type of learner ...

I think it worked quite well. But you need at least three hours to set up and take down a lecture performance like this, to be able to create an atmosphere using light and other elements which bears a resemblance to the sensory experiences and dramaturgy of a room. As the auditorium at the House of World Cultures, the venue of the DANCE CONGRESS, is a difficult place due to its size and the fact that the stage is open on all sides, it took a courageous decision to present HAUTSACHE BEWEGUNG in spite of the odds. But many in the audience welcomed it.

During the performance you act as the speaker, but also do some dancing yourself. No doubt many in the audience found it unusual to see the dean of a university dancing ›skin on skin‹ with his students.

This ›acting together‹ is part and parcel of contact improvisation. For this type of ›improvising together‹ to evolve, a different teacher-student relationship is required. From the very beginning of the first year of study, we ask students: »Can we touch you?« If not, we ask them: »Talk to us!« This is how to go about clarifying each individual's personal level of physical contact. This is a fundamental prerequisite for contact improvisation.

How would you define this special relationship between teachers and students?

It all starts with the fact that contact improvisation is not called the »Steve Paxton method« but that every knowledge bearer who practices it contributes to this open dance technique – which continues to develop even after 35 years. By the same token, everyone picks something up for themselves. This idea of developing something through a shared relationship has been an integral part of contact improvisation from the beginning. Consequently, the exchange going on during shared improvisation meetings is especially fostered – and not just the exchange among teachers but also between teachers and students. But more awareness needs to be raised about where the idea for a movement or exercise originates. If a student already has more extensive knowledge of contemporary dance and is fed information about where individual elements come from, then that person can see a given exercise in a very different light.

During the lecture performance, you also incorporate an exploration used by the choreographer Lisa Nelson or you explain what the term »skinesphere«[4] means and who coined it. Is it fair to say that HautSache Bewegung is also a lesson in dance history?

Yes, I believe that, in contemporary dance, there is a desire for terms used in dance practice to denote movement or techniques to be explained. If someone uses the term »rolling point«, do we really all mean the same thing? Or are we talking at cross-purposes? What about »counterbalance«, or »pivot«? It's a question of defining certain terms so that everyone involved in the same work has a similar understanding and can later pass on the meaning of these terms.

Let's now turn to the content of the performance itself: Why is it so impor-

---

4 | The term »skinesphere« is an integral part of the UNDERSCORE developed by Nancy Stark Smith. The performer, editor and improvisation teacher uses this term to describe the space within the skin. The »skinesphere« is the scope within the body, as opposed to the »kinesphere«, which is the space surrounding the body. Cf. Dieter Heitkamp: »Moving from the skin«, in: *Contact Quarterly* Vol. 28/2 (2003), pp. 38–46.

tant for contemporary dancers still undergoing training to concern themselves with the organ skin?

Within the body systems in dance, the ones that are most common are those linked to very specific qualities. In the »Body-Mind Centering« approach these are bones or joints, for example, used for focusing and articulating the body in the room or muscles responsible for providing dynamics. I find that working with the skin generates an even greater sensuous quality. If the task is, for example, to sense the skin across the entire body and not just wherever it touches the floor or a partner, then I undergo a 360° experience with the body. It changes the entire presence.

That means it also changes the dancer's presence on stage?

I see it like this: more volume is present in the body when this »skin-esphere« – as Nancy Stark Smith calls this area within the skin – is really completely filled out. The awareness is there then, and more room evolves in every direction.

Is it visible?

Yes, it is visible. But this in itself leads on to the next question: does this presence stop with the skin or does it spread further into the room? Sometimes, there is what we call a »bell effect«: something materialises between two improvising dancers but only between them, no-one else. What's important is how whatever happens can then be passed on into the room. How can it be communicated without coming across as false or demonstrative?

Does skin presence also have something to do with how swift dancers' reactions are?

Yes, because both the skin and kinaesthetic sense are the only senses found everywhere. In contact improvisation, you do not just communicate with hands and arms; the entire body is used and employed as a contact and communication area. The skin – along with the entire nervous system which sends feedback to the brain – is a good tool for doing this.[5]

Many exercises found in contemporary dance are similar to those used in body therapies which arose around the same time. The idea is to slow down the communication processes and make them microscopically visible – including communication within your own body, sensations, thinking and feeling. In other words, the idea is to discover self-definition, and your own thoughts and concepts. Do you see a gateway here to the social and philosophical relevance of contemporary dance?

---

5 | Since these senses are on hand as receptors on the entire body, certain movement decisions can be taken inside the body at a pre-conscious level and therefore more rapidly than through the conscious thought process in the brain (annotation G.W.).

I believe that immersing yourself at this level of body awareness plays a very significant role in contemporary dance – whether this occurs through »Body-Mind Centering«, »Feldenkrais«, the »Alexander Technique«, or »Ideokinesis«. Or through principles that have their origin in Asian martial arts and teach you how to be ›in the flow‹ and how to work with this flow of energy.

Or how you can set boundaries: say »no«. That boundaries can be seen as something flexible you can outgrow. Or even accepting that perhaps a certain boundary is there – and respecting this fact. Contact improvisation is also about how people deal with each other, what means of exchange are created during dance, in lessons or in jam sessions. It's about allowing everyone to speak out, even at contact improvisation festivals in large groups of 100 people, in feedback rounds and planning sessions so that everybody is heard. These days, some groups consist of even 200 people – this takes on a social relevance.

HautSache Bewegung – Moving from the skin
by Dieter Heitkamp, Dance Congress
Germany 2006

Photos: Thomas Aurin

Contemporary dance deals with numerous issues such as: where do the boundaries lie? What is the ego? What is the other? What really are definitions? A popular issue is that of perception, of listening to yourself while thinking. Just think of the works of Jérôme Bel, for example. Or the issue of not seeing yourself as a subject/object but as part of an ongoing communication process, as indicated by Xavier Le Roy in his use of the term »osmosis«.[6] All of these issues are reflected in many performances ...

This research is expressed in the works of a lot of choreographers. For this reason I would say that, in the relation between contemporary dance and certain body awareness methods, there are areas where scientific and artistic research coincide somewhere along the way. This is true of artists like Felix Ruckert or even Ka Rustler. But also of the Rubato Group and Anna Huber – it happens to all of them in a different way.

---

6 | Cf. Xavier Le Roy in his Self-Interview, in which he interviews himself on the concepts of the body, among other things.
Cf. *www.insituproductions.net/_eng/framesetl.html* from 12 May 2007.

What can we expect next for HautSache Bewegung?
I would like to rework the material in a completely different medium: turn it into a book with a DVD, with recordings of performances and video clips. A book not only containing photos, but also texts used on stage – in German and English.

And the next lecture performance? Will you also be looking at other body systems taken from »Body-Mind Centering«, the subject of »liquid«, for example?

No. I'd rather turn my attention to a lecture performance on the subject of dance and language. The inspiration for this came from your text DANCING IS NOT WRITING[7] and your essay that has just been published, JEDE FASER ATMET DEN ZUG.[8] This research work would also include HUMAN WRITES by William Forsythe – though with a different slant: his book deals with writing, inscribing, the connection between movement and words. This interplay is something I've been looking at more intensively over the past year, though I need more time to research it. But that will be the next area I will be researching.

Translation from German

---

7 | Cf. Gabriele Wittmann: »Dancing is Not Writing«, in: Gabriele Klein/Christa Zipprich (eds.): *Tanz Theorie Text, Jahrbuch der Gesellschaft für Tanzforschung* Vol. 12, Münster: LIT 2002, pp. 585–596.

8 | Cf. Gabriele Wittmann: »Jede Faser atmet den Zug«, in: *die deutsche bühne* 78, 1 (2007), pp. 24–28.

References

Anzieu, Didier: *The Skin Ego*, Yale: University Press 1989.

Heitkamp, Dieter: »Hautsache Bewegung. Moving from the skin«, in: Antje Klinge/Martina Leeker (eds.): *Tanz Kommunikation Praxis, Jahrbuch der Gesellschaft für Tanzforschung* Vol. 13, Münster: LIT 2003, pp. 125–146.

Heitkamp, Dieter: »Moving from the skin«, in: *Contact Quarterly* Vol. 28/2 (2003), pp. 38–46.

Le Roy, Xavier: »Self-Interview«, in: *www.insituproductions.net/_eng/framesetl.html* .

Wittmann, Gabriele: »Dancing is Not Writing«, in: Gabriele Klein/Christa Zipprich (eds.): *Tanz Theorie Text, Jahrbuch der Gesellschaft für Tanzforschung* Vol. 12, Münster: LIT 2002, pp. 585–596.

Wittmann, Gabriele: »Jede Faser atmet den Zug«, in: *die deutsche bühne* 78, 1 (2007), pp. 24–28.

About Risks and ›Side Effects‹ of Dancing

Dance Medicine in Dance Training

and the Professional Career

Eileen M. Wanke

Male and female professional dancers are the elite athletes of the performing arts. During their dance education and later during professional training, rehearsal, and performance, male and female dancers are subjected to extreme physical and psychological demands. Compared to other professions, the career of a female and a male dancer is exceptionally short in duration, particularly when contrasted to the necessary lengthy and dance-only period of education and training. The careers of both male and female dancers typically end before their fortieth birthdays. Especially for female dancers, epitomizing the physical ideal which is particularly, but not exclusively, defined by extreme slenderness and low body weight, is as important a requirement for professional training and a professional career as technical proficiency. Again in contrast to other professions, stage dance makes little or no use of tools or equipment to provide support to the body during the work process. The dancer's body, which expresses movement, emotion, and action, is both the tool and the sole capital of the professional dancer in his or her career. The strain of dance training and the subsequent professional career is exerted exclusively and wholly upon the body of the dancer.

As a rule, in order to practice his or her profession, a dancer requires a fundamentally functional physical organism. It is often difficult, even impossible, to compensate for even minor physical ›deficits‹ in dance. Even minor physical deficits can seriously hinder a dancer's professional career, and often will lead to temporary or permanent occupational disability. For this reason, the therapy and especially the prevention of injuries, regardless of severity and extent, is a matter of fundamental importance to the field of professional stage dance. Specific and targeted injury prevention and therapy requires specialised knowledge and understanding of the working conditions particular to professional dance. Key in this respect is knowledge of the occupational health risks as well as the mechanism of accidents that characterise professional dance.

The earliest isolated discussions of medical aspects of dance can be dated back to the nineteenth century. However, an additional 200 years would pass before the first professional organisations devoted to dance medicine were founded. Meanwhile, national as well as international dance medicine organisations have been founded in many countries across the world. The scope of dance medicine is broad, and requires a level of interdisciplinary cooperation similar to sports medicine, linking issues of physiology, biomechanics, traumatology, psychology, nutrition, injury prevention, and injury therapy. The goals of dance medicine include the improvement of medical care, the promotion of awareness and education among professionals in the field, the stimulation of research and teaching, and the overall improvement in communication within the field.

The status of professional dance[1] in Germany has changed dramatically in recent years. In the past ten years, the number of dancers in salaried professional positions has declined by nearly a third at the national level (see Fig. 1).

In Berlin, the change has been even more dramatic; over the past ten years, the number of dancers in salaried employment has declined by more than fifty percent.

Figure 1: Development in the number of salaried female and male dancers in Germany

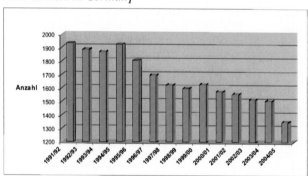

In the course of this development, two companies were dissolved, and two other companies were merged. This ›death of ballet‹ continues across Germany today.

---

1 | In what follows, dance shall be assumed to include classical and neoclassical ballet, revue dance, musical dance and dance theatre.

Unfortunately, this means it has become increasingly difficult for trained female and male dancers to find salaried employment. However, even as the number of professional dance positions has declined, the number of performances and premieres over this period has remained largely unchanged. The existing work load, which was already intense, has now been distributed among a significantly smaller number of female and male dancers. The work load for professional female and male dancers thus has increased exponentially. Moreover, over the course of the 20th century, the increased demands for technical perfection and virtuosity, the requirement to typify the physical ideal, and the boundless imagination of the choreographers continue to intensify and exacerbate the heavy physical demands of dance.

As a result, approximately half of all professional dancers today will experience at least one occupational injury during the course of a single season. This number is twice as high as it was only ten years ago. The injury frequency for professional dancers is directly related to the duration, type, and intensity of the burdens placed upon the male and female dancer. While occupational injury rates for other kinds of stage workers have remained constant in recent years, they have sharply increased for professional male and female dancers.

Sprains and pulled muscles are among the most common injuries to both male and female dancers. In the case of female dancers, approximately 20 percent of injuries are bruises resulting from lifts (holds and grips) performed by the partner. The most common sites of injury to both male and female dancers are the joints, which are affected by one-third of all injuries. The next most common site of injury, representing more than one-quarter of injuries in male dancers, are the muscles. In female dancers, one-quarter of occupational accidents result in injuries to the ligaments, while one-seventh of all accidents lead to muscle injuries. For male dancers, one-eighth of all accidents result in injuries of the bone; for female dancers, this figure is one-seventh of all accidents.

Depending on the form of dance, between 50 and 70 percent of injuries affect the lower extremities. The more removed the dance form from the techniques of classical ballet, the higher the rate of injury to other parts of the body. In dance theatre, for example, the head and neck region and the upper extremities are affected in one-third of all accidents. This divergent injury pattern is due both to the use of props and to the employment of movement patterns not typical of dance. These movement patterns often are only trained infrequently or not at all during daily rehearsals, which typically focus on classical dance technique instead. Movement patterns from outside the vocabulary of classical dance include movements such as leaps from high or unstable objects, cartwheels, and forward and backward somersaults.

The lower extremities are also the most common site of injury during the years of preparatory training. Although there are important differences in injury patterns to male and female dancers, the most common sites of injury are the hip, leg, and foot. Injury rates to young dancers increase during periods of physical growth. For all forms of dance, the most common injury during preparatory training and during a dancer's professional career is a supination trauma (»sprain«) of the ankle.

Depending on the form of dance, between 25 and 50 percent of accidents take place during the execution of a jump or jump combination. Leaps and jumps place the greatest demands on a dancer's physical condition and coordination skills. The different demands made on male and female dancers result in a marked difference in injury rates from jumps. Female dancers are much less likely to injure themselves during jump combinations and lifts, and are more likely to acquire injuries in the course of executing ordinary dance movements, such as smaller jumps or combinations of steps that are elements of the standard vocabulary of dance. This difference results from specific demands placed upon male and female dancers. For example, as a rule only female dancers wear pointe shoes, while male dancers perform the large jump combinations. Female dancers are more likely to be lifted than to perform a lift. The greater the distance from classical dance technique, the more these gender-specific patterns of injury dissolve.

Since the entire body serves as work material in dance, it comes as no surprise that a large number of injuries have multi-factorial causes. Multi-factorial causes include endogenous factors, such as the type and scope of the performance contract, the male and female dancer's role in the group, nutrition, training and performance planning, and more. Figure 2 depicts a characteristic distribution of injury causation for the different forms of dance.

Figure 2: Causes of occupational injury in stage dance

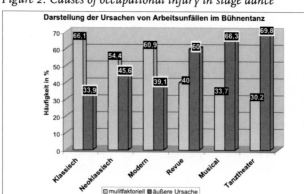

Wanke, Wolff 2005

In classical dance (ballet), approximately two-thirds of all injuries have multi-factorial causes. As the distance to classical (and thus highly defined) dance technique increases, the causality of injury also shifts. In revue dance, dance musicals, and dance theatre, the majority of injuries are caused by an ›outside object‹. These injuries thus conform more closely to the standard definition of occupational injury. The ›outside‹ influence or the object that results in injury to the dancers may include the following: flooring, costuming, other dancers or persons, props and the scenery, and in some cases movement sequences not specific to dance (see above).

In addition to other persons and to props (particularly in dance theatre and in musicals), statistically speaking the flooring is one of the most common causes of accidents. Why should this be the case? Flooring plays a ›lead role‹ in dance. Often the floor represents the only reliable grounding for the dancer apart from his or her partner. Ensuring optimal floor surface conditions thus should be a matter of highest priority. Here it is important to note that flooring requirements differ for male and female dancers. Because of their work en pointe, female dancers prefer flooring with high slip resistance. This is not the case for male dancers, however. Overly slip-resistant flooring, for example, may make pirouettes much more difficult or even impossible. Also, flooring with excessive slip resistance may sharply increase the risk of injury due to ›jamming‹ on the floor during jump combinations, which place the utmost demand upon the male and female dancer's coordination skills. Other problems associated with flooring are unevenness, the presence of stage wagon tracks for multi-functional stage technology, fissures or discrepancies in floor level, dirt and foreign substances, and curling edges in the case of glued floor coverings.

While props are less common in classical, modern, and revue dance, they are quite common in dance theatre. In dance theatre, one in three accidents is caused by props. Props might include, for example, objects such as cabinets used in the choreography, cages made out of wood laths, which can lead to splinters, and metal chains that might be used to bind male and female dancers to chairs. Other props might include dentures and nails to be inserted into the mouth, other sharp objects, metal beds, or any other object that might be used in implementing the choreographer's boundless imagination, all of which can lead to injury.

In classical dance, the causes of accidents are quite different. More than 70 percent of all accidents in classical dance have multi-factorial causes. Indeed, in many instances it is impossible to determine the precise combination of factors which led to a specific accident.

Among the many factors that may promote or cause injuries in dance
are:
- training and nutritional status;
- hydration levels;
- fatigue levels;
- status within the troupe and the pressure of competition;
- the time of day;
- technical skills and physical ability;
- the planning of the season with its rehearsal and performance
  schedule;
- and conditions in the employment market.

It is comparatively easy to identify outside objects that may lead to accident. However, although they are equally important to the prevention
of injury, the factors cited above require special knowledge about dance
and the situation of the dancers. One of the key factors worthy of particular mention is the nutritional factor. In addition to the technical skills
required by dance, the aesthetics of dance require that male and female
dancers epitomise a particular physical ideal. Although the specifics of
this ideal vary slightly among the different forms of dance, in all forms
of dance the ideal makes extreme demands on the male and female
dancer. The physical ideal is excessive, in a negative sense, and over the
medium and long term may result in serious and permanent physical
damage. As a male and a female dancer's physical appearance is also
genetically determined, eating disorders are the norm if the physical
ideal does not match reality. Indeed, eating disorders are often encouraged, even required, during dance training and the search for professional employment. Such disordered eating problems *(anorexia athletica)*,
and full-blown eating disorders *(anorexia nervosa, bulimia nervosa)* are
rarely addressed openly, even though they may result in life-threaten-
ing complications and death. Given the growing media attention paid
to eating disorders, it is hard to imagine that individuals in positions of
responsibility in the world of dance, and the students of dance and their
parents, remain unaware of the health problems caused by constant
dieting, particularly in the sphere of dance. Today, the physical ideal is
still largely measured by body weight in kilograms. It can only be hoped
that individuals in a position of responsibility in the world of dance, as
well as students and parents, will begin to tolerate and accept instead the
use of body composition measurements in assessing conformity to the
physical ideal. Body composition rather than body weight in kilograms
is a comparatively more health-promoting form of measurement, as the
current state of knowledge in the field has demonstrated. An insistence
on a rigid physical ideal is frequently associated with a negligent attitude towards the health of young male and female dancers, who are still

growing, and to their later health as adults. The results are immediately evident in the form of increased injury rates, but may often not be fully experienced until after the end of the male and female dancer's career, when bone loss leads to severe impairments to the quality of life.

All dance is not alike. Just as the forms of dance differ greatly, so too do the causes of injury. This in turn affects the preventive measures that should be undertaken in professional stage dance. Preventive measures should take into account work conditions, the sex of the dancer, improved prevention techniques (for example, regular screening), and the possibility of extended therapy (for example, transitional training). Finally, preventive measures must take into account the process of gaining recognition for the reality of occupational accident and illness in the field of professional dance. This requires a great deal of specialised knowledge, interdisciplinary cooperation, and especially education efforts aimed at those responsible for and affected by the work conditions specific to dance, and the unusual work and life circumstances of professional male and female dancers.

Translation from German

References

Arendt, Yasmin D./Kerschbaumer, F.: »Verletzungen und Überlastungserscheinungen im professionellen Ballett«, in: *Zeitung für Orthopädie* 141 (2003), pp. 349–356.

Bronner, Shaw/Brownstein, Bruce: »Profile of dance injuries in a Broadway show: a discussion of issues in dance medicine epidemiology«, in: *The journal of orthopaedic and sports physical therapy* 26 (1997), pp. 87–94.

Cohen, J.L./Segal, K.R./McArdle, Willam D.: »Heartrate response to ballet stage performance«, in: *Physician Sportsmed* (1982), pp. 10, 120–133.

Kelman, B.B.: »Occupational hazards in female ballet dancers. Advocate for a forgotten population«, in: *AAOHN Journal* 48 (2000), pp. 430–434.

Ravaldia, C./Vannacci, A. et al.: »Eating disorders and body image disturbances among ballet dancers, gymnasium users and body builders«, in: *Psychopathology* 36 (2003), pp. 247–254.

Schantz, P.G./Astrand, Per Olov: »Physiological characteristics of classical ballet«, in: *Medicine and science in sports and exercise* 16 (1984), pp. 472–476.

Stretanski, M.F./Weber, G.J.: »Medical and rehabilitation issues in classical ballet«, in: *Am J Phys Med Rehabil* 81 (2002), pp. 383–391.

Unfallkasse Berlin (ed.): *Tanzmedizin – Ausbildung und Arbeitsplatz*, Berlin 2005.

Wanke, Eileen M.: *Leitlinien zur Prävention von Unfällen im professionellen Bühnentanz*, in print.

Dance History and Reconstruction

*Martin Nachbar in his reconstruction of Dore
Hoyer's AFFECTOS HUMANOS,
Photo: Kathrin Schander*

Capturing the Essence

A Personal View on Dance History

and Reconstruction

Jason Beechey

Addressing such monumental issues as the history of dance and reconstruction is a very imposing task. Conjuring up images of bespectacled scholars delving into great volumes of history books in sacred libraries, scouring the earth for lost video footage and stumbling across long forgotten scripts and love letters revealing the inner-most secrets and driving passions behind the great creative minds of the dance world. These knowledgeable souls then setting forth after thousands of hours of painstaking research to breach the door of a dance studio with a fresh young bunch of dancers to relive, revive and recreate the glories of the past. A labour of love, involving the most precise attention to minute details and going over harrowed ground with a fine-tooth comb. A necessary labour so the future generation can experience the fruits of the past. To see with their own eyes exactly what the statements, discoveries and tastes of the past were.

Is this reconstruction accurate? Is this the way it was intended? One only has to watch a video of how something was danced twenty years ago to have the confirmation that ballet technique is more alive and evolving than ever. Peoples' perceptions are constantly changing – what was modern is now old-fashioned. Cutting edge becomes dull and experimental becomes a re-run.

Can a ballet ever really be reconstructed or is it not in permanent evolution? When so many elements come into play – not least of all who is dancing the work or how they have been trained; are these uncontrollable factors not exactly the elements that make dance such an exciting, live art form? The fact that every live performance is unique, special and cannot be reconstructed – is this not the cornerstone of the art of dance? How can we reconstruct something that was alive? How are we to not miss the essential?

I hope and believe that for many generations of dancers to come they will have the pleasure of testing their mettles (and also thrilling audiences) with the small existing canon of classical ballets in the likes of Swan Lake and Sleeping Beauty, but I also hope they will keep them alive – not by reconstructing them, but rather by reinventing them with every single performance and interpretation.

At the same time, the true creative geniuses in generations past were all artists who had irrepressible talents that found their ways to expression and in so doing they set the course for the future. The way the choreographer George Balanchine reconstructed the classical vocabulary and developed it into something new.

We also need to create an atmosphere where such creative talents are able to flourish. Is this not the actual act of reconstruction that we should be focusing on? Creating the time and place for such creative acts to take place? Rather than stifle by comparison, a way to learn and respect the past and give room for the future?

Toronto 1986

Let's go back until 1986. The cold war was thawing out and the fresh winds of glasnost were amongst us and the Kirov Ballet had just set foot into the West after an absence of almost twenty-five years. I was a student and you could not force me to sit still in classes for about two weeks prior to their visit. On the day of the performance I was there hours ahead of time and after a great delay, the lights dimmed and the performance began.

After Chopiniana, a mixed bag of diverts and Paquita my perception of dance had been altered forever. Here was the ›temple‹ of Petipa[1] the historical birthplace of most of the great classics doing absolutely everything that represented ›cardinal sins‹ according to the training I was then receiving. And yet, it was exactly why I was driven to dance. It was inspiring! Here was history at its most alive and kicking.

How was this possible? I was in an excellent school, working with teachers, some of whom had come from this very School and yet, this seemed so completely different.

For me at that time, ballet training was focused on a ›form‹, a rather polite, correct manner of moving where for each step you had to learn the exact form from the fingernail to the eyebrow. You had exams and we all had to be identical in our phrasing, timing and execution. You had to

---

1 | The French-Russian ballet dancer and choreographer Marius Petipa is considered to be the ›father of the classical ballet‹ as he combined French and Italian influences with the Russian ballet.

memorize entire classes only to have the adjudicator decide whether you would do adage number one, two or three. The focus was on learning the correct physical positions and the details. The phrase ›one clean one was always better than three sloppy ones‹ pretty well sums it up. It was a very politically correct, body-friendly approach towards learning ballet. But yet, had we not lost part of the essence?

How come their *épaulement* looked so different from mine? How did they seem to be not performing but they seemed to be rather simply breathing life and artistry from their very pores? The dancers of the Kirov Ballett were full of passion, exuberance, power, elegance and above all – artistry. This was the generation of Lyubov Kunakova, Altynai Asymulratova and Irina Kolpakova. It seemed they oozed freedom, expression, and despite such a seemingly carefree approach could execute the most astounding technical feats. But what cost had they paid to learn this? Where they thinking as they danced? Had they been born with a super-human talent, all of them?

What astounded me even more was that returning the next night I found a completely new set, not only of dancers, but of variations too. This was sacred ground, this was *the* PAQUITA and yet they seemed to be playing free range with it. What was the ›real‹, the historically correct version? Seeing the same variation danced with a completely altered pirouette section or with a different coda and, yet underneath it all, it all seemed so right. As if they understood some underlying current that regardless of what they did, they still captured the essence. It was as if each person possessed their own, personal version, of the ballet.

Was this the true and accurate form, with so much leeway and freedom? How had these certain elements become lost in the translation to the western world? Or had we adapted them to suit our tastes and styles? Or had they continued to evolve (or possibly preserve) them under the Soviet regime? Had they begun to tinker with the choreography out of a lack of inspiring new work? What were the roles and effects of history and reconstruction on both sides of the fence?

Leningrad 1989

Two and a half years later I found myself living on Theatre Street in Leningrad and in one of the graduating classes of the Vaganova Ballet Academy. Here, at the heart of the matter, I wanted to soak up all I could. Far from the warning I had been given prior to going that I would be told all my training was ›wrong‹, I discovered a wonderful openness to go forward. To work with what existed, which in my case meant, working with what I had already learned in the West and to build (not deconstruct) from there. The training at that time in the Vaganova School seemed to stem from the basic »qualitative« principles, such as turn, jump, extend, feel, believe, and the positions were but codified elements to illustrate these principles. A series of exercises designed to test one's basic understandings of these principles, not learning static forms or shapes. You worked from the inside out. And yet the forms and shapes they created were by far more physically extreme than I had previously seen, but yet also so much more expressive and with an inbuilt artistic sense. They did not ›take‹ a position they ›spoke‹ it, in a physical language.

Fascinating for me was how the artistic and technical were so fused. As we hear more and more about dance sciences, technique and performing qualities as separate items – back in Leningrad in 1989 they were most definitely one and the same. The technique was artistic.

Parallel to the ballet training in the West, learning all the traditional dances so integral to the classics seemed so foreign, at least in my opinion. Dancers from the West moved differently, we had different rhythms, no matter how hard we tried; a group of children that grew up listening to pop music did not have the same weight to the movements as one who had attended folk festivities. It was as different as the sounds, sentence structure and speed of a language. It really boiled down to the physical expression of a different mentality. Can you teach this to someone who does not come from the same cultural background? Can such a thing be transposed? How can you pass this on to the next generation? Or does each generation have a language of its own?

For my classmates, it was their history and rhythm they were learning. It was not some foreign character dance, it was the same rhythms they would hear on many festive occasions or official events. It made perfect sense to them and they danced it as such. There was nothing historical about it, or at least not to them; it all seemed perfectly relevant.

I grew up on a diet of Balanchine works at Pacific Northwest Ballet in Seattle and I was absolutely hooked on the physicality of the movement. Streamlined to the pure, nothing extra, speaking with the body, nothing added, no frills or fuss, pure dance.

Some elements in the Vaganova School did strike me as being rather old-fashioned compared to what was then being done in the west. Almost exclusively slow tempos, an indulgent musicality and very clunky pointe work. But are these not three of the defining elements of Balanchine's work? This was where I really began to wonder how much of his work was based on what was in Russia when he was there, both the strong points that he saw could be developed further.

Further questions over this evolution and stagnation were very clearly brought to the forefront by the visit of the répétiteurs of the Kirov Ballet, Suzanne Farrell and Francia Russell, who staged the first Balanchine evening during my stay. Having the chance to speak with Francia Russell, she mentioned dealing with dancers unused to such quick tempos, precise musicality and exact choreography. However, seeing the Kirov Ballet dance their first SCOTCH SYMPHONY, theme and variations did feel like they had been jet- launched into the future, but yet, they were still speaking exactly the same language. Like they were trying to bring their history forward, to catch up what they had missed over the past fifty years in the space of two ballets.

The best way for me to sum up my brief six-month study period was one of intense appreciation and awe. A place built upon pure focus and dedication all stemming from an artistic inspiration for an art form that they truly believed in with their heart and soul. Here lived history, very stifled for new creative outlets under the political regime, but yet dance was revered and respected and the artists danced what they were allowed to dance with total dedication

New York 1990

I went straight from Leningrad to New York. Here was the School of American Ballet founded by Balanchine based upon the School of his childhood and a teaching method that he set out to bring ballet to America with; to create an American way of doing ballet. In many ways, his aim was to break free from tradition, to set forth and to explore.

In the teaching of Stanley Williams, ballet teacher at the School of American Ballet, all the corrections were built into the exercises. In order to do the exercises properly, you had to understand and integrate all the corrections. You could only get the point by letting your physical intelligence figure it out. You could not understand by watching or reading about it, you had to do it. Was this his idea or a reflection of the ideals of Balanchine?

Was this method, so focused on details and the fine-tuning elements better suited for students generally coming from the USA? Was this more competitive environment necessary to stimulate this new generation to strive for the best? Or was this an economic factor? In the Soviet Union each class had between eight to twelve students and in New York we were triple this amount. Was it due to a lack of time or a new teaching method? I believe it was a teaching method built on giving the space to let the body think. He was simply giving us the tools and headspace for us to learn to teach ourselves.

The accent was exactly like at the Vaganova Ballet Academy. Sure, the style was different, but each School suited its location and was a product of the people and place in which they existed. I believe each method has its advantages and disadvantages but yet seemed extremely complementary.

With the School of American Ballet Balanchine founded a new

School, in a new Country and seemed to embrace both the history with the contemporary and lead to a very creative and inspired period in New York.

Is this not the true historical act of reconstruction? The actual act of re-thinking, distilling and redefining of what previously existed? This was the theory being developed in the hands of the practitioners. Not history repeating itself, but rather history being used as a springboard, with a reconstruction through a fertile environment. Both Schools are working on capturing the essence of the movements in their similar, yet different ways, reflective of their native countries and mentalities.

Lecture Demonstration George Balanchine: See the Music Hear the Dance! by Colleen Neary, Dance Congress Germany 2006

Photo: Thomas Aurin

Berlin 2006

Having never performed a Balanchine ballet myself, my interpretation of his work remains that of a student who spent a year at the School of American Ballet and as an audience member at countless performances by a multitude of companies. But it always brings me back to the same point. When not reconstructing one of his ballets, from a written or recorded record, each and every performance can only live and be true if the dancers have the intimate knowledge and understanding of the work. Balanchine always claimed to be first and foremost a teacher, with his ballets crafted as learning tools, not as choreography. You learn by doing. The theory is in, and can only live through, the practical. The history can only live through the contemporary, a live performance.

As one of the principal répétiteurs of the George Balanchine Trust,

Colleen Neary began her presentation[2] at the Dance Congress by saying: »Don't think, just do.« She used the famous quote from Balanchine to set the tone. Having worked intimately with Balanchine for many years, here was someone standing before us who is literally ›Knowledge in Motion‹. But yet, she learned a lot of this knowledge by, apparently, ›not thinking‹.

What does it mean to think? At least in my mind knowledge is something that has to be learnt. Entailing hard work, you have to think to learn. Learning is the key to acquiring knowledge. But here, someone actually learnt *more* by actually consciously trying not to think. At least not thinking in such a cerebral way, but rather by letting her body think for her. Actually ›switching her brain off‹ and letting her body intelligence go to work. She acquired her knowledge, her physical knowledge through her physical instrument. How can we recognise such learned intelligence?

I hope as you have been reading this article that you have been breathing. Did you think about how to accomplish the act of breathing? On which exact second you would breathe in? When exactly you would exhale? I hope not. You could have had a much easier time with your breathing while you were attentively reading this. Maybe this is the principal Balanchine was getting at? Is our body more intelligent than our brain in certain areas? Or maybe when we try to use our brain it can complicate matters physically?

Working as a teacher, one thing I constantly have to ask dancers is to breathe. Not to hear them breathe, but to just let it happen. Why do such highly skilled dancers so often have to be told to breathe? Just as when you are reading this, your body breathes for you. It is also much easier to dance when you let your body do the same thing.

Is there a parallel here as to why many teachers and choreographers also have their best ideas while they are asleep and their conscious minds are ›turned off‹ rather than labouring away in a studio ›thinking‹ about it? Maybe many creative impulses are blocked out by our over-learned way of rational/learned thinking? Are these two basic examples of what Balanchine was trying to get his dancers to do in the studio by saying to them: »Don't think – just do«?

Now in her role as teacher and coach how is Colleen Neary able to pass on her knowledge? To reconstruct not the steps, but the atmosphere that led Balanchine to create and instil in his dancers exactly what he was looking for. But then has the transmission of this exact atmosphere, a

---

2 | In a lecture demonstration at the Dance Congress Neary provided an insight into the technique, methods and understanding of dance, music and style of George Balanchine.

creative one, not been lost? Has it now become an atmosphere of reproduction? Or can this creative atmosphere be reconstructed whereby the
dancer can approach this ballet as a creative act of self-discovery? I very
much hope for the latter.

I am very curious to see in the future how ballets being created today
will live on, or if they will live on at all. Works that combine a physical
act and an active, creative, spontaneous mind will and cannot look the
same when danced by other people. But maybe that is just the point? To
keep them alive the ›essence‹ must be caught and with the right coaching and training the future generations (both on the stage and in the
audience) can find as much excitement and inspiration in these works
as the past generations.

In my opinion, when referring to »dance history« I would like to think
that the best living example of dance history is not the reconstructed elements, but exactly the questioning, challenging new works of today. To
focus on the ›here and now‹ elements combing the best of the past with
a clear mind frame involving the ideas of the current generation.

Re-Constructions: Figures of Thought and Figures of Dance: Nijinsky's Faune[1]

Experiences with Dancing Competence

Claudia Jeschke

In dance, movement and the body are, on the one hand, functionalised into a medium themselves by means of choreographic procedures, and on the other, they interact with other media that are part of the production, such as the plot, the music, the stage design, the costumes and the conditions particular to each individual production. Beyond this, they are also reflected in documents, i.e. in written records and in technical storage systems (i.e. recordings, dance notations, reviews), and they are passed on by means of corporeal memories.

The re-construction[2] of Nijinsky's Faune is one example – one that has been amply discussed historiographically and theoretically – of the multi-faceted mediatisation of documents and discourses, memories and creative process of dance. By way of introduction, I will review the most important background information to these debates and activities, before turning to an account of the rehearsal process and to direct attention to a more liminal aspect of dance studies: the role of dancing and thus of the dancer and of »reconstructors«[3] in the complex, mobile (both in terms of

---

1 | This article discusses various aspects of corporeal mediatisation in dance using the example of a specific re-construction. The theoretical and historical parts are based on a lecture which I held at the DANCE CONGRESS; the description of the practical implementation refers to experiences I and my colleague had during rehearsals for Vaclav Nijinsky's L'Après-midi d'un Faune at Goucher College, Baltimore in February 2007.

2 | On the concept of re-construction, see for example Jean Michel Nectoux (ed.): Nijinsky. L'Après-midi d'un Faune, Paris: Biro 1989, and Ann Hutchinson Guest/ Claudia Jeschke: Nijinsky's Faune Restored, London: Gordon and Breach 1991.

3 | This professional designation for someone who works with dance history,

events and of evolution), but always specific arrangements of knowledge and dance-theatre practice that re-constructions ultimately are.

The dance historian Ivor Guest had the following to say on the re-construction of Nijinsky's FAUNE:

> L'APRÈS-MIDI D'UN FAUNE was recorded in 1915 by Vaslav Nijinsky himself using his own dance notation system. The score lay unused in the British Library for nearly 40 years after his death because nobody could read it. Restaging the ballet relied exclusively on dancers' memories and photographic evidence. With the inevitable loss of detail and distortions through personal movement preference, the piece lost accuracy. In 1988, Dr. Ann Hutchinson Guest and Dr. Claudia Jeschke deciphered Nijinsky's notation system and translated the score into Labanotation. This translation provides great insight into the creative genius of Nijinsky's choreography.[4]

Ivor Guest proposes a qualitative hierarchy of the sources which allowed the re-construction of FAUNE – the memory of the dancers and photographs on the lower rungs, and Nijinsky's own dance notation higher up. Guest's prioritisation, or even idealisation of the dance notation of Nijinsky's first choreography is evidence that notations are rare and highly significant sources of practical and theoretical re-constructions, yet it ignores the complex role dance historiography plays, with or without notations – the interrelationships between discursive sources (materials, texts, pictures) and kinetic information which arises *in actu* through the movements of the dance itself. The following recapitulates and reflects on the methodological difficulty of understanding kinetic ability and feeling as a perspective within trans-historical and trans-cultural dance practice and of defining literal »knowledge in motion«.

The Cultural Studies Approach to Dance Memory

The fact that re-constructions require forms of recorded memory is clear, and it is well known that the prevalent cultural studies definition of memory is based on the work of the Egyptologists and cultural theorists Jan and Aleida Assmann. Certain aspects of the Assmann system can – as an example of the situation of dance culture – be transferred to Nijinsky's FAUNE.

Jan Assmann called cultural memory a »collective term for all know-

---

theoretically but primarily practically, has become established in the US dance scene in recent years.

4 | Last published in Princeton University's programme »The Program in Theatre and Dance«, *Spring Dance Festival, 24–26 February 2006*, no page designation.

ledge which steers actions and experiences within the specific interaction framework of a society and which is initiated and learned again and again from generation to generation.«[5] Assmann sets this collective knowledge apart from »communicative memory«, on the one hand, and »science« as a highly specialised form of memory formation, on the other.[6] »Communicative memory« lives interactively in the attempts of individuals and groups to bring the past into the present, and, unlike cultural memory or science, it represents the short-term memory of a society – it is intrinsically linked to the living bearers and communicators of experiences and lasts around 80 years, i.e. three to four generations. In dance, communicative memory has most effect through the activities of contemporaries, especially in teaching and in the performative, oral communication of dance. The content of these memories can only be fixed through »cultural formation« – that is, through organised, ritualised communication about the past. In dance this happens in notations and in ›schools‹.

According to Assmann, one of the essential characteristics of cultural memory is »concrete identity«; cultural memory is based on a store of knowledge and on the constitutive significance of this store for the identity of a group, in this case people interested in dance. Nijinsky made a significant contribution to dance-culture formation and its concrete identity by truly choreographing his work, which was initially communicated purely physically; he attached his work to the tradition of the dance notation technique and it thus became a part of the cultural memory.

Assmann believes that »reconstructivity« is a further characteristic of cultural formation. The knowledge of the group is the knowledge of the present. »It may be fixed on firmly established figures of memory and stores of knowledge, but every present adds to it, assimilating and challenging, perpetuating and adapting.« Assmann believes that cultural memory exists in two different modes: in the potentiality of the knowledge stored in archives, images and patterns of behaviour and in the topicality of what is used from this store because it is of interest in the present. Every re-construction is an expression of cultural reminiscing which is formed in a perpetual interplay with communicative memory.

---

5 | This and all following Assmann quotes in Jan Assmann: »Kollektives Gedächtnis und kulturelle Identität«, in: Jan Assmann/Tonio Hölscher (eds.): *Kultur und Gedächtnis*, Frankfurt a.M.: Suhrkamp 1988, pp. 9–19. Cf. Harald Welzer: *Das kommunikative Gedächtnis. Eine Theorie der Erinnerung*, Munich: Beck 2005, pp. 13–18.

6 | I will not enter into the discussion on how »dance studies« are traditionally involved in re-constructions, for obvious reasons: this article represents the view that dance studies are not only formed through documents but through the experience of dance itself.

On Cultural Formation: Nijinsky's Notation
as Text and Artefact

As mentioned above, it is very rare for an important choreographer to be fluent in a dance notation system and to note down movements for an entire ballet. More frequently, choreographers document their works using a kind of »aide-mémoire« and there was only one who had done so before Vaclav Nijinsky: in the mid-19th century Arthur Saint-Léon noted down parts of his ballet LA VIVANDIÈRE using a detailed, more elaborated system. Both Saint-Léon and Nijinsky were much too busy with their daily lives as dancers and choreographers to be able to make any real, regular use of their notation systems, and certainly did not have time to popularise them. Yet, fate brought Nijinsky opportunities to invest more energy into the idea – first of all his internment in Budapest from 1914–16 during the First World War, and then again from 1917–18, when he and his family lived in Switzerland.

However, the four notebooks that Nijinsky filled with ideas for the written documentation of dance movements during his period in Switzerland are of little interest for the earlier notation of 1915 for his first choreographed work L'APRÈS-MIDI D'UN FAUNE. Here Nijinsky was experimenting with geometrically orientated concepts of motion.[7]

The notation which Nijinsky used for FAUNE has similarities to the Stepanov system which Nijinsky had learned during his period of training at the Imperial Ballet School in St. Petersburg (1900–1908), though. Vladimir Stepanov's notation was based on anatomical analyses of motion and used musical notes to portray movements. The method was sufficient to notate the ballet repertoire of the day but Nijinsky modified and expanded it to correspond to his own requirements. This meant that Nijinsky's system could not be decoded with the assistance of Stepanov's rules, although its composition and vocabulary of signs clearly derived from Stepanov's concept. And there was (and is) no evidence to suggest that Nijinsky drew up or left ›instructions for use‹ for the 1915 version of his notation. So the content of his choreography score for FAUNE remained inaccessible and it seemed that Nijinsky's personal documentation of the choreography for his first ballet was lost.

Although Nijinsky's widow Pulszky Romola always claimed her husband had taught her the notation, she was not versed enough to get the notebooks published herself, nor was she able to read the FAUNE score for purposes of reconstruction. She sought assistance. After a long and arduous search for decoders the notation specialist Ann Hutchinson Guest and myself decided, in the mid-1980s, to work together to deci-

---

7 | Cf. Claudia Jeschke: »Das ›Opus‹ Waslaw Nijinskys«, in: Staatsoper Berlin (ed.): LE SACRE DU PRINTEMPS, Berlin 2001, pp. 54–70.

pher the score, translate it into Labanotation (a frequently used notation, particularly in the United States) and to get FAUNE ready for production as a stage performance.

The New Establishment of a Communicative Memory Using the Choreographic Score

In his written version of 1915, Nijinsky uses a tripartite system with five lines placed over one another in each third. In the lower third he notates the movement of the legs, in the centre third the movement of the arms and in the upper third the movements of the torso and the head. As in Stepanov's system, the musical notes provide information on duration, direction and height. The notation is based on an innovative analysis of motion, which isolates the movements of the individual parts of the body and arranges them in a hierarchy. Nijinsky added verbal remarks (about the handling of props or unusually expressive gestures) and floor plans to his extremely detailed recordings.

The decoding process for the score relied particularly on the very musical approach which Nijinsky took to movement analysis. He seg-mented movements and gestures like sounds and created exceedingly complex temporal relationships between the individual body parts – these are so precisely timed as to be impossible for the human body to actually achieve in the way that a musical instrument can. This body-oriented concept was maintained in the idiomatic and syntactic construction of the Labanotation translation; it is a genuinely spatial approach, yet combines the perspectives of body and space with a great amount of flexibility. The rules behind the translated version of the notation must be aligned with the cultural background to Nijinsky's work and his notation. Only specialists in the field even know that the notation exists, the concept behind it is only accessible to the two reconstructors, Ann Hutchinson Guest and myself. And it (only) exists indirectly in the Labanotation as a kind of subtext. We have managed to preserve the knowledge apparent in the Nijinsky score; it has ›inscribed‹ itself into the stock of knowledge in the translation (which we in any case can perceive) and the way we have approached the movements in FAUNE.

During preparation for the production of FAUNE and during our work with students at Goucher College, Ann Hutchinson Guest and I realised that we need to consult the notation constantly to see how certain move-ments should be performed, while other movements appear to be firmly anchored in our physical memory. In our work with professional dancers in companies (who usually have no knowledge of notation) we rehearse the sequences mimetically, i.e. through demonstration and imitation. If the students are familiar with Labanotation, we try to refer to the score as much as possible and to encourage the dancers to show initiative in their own interpretation of the movements. This was the case at Goucher. Ann Hutchinson Guest's interpretation and representation of the score primarily emphasises narrative and metric aspects (such as the way the nymphs employ their veils), whereas I tend to focus on movement structures and musical correspondences (such as the choreographic themes in the opening and closing pieces). The varying strategies depend on personal preferences and one's professional history – they are thus the result of the complex interplay of cultural and communicative memory.

*Lecture RE-CONSTRUCTIONS:
STRATEGIES OF DOCUMENTATION AND MEMORY
by Claudia Jeschke, DANCE CONGRESS GERMANY 2006*

Photo: Thomas Aurin

Approaches to Dance Memory in Neurophysiological Science and Dance Studies

Movement has its own cognitive potential which allows ›understanding‹ in the sense of individual approaches which stimulate both sensual awareness and intellectual reflection and interpretation. These processes do not make the phenomenon any easier to describe in writing; they integrate information of a non-representative character and, at least initially, defy any fixed definition.

According to the neurophysiologist Wolf Singer[8] there are no percep-

---

8 | Cf. a.o. Wolf Singer in conversation with Dorothee Hannappel: »Keine Wahrnehmung ohne Gedächtnis«, in: *Theaterschrift* 8 (1994), p. 30. For questions on the construction of meaning and possible methodical answers see Bettina Schlüter: »Konstruktivistische Aspekte einer Korrelationsanalyse

tions which are not orientated around memories already stored in the brain. Information received by the senses arranges itself on the basis of this stored memory. The brain analyses the information for structures to fit over some patterns in the memory. It then creates additional constructs to fill the gaps.

Singer distinguishes between two types of memory which are called upon when the human brain perceives something. One is the »procedural memory« which stores motor and sensory functions and which is expanded through practice. This memory is activated when we learn new ways of moving. The other sort of memory Singer identified is the »episodic or declarative memory« which we use to chronologically order events and is where we store sequences, associations and thus contexts.[9]

So the particularly interesting thing about the perception and understanding of movement and dance is that the cognition process accesses both types of memory at once: the messages the brain receives are contextualised by the declarative memory and then, most importantly, are processed by the engrams in the memory dedicated to motor and sensory functions.[10]

All experiences of movement come from active movement of one's own body and/or through watching other people's movements, something which triggers similar reactions in the procedural memory of motion. Annette Hartmann relates the two types of memory analytically separated by Wolf Singer to each other to a much greater degree than he did himself. She describes them as an above all physical process. And she points out that it is not only performing movements oneself which forms the physical memory, but that (visual) perception and imagination also contribute.[11]

Dance historians and dancers regularly make reference to ›kinaes-

---

von Musik und Tanz«, in: Claudia Jeschke/Hans-Peter Bayerdörfer (eds.): *Bewegung im Blick. Beiträge zu einer theaterwissenschaftlichen Bewegungsforschung*, Berlin: Vorwerk 8, 2000, pp. 59–69.

9 | Wolf Singer in conversation with Dorothee Hannappel, l.c., pp. 24ff.

10 | As far as I see, in dance this second type of memory is usually characterised as ›kinaesthesia‹ or as ›muscle feeling‹, ›muscle sense‹ or ›feeling of movement‹. For the person perceiving them, kinaesthetic messages make ›sense‹ when they can be related to patterns in the memory. Although it initially is unimportant in which of the two types of memory the pattern is to be found. Movement can thus make sense both in a physical way and in an intellectual, reflective way (with the help of the declarative memory). Both contribute to the overall perception of the observer.

11 | Cf. Annette Hartmann: »Mit dem Körper memorieren. Betrachtung des Körpergedächtnisses im Tanz aus neurowissenschaftlicher Sicht«, in: Johannes Birringer/Josephine Fenger (eds.): *Tanz im Kopf. Dance and Cognition*, Münster: LIT 2005, p. 197.

thesia‹ as crucial for an appreciation of dance knowledge. ›Kinaesthesia‹ refers both to the physical process of perceiving one's own movements and to ›empathy‹ for the perceived movements of others.[12] Thus, from a dance-oriented viewpoint, kinaesthesia modifies the procedural and declarative memories postulated by neurophysiologists. In her article of 1984, Mary M. Smyth showed that there is a theoretical distinction between motor knowledge[13], i.e. knowledge about the classification and performance of movement, and kinaesthesia as the meaningful, sensuous experience of movement.[14]

Motor Knowledge and Kinaesthesia in the Practical Preparation of FAUNE

The Goucher College students demonstrated open and pluralistic approaches to the dance material. In the audition we asked them to experiment with the motor ›basics‹ of Nijinsky's FAUNE: with the »split front«, where the front of the body and the direction the eyes are looking is not identical with the direction the body moves in; with keeping their legs parallel when moving forward and thus having to immediately shift their weight with every step; with the articulated use of the feet; with the permanent body twist; with stylised arm and hand positions, which are partly taken from images (from Greek vases) and are partly original inventions by Nijinsky and which portray direct energetic content. This last point in particular was important for us when selecting our cast: which dancers were able to translate the specific positions into movements without losing the form? We were not interested in students who already knew about Nijinsky's FAUNE and were therefore able to call up typical positions from their physical memories. If they were not able to make these positions dynamic, the knowledge students already had was less important to us than their ability to make use of space and maintain sculptural hold in movement.

The dancers at Goucher had no or only little knowledge of Nijinsky and/or the first piece he choreographed. It was difficult for them to force their bodies to adopt these unusual positions and movements. Nijinsky's vocabulary of movement is riddled with coordination pitfalls and its

---

12 | For information on understanding of kinaesthesia throughout time see Sabine Huschka: *Moderner Tanz. Konzepte. Stile. Utopien*, Hamburg: Rowohlt 2002, p. 27, point 3.

13 | Of interest here would be training and aesthetic approaches to communicative dance memory.

14 | Cf. Mary M. Smyth: »Kinesthetic Communication in Dance«, in: *Dance Research Journal* 16/2 (1984), p. 21.

aesthetic was as strange in his day as it is in ours. In general, it is true that even if dancers are allegedly familiar with the style Nijinsky used in FAUNE (for example through their knowledge of Baron Adolf de Meyer's photographs), rehearsals for this version of FAUNE require them to un-learn all idiosyncratic dance behaviour and to concentrate on minimalist, slow, highly stylised movements which initially seem to ask too little of the energetic and expressive potential of all dancers.

However, it has always been our experience, and was the same at Goucher, that in later stages of the rehearsal process the complexity of coordinating the movements with the timing constraints of the music and the spatial configuration of the choreography turns out to be a real challenge for dancers, both physically and artistically. Movements must be created with a high level of concentrated awareness; they seem artifi-cial to the dancers because they do not follow any established technique. However, at the same time they reflect the abstract, continuous pulse of Debussy's composition and integrate the story about the faun and the nymphs through the interaction and specific use of space. Prior motor knowledge was of little importance for the preparation of FAUNE; kinaes-thetic perception was much more important. This means that the vocabu-lary of movement employed in this work is not primarily accessible via motor knowledge. Classically trained dancers may have fewer problems with the definition of form involved in this vocabulary, but they find its interpretative dynamic challenging. Dancers trained in other techniques, on the other hand, have to learn to restrict their desire to give free reign to their kinaesthetic feelings and must follow formal patterns.

As I have already mentioned, Ann Hutchinson Guest favours the communication of the storytelling, mimetic and metric aspects of the choreography, whereas I concentrated on the constellation of the move-ments and the musical pulse, the musical development, the theme, the instrumentation of the composition and on listening to the music. The two different strategies are based on our individual, separate kinaesthetic perceptions and I have noticed that they trigger moments of kinaesthetic identification in the dancers, although professional dancers (can) react more quickly to these moments and take them on board more easily and in a more focused manner, and are subsequently able to adapt them to their own interpretations.

Digression: The Continuous Exchange between Reception and Production of Movement

I believe that an important part of the discussion of motor and kinaes-thetic processes is the fact that the physicality of the memory reduces the gap between producers and recipients. This applies both to the process of learning and rehearsing and to the process of watching a perform-ance. The people watching the movement actually move themselves and vice versa. For the study of dance this means the revaluation of so-called recipients into performers through the perception of movement or, in other words, training in how to perceive movement turns the spectators, the recipients, the scientists, into performers. And the other way around: when training and devising choreography, dancers learn movements through observing them; this kind of perception has the potential for reception, for reflection, for transformation. Thus, when spectators, or the ›reflectors‹, study the re-construction of Nijinsky's FAUNE, their perceptive skills make them into potential dancers, and the dancers are to be seen as competent, even if acting somewhat unconsciously, reflectors. The work of dancers/researchers on the various cognitive and experimental levels of the re-construction has uncovered areas where the experience-oriented knowledge of dance, until now largely neglected, plays an important role.

Overlaps

To conclude my thoughts on the competence potential of re-constructions, I would like to once more direct my view towards the practitioners and their specific knowledge in motion. It consists of complex calibrations of personal movement skills (including studied dance techniques, motor knowledge and cultural, social and biographical experiences) with the declarative or declared information of the communicative and cultural memory and of both kinaesthetic qualities in the experience of dancing and of watching dance. Re-constructions make use of the traces, relics and indicators of stored and functional dancing histories.[15] In my work on the concept and practice of re-constructions I realised how much the material, i.e. texts of the choreography and about the choreogra-phy, changes with the physical interpretations and movement-oriented actions of the reconstructors and the dancers. With regard to the latter: is the performance of an experienced celebrity schooled in the Russian tradition, such as Irek Mukhamedov from the Royal Ballet London, who actually originally interpreted the Nureyev version, automatically better than the approach of a movement artist trained in Cuba such as Carlos Acosta, also a star of the Royal Ballet London, who, as rehearsals began,

---

15 | The distinction between stored memory and functional memory is based on the thoughts of Aleida Assmann in i.e. idem: »Zur Mediengeschichte des kulturellen Gedächtnisses«, in: Astrid Erll/Ansgar Nünning (eds.): *Medien des kollektiven Gedächtnisses. Konstruktivität – Historizität – Kultur-spezifizität*, Berlin/New York: de Gruyter 2004, p. 47.

asked me who composed the music to the ballet?[16] Dancing competence is visible, tangible, even though it has to date been difficult to truly comprehend via a methodical approach. What can be described – alongside individual ability – are the fields of technical and stylistic training, which are limited in content and time. Our communicative, functional memory seems to make someone's training history accessible and re-constructable. However, further traces or stores from cultural dance, movement and physical memory are lost in questions such as: how can historical periodifications be read in the act of dancing? And how does dance get passed on through the generations – through documentation or through people dancing today? My reflections do not go much further than to formulate the lack of a historical, practice-oriented dance research tradition. My awareness of an appreciation for the topic arises from a deep respect for dance ability and dance knowledge – a form of knowledge which I would like to see considered separately from personality and training – just as any sort of ability and knowledge should be. Or do I have no choice but to continue operating in a (albeit creative and auratic) vacuum in this constantly shifting overlapping field?

Translation from German

---

16 | Dance ability becomes even more important as a reference system in cases when re-constructions have to make do with less ›solid‹ reference material than in FAUNE.

References

Assmann, Aleida: »Zur Mediengeschichte des kulturellen Gedächtnisses«, in: Astrid Erll/Ansgar Nünning (eds.): *Medien des kollektiven Gedächtnisses. Konstruktivität – Historizität – Kulturspezifizität*, Berlin/New York: de Gruyter 2004, pp. 45–60.

Assmann, Jan: »Kollektives Gedächtnis und kulturelle Identität«, in: Jan Assmann/Tonio Hölscher (eds.): *Kultur und Gedächtnis*, Frankfurt a.M.: Suhrkamp 1988, pp. 9–19.

Hartmann, Annette: »Mit dem Körper memorieren. Betrachtung des Körpergedächtnisses im Tanz aus neurowissenschaftlicher Sicht«, in: Johannes Birringer/Josephine Fenger (eds.): *Tanz im Kopf. Dance and Cognition*, Münster: LIT 2005, pp. 185–199.

Huschka, Sabine: *Moderner Tanz. Konzepte. Stile. Utopien*, Hamburg: Rowohlt 2002.

Hutchinson Guest, Ann/Jeschke, Claudia: *Nijinsky's Faune Restored*, London: Gordon and Breach 1991.

Jeschke, Claudia: »Das ›Opus‹ Waslaw Nijinskys«, in: Staatsoper Berlin (ed.): LE SACRE DU PRINTEMPS, Berlin 2001, pp. 54–70.

Nectoux, Jean Michel (ed.): *Nijinsky. L'Après-midi d'un Faune*, Paris: Biro 1989.

Princeton University: »The Program in Theatre and Dance«, *Spring Dance Festival, 24–26 February 2006*.

Schlüter, Bettina: »Konstruktivistische Aspekte einer Korrelationsanalyse von Musik und Tanz«, in: Claudia Jeschke/Hans-Peter Bayerdörfer (eds.): *Bewegung im Blick. Beiträge zu einer theaterwissenschaftlichen Bewegungsforschung*, Berlin: Vorwerk 8, 2000, pp. 59–69.

Singer, Wolf: in conversation with Dorothee Hannappel: »Keine Wahrnehmung ohne Gedächtnis«, in: *Theaterschrift* 8 (1994), pp. 21–34.

Smyth, Mary M.: »Kinesthetic Communication in Dance«, in: *Dance Research Journal* 16/2 (1984), p. 19–22.

Welzer, Harald: *Das kommunikative Gedächtnis. Eine Theorie der Erinnerung*, Munich: Beck 2005.

What the Body Remembers

How Pina Bausch Keeps Her Repertoire in Shape

Norbert Servos

Pina Bausch has choreographed almost 40 works in and for Wuppertal, including those she created while she was still a guest choreographer before taking over the Tanztheater directorship in the 1973/74
season. Her productivity was especially impressive in the early years.
At times, this pioneer of Tanztheater created up to three new works a
year. From the very start she made a point of preserving her rapidly
growing repertoire and also keeping the older pieces in the public eye.
This was facilitated by the fact that the significance of the work in Wuppertal rapidly became apparent, which meant an increasing number of
inquiries for international guest performances. The desire to provide
an overview of the development of Tanztheater in concerts soon arose,
for example in 1981 at the Theater der Welt festival in Cologne, when
the ensemble presented no fewer than seven productions in quick suc-
cession. In some years, Wuppertal had a repertory of over ten pieces
ready for performance. This achievement is all the more remarkable
because the Tanztheater Wuppertal is not a large ballet ensemble made
up of 80 to 100 dancers, but rather a comparatively small company.
Double and multiple castings of roles were not and are not possible,
even today. Accordingly, virtually every member of the ensemble per-
forms in every piece. Under these conditions, keeping the repertoire
in shape requires an excellent memory as well as resilience on the part
of the performers.

From the mid-1980s onwards, Pina Bausch curtailed her productivity. From then on, she created only one new piece a year, accompanied
by a revival. Year by year she took one step backward into the past. By
now, the entire repertoire has been revived, including the early Gluck
operas IPHIGENIE AUF TAURIS and ORPHEUS UND EURYDIKE. This keeps

the creative potential of the choreographer and the ensemble from being overstrained. At the same time, it gives the audience a minutely detailed reconstruction of the complete development process, from its beginnings to the present. Every revival represents an acid test as to whether a piece that was created ten, twenty or more years ago can stand up to the changing times.

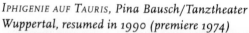

IPHIGENIE AUF TAURIS, Pina Bausch/Tanztheater Wuppertal, resumed in 1990 (premiere 1974)

Photo: Bernd Uhlig

However, Wuppertal revivals face particular challenges. On the one hand, these are due to the choreographer's own high expectations. Reconstructing sequences, no matter how perfectly and proficiently, is not enough. On the contrary: »The performances must never become routine. It would be the death of my pieces if they were to become routine«[1], says Pina Bausch. The *what* of a performance simply acts as a kind of rough script; what is more important is *how* something happens, for example, the quality of the performer's execution: »Of course the pieces remain the same. But the performers sustain the pieces and make us feel them – and sometimes you can't feel a piece properly, and sometimes you feel it absolutely properly, so what is it?«[2] Delving into the origins of a certain quality so it can be re-established is a lengthy and complex process.

---

1 | Pina Bausch op. cit. Norbert Servos: *Pina Bausch – Wuppertaler Tanztheater oder Die Kunst, einen Goldfisch zu dressieren*, Seelze-Velber: Kallmeyer 1996, p. 296.

2 | Ibid., p. 300.

It's a lot of work maintaining a performance so that it really is as though it had just been born. You can't just carry things along and say: ›We'll do that then.‹ It has to be fresh and new, every time.[3]

What applies to the current season's new pieces is especially applicable to the revival of older pieces. How does one pass on the body knowledge from one generation of dancers to the next? Do altered and new casts change the pieces? Pina Bausch says:

Certain things ought to remain. The performance ought to ensure that the piece can be seen, even on a poor night. Of course it is sometimes very difficult to recast the piece, or it takes longer for it to develop until it is nice and well-rounded again. Sometimes it happens very quickly, and sometimes it is much better afterwards. Many things have become much better through casting changes as well. There is no recipe. I haven't even dared to recast some things. Doing so would make the piece superfluous.[4]

Thus revivals always harbour two possibilities: either they make the process lengthy and complicated until the context of activities, the empirical knowledge behind them, is restored; or working through the material again and clarifying it results in an unexpected leap in quality.

Pina Bausch depends on her dancers' qualities as performers in a special way. One of the reasons for this is a distinctive concept of dance, which forms the basis of her entire work: »Almost anything can be dance. It has to do with a certain kind of awareness, a certain inner, physical attitude, and extreme precision: knowledge, breathing, every tiny detail. It always has something to do with the ›How‹.«[5]

And the choreographer specifies: »It's not as though dance is a specific technique. Moreover, I feel that many very simple things can be done only by a very good dancer.«[6] However, if the dance in dance theatre is not primarily defined through technique, a reconstruction is not achieved merely by restoring movements, directions in space, dynamics and phrasing. In addition, a certain consciousness, an attitude towards the movements, and a certain range of experience must also be reawakened. It can be found in the sources of the movements, which in dance theatre are different from the customary ones. The choreographer humorously points out that this also applies to the choreographed sequences of her

---

3 | Pina Bausch op. cit. Norbert Servos: *Pina Bausch. Tanztheater,* Munich: Kieser 2003, p. 237.

4 | Ibid., p. 237.

5 | Pina Bausch op. cit. Servos: *Pina Bausch – Wuppertaler Tanztheater,* l.c., p. 305.

6 | Ibid., p. 304.

pieces. »The steps always came from somewhere else; they never came from the legs.«[7]

Using this enhanced understanding of dance as a starting point for acquiring other stage and choreographic material, it seemed logical for Pina Bausch to alter her working methods as well. The occasion arrived in the late 1970s, when Peter Zadek invited her to develop an adaptation of Shakespeare's Macbeth for his theatre in Bochum. At the time, she was in a state of double conflict. Despite international recognition, she continued to be in the crossfire between critics and audiences; opposition and doubts about the work also began to stir within her own ensemble. Pina Bausch cast her piece, which premiered in Bochum on April 22, 1978 under the title Er nimmt sie an der Hand und führt sie in das Schloss, die andern folgen (He takes her by the hand and guides her to the palace; the others follow), with only four ›loyal‹ dancers from Wuppertal, five actors and a singer. As a result of this mixed cast, a purely choreographic approach was out of the question from the outset. Instead, Pina Bausch began to ask her performers questions that centred on several sets of themes evoked by Shakespeare's drama. To be able to answer them, the performers had to draw on their personal experiences. The answers gradually produced material that brought forth movement sequences and series of scenes, which were then again joined together to form a piece. Through the process of careful form-finding, the initially personal, but by no means private, answers became examples of human behaviour that transcended the personal. By incorporating the everyday experiences of her performers, Pina Bausch not only added to her own range of experience as a source of material, she also ensured that movements were found that did not »come from the legs«. The pieces grew, as the choreographer wanted them to, from the inside out.

From 1978 onwards, working by asking questions became the key to all her following productions. This method of working poses a particular challenge, however, when pieces are reconstructed. When reproducing the piece onstage, the original performers can fall back on their personal experiences time and again because they were ›co-authors‹ in finding reasons for their movements. Whoever else takes over a part has to generate a similar, comparable experience to establish the appropriate motivation and emotional depth. This applies not only to the staged theatrical sequences, but also to the dances, because in dance theatre they also arise not from an abstract idea for movement but from dealing with specific questions. Movement by movement, every dance tells its own small story. If this is not communicated to the new dancer when the part is passed on, the essence of the message is missing. The aim is not to make this particular internal story visible to the audience. It is meant

---

7 | Ibid., p. 298.

to bring about a certain quality and precision in the performance. The members of the audience have another interpretation in any case, because they relate the experiences presented on stage to their own experiences and reach their own conclusions.

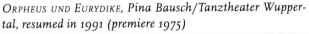

ORPHEUS UND EURYDIKE, *Pina Bausch/Tanztheater Wuppertal, resumed in 1991 (premiere 1975)*

Photo: Bernd Uhlig

It becomes clear that properly preserving a choreographic work, especially in the case of Wuppertal, is linked to the knowledge of individuals: to the dancers of the original cast, to assistants and last but not least to the choreographer. She is the only person who knows all the sequences of motivation and who made them the basis of her compositional decisions. This might be one reason why George Balanchine distributed his choreographic legacy to various dancers who were original cast members of his pieces, with the obligation to stage the respective pieces on demand. Balanchine seems to have realised that the dancers with whom he first created the works have a knowledge that no medium can replace.

Choreographic notebooks can indeed document sequences of scenes, cues, texts used, costume lists and much more. Sequences and movement patterns can be reconstructed with the help of video recordings. If an especially successful performance has been documented, even the desired performance quality can be visually preserved. What is not captured, however, is the pathway that led to this quality. Every performance is preceded by weeks, sometimes even months, of rehearsals in which the piece is perfected in a process of hundreds of corrections and extensive fine-tuning. Every person involved in the creation of a piece stores a vast wealth of detailed information in his or her physical and mental memory, and knows about the system of their complex connections. Only those who know how to create this complex richness and its interactions can revive the spirit of a piece. In this sense reconstruction does not mean construction so much as it means the knowledge of a complete creative system that expresses an approach to the world in hundreds of predetermined details. Since choreographers nowadays always develop their own ›vocabulary‹, every reconstruction involves re-establishing that vocabulary, including its intended connotations. In the case of Wuppertal, with its emphasis on the ›How before the What‹, it becomes clear that notations, whether written or visual, and audio recordings allow only limited access to a choreographic work.

Like most ensembles, Tanztheater Wuppertal has at its disposal extensive audio-visual documentation, which has grown to comprise over 6,000 videotapes. Since 1998, Grigori Chakhov has been filming not only the premieres, but also subsequent performances, because as a rule, Pina Bausch returns to work on her pieces after the opening night. Shooting always takes place from different perspectives: once in long shot, to capture the overall impression, and additionally in close-ups, to record details and to give precise original material to the new dancers who take over the parts at a later date. Favoured versions – those that yield the final version of the piece or a performance of particularly good quality – are provided with written information: this includes the date and location of the performance as well as information about the cast, and comments about whether the technical realisation of a performance was successful and faultless. A dancer taking over a part has access to both the long shot and the close-ups. Specially edited tapes documenting different performances are available for some pieces, making individual dances comprehensible. As a rule, a role is handed over from the predecessor to the dancer who will be rehearsing the role anew.

But the dancers of the ensemble are not only involved in preserving the pieces by passing on roles. Pina Bausch has appointed one dancer each to certain pieces, and they are held responsible for revivals of their respective pieces. These are usually dancers who have belonged to the ensemble for many years. Over the years, a network of assistants has evolved (among them, Benedicte Billiet, Jo-Ann Endicott, Barbara Hampel, Beatrice Libonati, Helena Pikon, Daphnis Kokkinos, Ed Kortlandt, Dominique Mercy, Robert Sturm), who keep track of the choreographic notebooks together with Pina Bausch. These notebooks also contain the texts that are spoken on stage, in all the languages in which they are spoken, depending on the country in which they are performed. In addition, there are precise inventory lists for costumes and staging, as well as lighting plots and records of cues for lighting, sound and projections. Even during the rehearsal phase the assistants (currently Robert Sturm) document every step of the work, sometimes daily.

Chakhov had begun to standardise and copy the material initially recorded in the most diverse formats – from VHS to U-matic – as early as 1993. As a result of the repertoire policy mentioned before, in which a premiere was always combined with a revival, the entire work of the Tanztheater has since been documented in numerous recordings. The company's ›own‹ material is supplemented by archived external material. Wuppertal has a copy of nearly everything that has been filmed about Pina Bausch's work. The next step will be to digitise the entire archive material to preserve and protect it in an »eternal data base«. In order to do this, there are plans to catalogue the entire material again and then scan it into a computer. It would then be compactly stored and quickly accessible to the company for their daily work as well as for research purposes.

With this extensive archive the Tanztheater has a good starting position for reconstructing its pieces. But even such a complex system of safeguards cannot replace the choreographer's eye. She possesses a remarkable memory for every detail of a production, even the tiniest, and she knows how to convey the meaning of her pieces. Only she can revive the spirit of a piece that has not been performed for years, and in the end make it appear as fresh and new as if it had just been born.

Translation from German

References

Servos, Norbert: *Pina Bausch – Wuppertaler Tanztheater oder Die Kunst, einen Goldfisch zu dressieren*, Seelze-Velber: Kallmeyer 1996.
Servos, Norbert: *Pina Bausch. Tanztheater*, Munich: Kieser 2003.

Reconstructing Dore Hoyer's

AFFECTOS HUMANOS

Yvonne Hardt on a discussion with Waltraud Luley,
Susanne Linke and Martin Nachbar[1]

The reconstruction or preservation of contemporary dance pieces usually
ekes out a niche existence in the world of dance and performance, particularly in a German context. The panel discussion on the reconstruction
of Dore Hoyer's AFFECTOS HUMANOS (1962)[2] at the Dance Congress
showed, however, that any prejudices seeking to associate reconstruction with a dry, artistically less relevant dance practice, can easily be
proved wrong. Reconstruction in no way simply means the emulation
or copying of movement that is as true as possible, but is primarily an
artistic as well as an analytical task, which the panel guests emphatically
demonstrated. Waltraud Luley (born in 1911, former personal assistant
to Dore Hoyer and executrix of her estate), Susanne Linke (one of the
most important dancers and choreographers in German dance theatre)
and Martin Nachbar (contemporary dancer and choreographer), who
represented three generations on the panel, provided an insight into the
scope, problems and controversy surrounding the subject of reconstruction. They also showed through their on-going examination of the ›late
work‹ of expressionist dancer Dore Hoyer her continuing importance for
the contemporary dance scene.

---

1 | The discussion lead by Yvonne Hardt took place on 21 April 2006 as part of
the Dance Congress at the House of World Cultures in Berlin.
2 | The date refers to the film recording of AFFECTOS HUMANOS.

Dore Hoyer in AFFECTOS HUMANOS

Photo: © Siegfried Enkelmann/VG Bild-
Kunst, Bonn 2007; Deutsches Tanzarchiv
Köln

The discussion was not just about her specific reconstructions in AFFEC-
TOS HUMANOS, but generally about the question of what an appropriation
of past dances can achieve, not only for dancers and choreographers,
but also for audiences and dance scientists. Even if reconstruction does
not allow fulfilment of the frequently fostered wish to maintain and
preserve the past, it can illustrate the importance of the history of dance
for dance today.[3] At the same time the interest in reconstruction also
highlights the desire to politically upgrade dance, to provide it with a
foundation. Performance theorists point out that any effort to hold on
to things, to preserve them and exhibit them as products are subject to
levels of subliminal meaning and power.[4] Hence the aims of the panel
at the DANCE CONGRESS consisted not only of reflecting on dance history
content and on a technical tool for reconstruction purposes, but also of

---

3 | Cf. Yvonne Hardt: »Prozessuale Archive. Wie Tanzgeschichte von Tänzern
geschrieben wird«, in: *tanz.de. Zeitgenössischer Tanz in Deutschland – Strukturen im Wandel – eine neue Wissenschaft*, Berlin: Theater der Zeit 2005, pp.
34–39.

4 | Cf. Mark Franko/Annette Richards: »Actualizing Absence: The Pastness
of Performance«, in: idem (eds.): *Acting on the Past. Historical Performance
Across the Disciplines*, Middletown: Wesleyan University Press 2000, pp.
1–9.

upgrading modern dance as part of a political venture, socially and in a cultural environment. It also clarified the fact that another review of dance history is needed inasmuch as it works with clear caesuras and grants expressionist dance little influence on the contemporary dance scene in Germany.

Dore Hoyer (1911–1967) belonged to the second generation of expressionist dancers who have gone down in dance history as less successful because their careers had been hampered by National Socialism, the war, and a subsequent blatant avoidance of modern dance in the postwar period. Taught originally by Mary Wigman, Hoyer was influenced by expressionist dance. However, at the same time she also broke new ground. Her highly technical and abstract movement composition set her apart from the rather empathetic and ecstatic work of her teacher. This had both a spectacular and a provocative effect on her contemporaries. As dance scientist and head of the German Dance Archive in Cologne, Frank-Manuel Peter, showed in his study on Hoyer's early work, something of a ›post-modern‹ dance style was emerging from this work.[5] Gabriele Brandstetter demonstrated similar tendencies in dances in the postwar era using the further development of Hoyer's DREHTANZ (»turning dance«) as an example.[6] This applies all the more to AFFECTOS HUMANOS, which both Susanne Linke and Martin Nachbar were enthusiastic about because of their consistent research into movement.

This research was not primarily about – even though the title of the piece perhaps leads to this assumption – looking for suitable forms of expression for inner emotions, but (almost in the sense of the artistic avant-garde of the 1960s/70s) a formal search for movement's sake. Hence reconstruction can provoke an examination of the history of dance that questions boundaries and caesuras between modernity and postmodernism. The examination and inclusion of older pieces and the exchange of opinions with those who danced in them, led to a reassessment and a different understanding of the choreographic creative process.

The reason for examining Hoyer's choreographic »cycle«, which consists of five dances called EITELKEIT (vanity), BEGIERDE (lust), ANGST (fear), HASS (hatred) and LIEBE (love), was a declared interest in this compelling form, for Linke as well as for Nachbar. The respective approaches were, however, different. In Linke's case, the reconstruction was initiated by Iris Scaccheri, an Argentinean dancer, who learned these dances shortly before Dore Hoyer committed suicide in 1967. Linke had

---

5 | Cf. Frank-Manuel Peter: *Zwischen Ausdruckstanz und Postmodern Dance: Dore Hoyers Beitrag zur Weiterentwicklung des modernen Tanzes in den 1930er Jahren*, dissertation, Freie Universität Berlin 2003.

6 | Cf. Gabriele Brandstetter: *Tanz-Lektüren. Körperbilder und Raumfiguren der Avantgarde*, Frankfurt a.M.: Fischer 1995, pp. 266–270.

already been an admirer of Hoyer's work; this inquiry was unexpected, however, and initially represented problems that seemed insurmountable. Although Linke was trained by Wigman at the start of her dance career, she had, in her own words, forgotten her and initially approached the material via the external form. Finally, together with Waltraud Luley she rediscovered the sources of movement, which emanated from a strong, restrained core, while, for example, the arms moved easily, energetically and charged with tension. Linke illustrated this emphatically during the panel discussion by demonstrating the difference between a movement where the body follows the direction of the arms and what it looks like when the rest of the body resists this tension in the arms.

It is these small details and problems encountered when learning movements which Martin Nachbar also addressed when saying that Hoyer placed energies and movements in very specific areas of her body. Unlike Linke, his background as a contemporary dancer, who was trained at the School for New Dance Development in Amsterdam, is character-ised, as he describes it »as being as relaxed as possible«. Consequently, he initially found Hoyer's tension-filled movements at odds with his release-based body training.

It was clear in dealing with the reconstruction that dance technique not only means the execution of different movements. Each training session also involves body shape and verbal reflection, so that through daily training a »body of ideas« emerges.[7] Learning movements occurs in conjunction with imaginary images, abstract constructs of spatial focus and anatomical instructions, as well as by using references to the degree of tension in the body. The more stability or continuity these verbal descriptions have, the more coherent the continuation of a spe-cific physicality. This means that knowledge of these notional aspects of dance is of central importance to a reconstruction over and above the form of a movement.[8]

---

7 | Cf. Susan Leigh Foster: »Dancing Bodies«, in: Jane D. Desmond (ed.): *Mean-ing in Motion. New Cultural Studies of Dance*, Durham: Duke University Press 2003, pp. 235–257.

8 | Cf. Hardt: »Prozessuale Archive«, l.c.

*Waltraud Luley and Martin Nachbar on the panel »The
Reconstruction of Dore Hoyer's* AFFECTOS HUMANOS«,
DANCE CONGRESS GERMANY 2006

Photo: Thomas Aurin

How important contact with Luley therefore was for Nachbar, who could communicate these images and principles, is made clear through the story of their first meeting: Nachbar introduced Luley to his version of HASS. This dance begins with tightly clenched hands, where one hand suddenly moves downwards and the other moves up. At first, Nachbar executed this movement in a rather relaxed, almost ungainly fashion, at which point Luley started attacking him verbally and shouted: »Mr. Nachbar! This is hatred! The whole body is in tension!« This was the beginning of a work process in which Nachbar attempted to embody the choreographies down to the very last detail. From movements of his little finger down to holding his head in a specific manner new things were discovered that could be worked on. Nachbar said about this:

You never know what the body will do with such a transfer, but that's what makes the work exciting. Luley and I are always discovering new details and approaches. Last week we established that I use the middle section of my body much less than Dore Hoyer. At the beginning of the year we discovered something new primarily about the use of the head and neck in »Begierde«.[9]

It is this total commitment that Luley demands from those who want to learn this material. Those who think that it doesn't look that difficult and believe that ›they can do it, too‹, are, in her opinion, not motivated enough. Here Luley represents a standpoint in the reconstruction debate which insists on service to the work, which cannot be changed formally. However, she also states enthusiastically that those who reconstruct Hoyer

---

9 | Martin Nachbar: unpublished manuscript of his lecture.

have always also created something new out of this material. Susanne Linke and Martin Nachbar went down different roads in the context of their respective individual contemporary movement practices.

This brings the subject to the context, which is crucial to reconstruction. Dance is more than pure execution of movement and modern dance has expressly declared it part of its agenda to call into question established forms of dance presentation and representation. Modernity plays with breaks, wants to disturb the viewer's perception or calls into question the respective understanding of what constitutes the virtuosity of a choreographic sequence. Hoyer should be considered part of this tradition of critical analysis of what has gone before and the search for one's own style. This conception of self is part of the significance and meaning of an artistic work. Consequently, it also constitutes one of the central problems of reconstructions if the aim is not to view them as museum pieces. In order for reconstructions to ›function‹ they must continue to live and not become an »illustrated corpse«, as dance scientist Ramsey Burt describes it.[10] Therefore, not only must the question be asked which body techniques and movements Hoyer demonstrates in AFFECTOS HUMANOS, but the question of the extent to which her dances were influenced by the *Zeitgeist* must also be examined, and even more so, why they provided such a source of friction at the time. A dimension of meaning to her choreography lies in this regenerative potential, in this confrontation with the *Zeitgeist* and conventions. How can this be incorporated into the reconstruction?

Both Susanne Linke's and Martin Nachbar's »reconstructions« of AFFECTOS HUMANOS have received a good deal of positive critical acclaim and also stimulated discussions, and this has been the case – in theory – because they have not treated the dances in AFFECTOS HUMANOS as isolated units, but because they have each included their own working style and have staged the dances differently for their respective context. These approaches are very different for historical reasons.

When Linke showed the reconstruction for the first time in 1987 on the anniversary of Hoyer's death, the reviews, on the one hand, referred seemingly without difficulty to »Hoyer's dances«, so faithful and perfect was Linke in approaching her role model. On the other hand, they stated without any apparent feeling of contradiction, that Linke gave clear formalism a physical sensuousness developed through dance theatre. In addition, she added a composition of her own to the dances devised with her partner, Urs Dietrich, in which she picked up the themes of AFFECTOS HUMANOS again and reshaped them using her own dance

---

10 | Cf. Ramsay Burt: »Reconstructing the Disturbing New Spaces of Modernity: The Ballet Skating Rink«, in: Stephanie Jordan (ed.): *Preservation Politics. Dance Revived Reconstructed Remade*, London: Dance Books 2000, pp. 21–30.

language. Thus homage was paid to Hoyer, in an evening that was not historical in nature, but contemporary.

In an even more striking fashion Nachbar did not stage a recon-struction in the traditional sense, but made the act of reflection and the constant changing of this work the theme on stage. Such production strategies clearly place him in a contemporary performing arts setting, in a »conceptual dance« context. He tried to reproduce three of the five dances in technical detail in terms of movement, but broke with this approach on stage in two ways: firstly, because he learns these dances as a man and thus automatically carves out something different, and secondly, because in URHEBEN UND AUFHEBEN (as the current version of this performance is called, while it was originally created with his dance colleagues Thomas Plischke and Joachim Gerstmeier under the title AFFEKTE), the reflection of the reconstruction process is in the fore-ground. Presented as a demonstration lecture, the presentation of Hoyer's dance movements is only a small aspect of the performance. Nachbar does not want to create the illusion of an original on the stage:

Such a type of re-enactment is, according to Elisabeth Grosz, never a reproduc-tion of the same thing, but a driving force for something new. The ›AH‹ dances, Luley's reminiscences, my reconstruction and your perception transfer in and out of each other and become something that was not there before.[11]

Susanne Linke and Yvonne Hardt on the panel »The Recon-struction of Dore Hoyer's AFFECTOS HUMANOS«, DANCE CONGRESS GERMANY 2006

Photo: Thomas Aurin

---

11 | Cf. Martin Nachbar: »ReKonstrukt«, in: Janine Schulze/Susanne Traub (eds.): *Moving Thoughts. Tanzen ist Denken*, Dokumenta Choreologica 2003, Berlin: Vorwerk 8, 2003, pp. 89–95.

Such interruptions are also present in Linke's interpretation in those moments when she gets changed on stage for each new part. This approach may have been just as provocative for some members of the audience at the end of the 1980s as Nachbar's current learning approach from the perspective of a contemporary audience. It may also have corresponded to irritation which some of the audience felt in the 1950s and 1960s because they were not able to deal with the abstract dance compositions and the new manner of meaning in Hoyer's dances. Consequently, it seems primarily that these »re/constructions« can provoke cracks in the way we usually perceive things. This reflects the ›spirit‹ of Hoyer's dances and in this sense »re/construction« should not be tackled in a fearful manner as if it were a service to a work of the past. On the contrary, memory culture appears exciting when it clearly displays the difference, namely the historical approach, in order to nevertheless cast a spell over the audience as an independent performance.

Translation from German

References

Brandstetter, Gabriele: *Tanz-Lektüren. Körperbilder und Raumfiguren der Avantgarde*, Frankfurt a.M.: Fischer 1995.

Burt, Ramsay: »Reconstructing the Disturbing New Spaces of Modernity: The Ballet Skating Rink«, in: Stephanie Jordan (ed.): *Preservation Politics. Dance Revived Reconstructed Remade*, London: Dance Books 2000, pp. 21–30.

Foster, Susan Leigh: »Dancing Bodies«, in: Jane D. Desmond (ed.): *Meaning in Motion. New Cultural Studies of Dance*, Durham: Duke University Press 2003, pp. 235–257.

Franko, Mark/Richards, Annette: »Actualizing Absence: The Pastness of Performance«, in: idem (eds.): *Acting on the Past. Historical Performance Across the Disciplines*, Middletown: Wesleyan University Press 2000, pp. 1–9.

Hardt, Yvonne: »Prozessuale Archive. Wie Tanzgeschichte von Tänzern geschrieben wird«, in: *tanz.de. Zeitgenössischer Tanz in Deutschland – Strukturen im Wandel – eine neue Wissenschaft*, Berlin: Theater der Zeit 2005, pp. 34–39.

Nachbar, Martin: »ReKonstrukt«, in: Janine Schulze/Susanne Traub (eds.): *Moving Thoughts. Tanzen ist Denken*, Dokumenta Choreologica 2003, Berlin: Vorwerk 8, 2003, pp. 89–95.

Peter, Frank-Manuel: *Zwischen Ausdruckstanz und Postmodern Dance: Dore Hoyers Beitrag zur Weiterentwicklung des modernen Tanzes in den 1930er Jahren*, dissertation, Freie Universität Berlin 2003.

Digestion and Infusion

Ways of Interpreting Dance

Julia Cima in dialogue with Alexandra Baudelot

Julia Cima is well-known for her work interpreting choreographers such as Boris Charmatz or Laure Bonicel. Time and again, she lends pieces a light and, at the same time, disturbing presence with forms of expression developed from states of movement. Up until now, there had been no indication of the bond which this intensely contemporary dancer felt with more virtuoso, older forms of expression. Yet it is precisely these forms which Julia Cima is now exploring in her nine solos in Visitations. The nine solos provide new productions of choreographic fragments from pieces by Vaslav Nijinsky, Merce Cunningham, Isadora Duncan, Valeska Gert, Tatsumi Hijikata and Dominique Bagouet, among others. Cima's body is the thread which connects these otherwise widely differing worlds of dance. It is a thread which symbolises the fact that dance – above and beyond its historical dimension and forms of expression – is primarily concerned with appropriation and updating. It is a game of listening and (re)creating.

Alexandra Baudelot: Visitations is a challenging piece for performers who have to interpret its various choreographic languages as well as the creative dimension of appropriating these languages on a personal, intimate level. How did you approach it?
Julia Cima: I must admit that I didn't give the issue of appropriation much thought. I restricted myself to working quite intensively on each solo over a fairly long period of time (two years have, after all, passed between when I began to work on the first solos and the final creation of Visitations). I took the time to ›take in‹ each solo, left it for a while and then returned to it once I had gained some distance. That allowed me to make my own way of reading and interpreting the pieces more

precisely. I thought it important to respect the movements which I saw on my screen as far as possible. Similarly, I wanted to remain as close as possible to the image of the choreographer's way of thinking (at the time when their solos or pieces were created) which I had developed or read about. The way the pieces were produced was equally important because that's something that can lead to very different interpretations. I wanted to be cautious and, if possible, create very immediate access to the movements. That's why I opted for one single costume, kept very neutral, so as not to influence the audience. But to get back to each solo's individual language: that was something I didn't need to spend much time thinking about. My body has been shaped by dance and my choreographic training and I have the feeling that all of these different languages had already been ›written into‹ my body. All I had to do was reactivate this slumbering ›basic knowledge‹ and, of course, I had to work on making my body language, facial expressions and rhythm more precise.

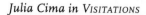

Julia Cima in VISITATIONS

Photo: Raphaël Pierre

Why did you want to explore the history of dance? And is it really history, as you understand it, when you say that it had already been written into your dancer's body? Or to put it another way: did you want to deal with the historical and cultural dimension of these works? And if so, how?

At the beginning of this project, my intention had absolutely nothing to do with exploring the history of dance. I simply had an irresistible urge to work on existing dances, which were both very exactly defined and stylistically very different. And it was something I wanted to do alone in the studio, for no other reason than to experience the joy of dancing. I very quickly came to enjoy exploring such striking styles and choreographies. And on top of that, there was the enjoyment of measuring my work against the standards set by solos which have shaped the history of dance. I believe it's a great luxury to be able to perform works by Nijinsky, Cunningham and Hijikata just as actors simply have to perform in plays by playwrights such as Racine, Molière or Shakespeare.

But I admit that I wasn't particularly timid. I never reached the point where I felt I was about to degrade the work of these choreographers. In fact, the whole time I was working on the dances, I had the feeling that they somehow belonged to me and that I was completely justified in reinterpreting them (at least once everything had been sorted out from a legal point of view!). I've worked for so many years and developed so many techniques in the studio that I think I've earned a certain amount of autonomy with regard to these solos, no matter how legendary they are! And, besides, it felt very natural to me that performers should have this enormous ›power‹ to reinterpret pieces in their own way, contributing everything which makes them who they are and all of their cultural baggage.

Of course, that wasn't something I could do without parallel documentation to allow me to really understand the choreographers' way of thinking and the context in which their pieces were created.

But weren't there, nevertheless, historical elements, political, social and cultural elements, which influenced the way you saw the choreography, giving it another meaning which made the movements appear different to what they would have signified in their original historical context?

Yes, the way you see the movements gains another dimension if you know, for instance, that Isadora spent several years in Moscow setting up a school there, or that her REVOLUTIONARY ETUDE was created shortly after the October Revolution. I certainly incorporated the events and contexts which influenced the choreographies into my work and made use of them in my own way. I know that I've forgotten a lot of what I read but the dances are steeped in what I read and in the feelings I had when I read the autobiographies, for instance, and really felt a part of these people's lives and energy. But that's precisely what interpretation means to me – ›working through‹, ›processing‹ ›taking in‹ and ›clarifying‹ a whole series of old and new information which has had an influence on me and which I then eternalise in my body language.

Besides your appropriation of the choreography with the help of your own history as a dancer, you want to establish continuity between your solos, your costume and your stage set as well as creating a contemporary environment and similar aesthetic look. Which contemporary images did you want to draw on?

I don't want to develop or construct a particular contemporary image. My aim is to show off the movements to their fullest advantage and draw the audience's attention to them. The costume is neutral and original at the same time. I couldn't imagine forever dancing in a tracksuit, that's far too dull! The stage set essentially consists of a screen onto which slides and a short film are projected. I wanted a background on which my presence would resound, which ›lived‹ on stage together with me, rather than just a screen. All of these elements arose from the necessity, but also the desire, to maintain a pure aesthetic look which didn't influence the way the audience saw the origin of the dances.

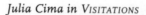

Julia Cima in VISITATIONS

Photo: Raphaël Pierre

The different narrative forms which you have developed for each solo with the aid of images, films and texts also distinguish the choreographic languages from each other. They add supplementary interpretations, open up new levels of expression and give the dance a different impact. How did you want to work with these narratives?

The point is to lend the dance an additional vitality, a different tone. Many of these choreographers have also written something, be it for an autobiography or for texts about their work or ideas. That's why it seemed important to me to use words to emphasise this almost permanent inter-action between mind and body. I like the idea of inviting an audience, which has come to watch a dance performance, to read words. Because reading is, by definition, the antithesis to the physical work which dance involves. There is a period of quiet when people read the words which I have chosen to suggest an interpretation for the preceding/subsequent dance. That opens the door to a world of ideas which would otherwise remain completely closed off or forgotten. The short film shows one of Isadora Duncan's students, Lisa Duncan, capering around happily. With this short film solo I am making a very direct and drastic link between these dances from another time and myself, the modern-day performer, who really doesn't have the feeling that contemporary dance is characterised by the joy which is so apparent in the film. I wanted to show the difference which, in my opinion, exists between the simple enjoyment of dancing and the enjoyment of thinking about how movement can be brought onto the stage with the help of ever more complex concepts. This film says a lot about the ideas which went into the conception of this performance. I wanted to return to something almost ›primitive‹.

Where do you see yourself as a performer as regards the choreographers of your generation? In which direction do you think body-based artistic creativity is moving? Towards the constant questioning of choreographic forms or the search for new forms of expression?

Performers must question what choreographers want on every level – with the help of their bodies, the physical means of expression available to them and also verbally. They must contribute sufficient input to help move the project forwards. I'm not talking about influence here, but rather about the ability to make suggestions to help solve all kinds of problems, so that the choreographer doesn't get stuck in familiar systems or ›formulae‹. It's not about claiming everything for yourself. It's about establishing real dialogue which everyone can contribute to in a creative way. Then I don't think it really matters anymore whether the dialogue is about choreographic forms or new forms of expression. If choreographers are talented and surround themselves with the right people, they can transform the simplest of ideas into an incredible performance. I'm absolutely convinced of this. But to do that you need talent, in particular the ability to give a group the self-confidence to allow everybody in it to be as creative as possible.

Translation from French

The Body as Archive

On the Difficult Relationship

between Movement and History

Inge Baxmann

Today what used to be seen as a deficiency has become an opportunity:
the ›speechlessness‹ of dance prevented it from becoming relevant to
the cultural memory of modern European societies. The historian Alain
Corbin criticised those archives of memories that are based essentially
on written language: »Western history, as a merely written one, has no
odour.«[1] One might add that it also has no rhythm.

With the current restructuring of the cultures of knowledge, the body
has been rediscovered as a seat of memory, because sensory, emotional
and cognitive experiences are stored in movements, gestures, and rhythm.
This knowledge is based on oral and gestural traditions and is manifested
in non-verbal expressive forms or artefacts. This tacit knowledge[2] was
never integrated into occidental historiography and remained marginal
to the European concept of culture. But how can this desideratum be
productive in writing dance history?

In the 1930s, the ethnologist Marcel Mauss developed the idea of
an archive of body techniques.[3] Mauss began his career with a scandal:

---

1 | Alain Corbin: *Pesthauch und Blütenduft: Eine Geschichte des Geruchs*, Frank-
furt a.M. 1988, p. 2.

2 | The expression »tacit knowledge« originated from the chemist and philoso-
pher Michael Polanyi. This knowledge is interpreted as a dynamic entity
and, with its own forms of activity and communication, a knowledge that
is constantly in flux. Cf. Michael Polanyi: *The Tacit Dimension*, New York:
Anchor 1967, and Mikhail Dua: *Tacit Knowing: Michael Polanyi's Exposition
of Scientific Knowledge*, Munich: Utz 2004.

3 | Through a closer connection with ethnology and psychoanalysis, Mauss
developed an anthropologically-orientated sociology (partly together with

in 1901 he was appointed to head the chair of l'Histoire des religions des peuples non civilisés (history of the religions of uncivilised peoples) at the École des Hautes Études in Paris. In his inaugural lecture he presented the fundamentals of his methodology, which were based on the assumption that there were no uncivilised peoples, but simply peoples with differing civilisations. Thus he said that an Australian society was neither simple nor primitive, but instead had just as long a history as modern western European cultural communities, even though the cultural memory of this civilisation had not been handed down in writing.

In his lecture »The Techniques of the Body« delivered in 1934,[4] Mauss showed how the various techniques of the body, that is to say, the modalities of physical habits (ranging from running to sexuality to techniques for falling asleep) depend on differing neural and muscular synergies shaped by different cultures. According to Mauss, conscious and unconscious individual and collective representations can be ascertained from these systems. He says that each body technique has its own specific form, is handed down, is acquired, links conscious and unconscious and encodes bodily perceptions as social experience. In Mauss's words, it presents a »physio-psycho-sociological montage«, in which the experience of the body is inextricably intermingled with its psychological and sociological context. Mauss's idea of an archive of body techniques is revolutionary because it does not assume a dualism between body and culture. The body memory is itself a cultural form that is always historically specific.

The »Archives Internationales de la Danse«

Mauss's concept of body memory was taken up by the »Archives Internationales de la Danse« (AID), which was founded in Paris in 1931 by Rolf de Maré, the patron of the Swedish Ballet. De Maré wanted to establish movement as an independent form of knowledge as opposed to the verbalisation of dance, which reduces it to the procedures of the written word. The »Archives Internationales de la Danse« gave this implicit knowledge a venue. The aim was to create a repository, a new sort of institution for the dance,

---

Émile Durkheim and Henri Hubert), which focussed its research on the question of the cohesion of societies beyond rational compacts. Together with Lucien Lévy-Bruhl and Paul Rivet, he founded the Institut d'Ethnologie at the Paris Sorbonne in 1925.

4 | Marcel Mauss: »Techniques du corps«, in: idem: *Sociologie et anthropologie, précédé d'une Introduction à l'oeuvre de Marcel Mauss par Claude Lévi-Strauss*, Paris: Presses universitaires de France 1950, pp. 380f.

[...] which centrally concentrates all the important documents on dance from all countries, and to establish a library, a museum and a documentation centre that collects books, pictures, engravings, and drawings, in a word, all the artworks there are that have anything to do with dance.[5]

The idea was not just to collect knowledge about dance, but also to make it productive in practice, through exchanges between practitioners, theoreticians of all sorts and interested amateurs. The AID organised exhibitions, choreographic competitions, lectures and dance performances of the most divergent styles and origins, and it published a magazine aimed at a broad readership, from dancers and choreographers to scholars and interested amateurs. In the process, old-fashioned disciplines or genres were given little consideration: here, sociologists, ethnologists, dancers, painters, writers and film-makers met directly.

Cover of the special issue »La danse dans la peinture« of the magazine »Revue des AID«, no. 5, 1933

© Bibliothèque Musée de l'Opéra de Paris

---

5 | *Les AID*, undated and unpaginated brochure, Bibliothèque Musée de l'Opéra (BMO Sign. Pro. 6.1). In cooperation with the Centre Nationale de la Danse and the Bibliothèque Musée de l'Opéra in Paris, Claire Rousier, Patrizia Veroli and I conducted a three year research project on the AID. Cf. Inge Baxmann/Claire Rousier/Patrizia Veroli (eds.): *Les Archives Internationales de la Danse 1931–1952*, Paris: Editions du CND: 2006. A revised German version of this book is to be a publication focussing on the cultural studies aspect: Inge Baxmann (ed.): *Kulturgeschichte als Körperwissen: Die Archives Internationales de la Danse (1931–1952)*, Munich: Kieser 2007.

In a lecture on »The position of Dance in Sociology«, the AID's archivist, Pierre Tugal, explored the range of theories on dance made available by Marcel Mauss and Emile Durkheim's school of sociology. »With regard to primitive dance, two eminent French sociologists, HUBERT and MAUSS, emphasise that dance is a powerful manifestation of the social instinct. According to these authors the entire social body is gripped by the same movement.«[6] In France at this time, *recherches collectives* became a privileged field of study which established new social scientific methods that were also productive in dance research. The historians Lucien Fèbvre, Marc Bloch and Maurice Halbwachs, who, with the Annales School, founded the study of mentality,[7] were interested in the myths, rituals and oral traditions of modern European civilisation. This made the most diverse physical practices the subject of a sociological investigation of modern European societies. It is no coincidence that within the AID a Départment sociologique et ethnologique, (sociological and ethnological department) was created, with the task: »[...] not only of collecting the immense amount of material on dance uncivilised peoples possess, but also, beyond it, to do comparative work from a sociological perspective and to further aesthetic, psychological and physiological work on dance and movement.«[8]

This academic department arranged conferences and exhibitions, showed films and functioned as a link between scholars and artists by organising *conférences-démonstrations* (conference demonstrations). The sociological and ethnological department was headed by Alfred Smoular, who had studied at the Institut d'Ethnologie de l'Université de Paris and was on the staff of the Trocadéro Museum (later on called Musée de l'Homme). Smoular found that only ethnology with its methods of observation and comparison offered answers to the questions that dance posed. Only ethnological studies, he said, were capable of fathoming the »secret depths«, that hidden sense which dance finds in the »network of social ideas.«[9]

The AID viewed dance from a social and art historical perspective. It saw it as more than just an aesthetic phenomenon, an art form or leisure time activity for an audience of aficionados. The variety of the collected materials went far beyond artistic dance and ranged from dance-related

---

6 | Pierre Tugal: »La Position de la Danse dans la Sociologie«, manuscript *AID*, p. 1 (emphasis in the original text).

7 | They belonged to a group of French historians who established a new methodology and practice in studies of history (the *nouvelle histoire*). The name is derived from their journalistic mouthpiece, »Annales D'Histoire Economique et Sociale«.

8 | *Revue des Archives Internationales de la Danse*, Paris, no 1/1932, p. 3.

9 | Alfred Smoular: »La Danse sacrée«, in: *Revue des AID* (July 1934), p. 86.

performances in the arts to records of choreographic works, dance and music notation, ethnological material and folk dances all the way to documents of the dance techniques of all cultures. The body as a seat of memory, a storehouse for knowledge about movement, sensory experiences and alternative sensory arrangements essentially called into question old-fashioned ideas of the archive and the corresponding cultural models. What is a document in dance? The practices of collection, preservation and documentation had to be rethought in order to create an archive of movement and dance.

Museology and Josephine Baker: In the Beginning was the Dance

The success of the AID lies in the fact that it was part of a contemporary current which called into question concepts of European culture and society that had prevailed for centuries. Like the oral traditions of non-European cultures, dance was considered to be the gateway to society's unconscious, to ›origins‹ and hidden drives. It was hoped it would generate impetus for cultural renewal, much like tendencies of primitivism in modern art, something with which Rolf de Maré, as a collector of avant-garde art, was familiar. But the industrially increased dynamism in daily life and the acceleration of its rhythms also engendered a new fascination with movement. The enthusiasm of the masses in the big cities for jazz rhythms as well as the rhythm, movement and simultaneity aimed at in variety theatre and music hall productions expressed a new collective awareness. Oriental, Indian and Latin American dances found their way into the movement repertoire of European dancers and into the dance halls. The »exotic« performers became a favourite projection surface for the yearnings of modern Europeans. It was none other than Rolf de Maré who organised Josephine Baker's first tour of Europe and her appearance in Paris. The exploration of non-European music and movement cultures was a fundamental motivation for developing new concepts of museology.

The question of the status of a document, its collection and presentation also concerned the group of avant-garde artists and theoreticians whom Georges Bataille (who was not only active as a writer) had assembled in connection with a magazine under the programmatic title »Documents. Doctrines, Archéologie, Beaux-Arts, Ethnographie«, which first appeared in Paris in 1929.[10] Bataille was the editor of this magazine,

---

10 | The first three issues appeared under this title. After the fourth, it changed to: *Documents. Archéologies. Beaux-Arts. Ethnographie. Variétés.* See also *Documents. Archéologies. Beaux-Arts. Ethnographie* I (1929ff.), Réédition by Denis Hollier (Paris, 1991).

which in the mere two years (and fifteen issues) of its existence between 1929 and 1931 propagated a new understanding of the archive, the document and knowledge while dealing with an extremely diverse range of topics, an understanding that also exerted an influence on the work of the AID. Several associates from the AID, Paul Rivet, Georges-Henri Rivière and Georges Wildenstein,[11] were on the editorial committee of the magazine. Artistic and ethnographic documents were accorded equal weight. In Bataille's approach a document understood in this way put the aesthetic self-image of western European culture into a wider context.[12] These documents were neither objects of aesthetic contemplation nor museum or art objects with a corresponding market value; it was their ›practical value‹, that is to say, their social function in their respective cultural contexts, which was of primary interest.

André Schaeffner (head of the musicology department in the Trocadéro and advisor to the AID on numerous exhibitions) had published a programmatic article »On Musical Instruments in an Ethnographic Museum« in »Documents«, which was a polemic against the isolation and removal of exhibits displayed in museums outside their context, which was usual at the time.[13]

Schaeffner considers an isolated musical instrument to be an abstraction. It must be accompanied. Photographic or phonographic documents must make it possible for the instrument to return to the concrete: the position of the musician, the place where the tones are being produced, etcetera. There is, however, a whole range of performances which use no other instrument than the (mortal) body of the musician, which consist of gestures and which would disappear if photography did not preserve their proceedings.[14]

Thus a photograph of the player next to the instrument exhibited should show how he held the instrument in his hands, to present the physical technique connected with playing the instrument. The central concept of this sort of museology is, not coincidentally, Mauss's concept of body techniques. With it emerged an approach to art, the museum and archives, which provides a vivid image to the senses and physically involves the visitor.

---

11 | Among those who delivered articles regularly were Roger Caillois, Michel Leiris and, with Curt Sachs and André Schaeffner, further important associates of the AID.

12 | Cf. *Documents. Doctrines. Archéologie. Beaux-Arts. Ethnographie* 1 [1929] 1991, Denis Hollier, Préface, p. VIII.

13 | André Schaeffner: »Des instruments de musique dans une musée d'ethnographie«, in: *Documents* 5 (octobre 1929), pp. 252f.

14 | Ibid., p. 254. Cf. Denis Hollier: *La valeur d'usage de l'impossible. Préface de la réédition de »Document«*, Paris 1991, p. XI.

Paul Rivet and Georges Henri Rivière had been developing a similar programme in the Musée d'Ethnographie since 1929. Rivière had listened enthusiastically to Marcel Mauss's lectures. There he found the inspiration for musée laboratoire, an ethnographic museology that linked research and documentation directly with preservation and exhibition. For this purpose he developed new forms of presentation, which – very much in the spirit of Mauss – exhibited non-European cultures using an all-embracing notion of culture as a starting point. This desire also characterised the AID. AID's exhibitions addressed a broad audience with quite varied interests. The exhibition »To the Glory of Pavlova« (1934) basically presented – from swan costume to pointe shoes or the artist's theatre box reconstructed down to the last detail – objects of contemplation for enthusiasts. Another major focus in the AID exhibitions was the relationship between dance and other arts, like, for example, in the exhibition »Dance and Movement« (1933/1934)[15], which dealt with dance in sculpture, ceramics and painting. The exhibition on marionettes (1934) offered an overview of the entire spectrum of the art of puppetry, ranging from the shadow theatre of Java, to folklore European puppet plays to modern marionette theatre. In accompanying the exhibition by performances of plays using marionettes, the AID contributed to the reconstruction of folk traditions. Puppets and marionettes belong to an oral culture, to songs or fairy tales as they are told in villages. The exhibition of pictures on festival traditions from antiquity to the modern era, which took place in 1935, also dealt with a subject which was extremely topical at a time when people were searching for community.

A couple (presumably Solange Schwarz and Claude Assenat) dancing at the LA NUIT DE DANSES *gala in Paris on 27 June 1935*

Photo: © Arax und Henry/Bibliothèque Musée de l'Opéra de Paris

---

15 | »Dance and Movement« was part of the international photography exhibition.

A Connection between Art and Science:
Conférences-Démonstrations

The AID functioned like a sponge soaking up contemporary tendencies. Its contribution to opening up a new field of discourse on dance and movement traditions lay in just this quality. Its activities covered broad areas in which completely new forums on documenting, presenting and collecting knowledge about movement emerged. The spectrum ranged from choreographic competitions to scholarly conferences, exhibitions, lecture-demonstrations and even using surveys to acquire data. Not the least of the AID's achievements was that it brought together people from very diverse cultural fields and created new synergies: scholars, artists, amateurs and politicians met through the topic of dance. In collating the knowledge on movement traditions from extremely divergent perspectives and systematically confronting academic theories of the most widely differing provenance with dance in practice, with the techniques and experience of dancers and choreographers, the AID made an original contribution to developing new forms of knowledge that is still valid today. In doing so, it blurred the boundaries between art and science and called into question both the exclusivity of art and the coherence of academic disciplines. The AID's dual scholarly-artistic approach is particularly evident in the *conférences-démonstrations* mentioned before, which dealt not only with dance and movement traditions, but also with theoretical models.

Lectures and »chats« on classical, exotic and modern dance[16] in its aesthetic, anthropological and sociological implications, combined with examples of dance and music (in addition to her dancers the choreographer Suria Margrite brought along an entire orchestra consisting primarily of percussion instruments), attracted a large and multifarious audience to the Rue Vital. The ethnologist Claire Holt had just returned from a research trip to Java when she delivered her lecture on June 18, 1936. »Mme Claire Holt [...] spoke about courtly, religious and theatrical dances, as they are preserved in both large royal courts on the island; numerous slides gave this lecture an unusual documentary value.«[17] On the basis of illustrative material from antiquity to modern times, problems in writing dance history were dealt with in both the magazine and

---

16 | The lectures and demonstrations also included other movement forms such as mime, gymnastics, and acrobatics from both within and beyond Europe. Thus there was a conference presentation on Mensendieck gymnastics (25 March 1935), on physical culture and hygiene (14 March 1935), and masks and pantomimes (15 April 1935).

17 | *Les Conférences des Archives Internationales de la Danse, Tribune de la Danse* 3, 16 (March 1935).

the lectures. The role of dance in the cultures of antiquity as well as the Christian and Jewish liturgies, each of which were accompanied by the reconstruction of these dances, was regarded with special interest.

The series of conferences on dance techniques, which presented a broad spectrum of dance styles and dance forms, from classical ballet to the many diverse variations of modern dance all the way to ›exotic‹ dance, were especially successful. »The success exceeded all expectations and often a disappointed public waited outside a completely filled hall,« reported the March 1935 edition of the »Tribune de la Danse«.[18] Without taking a position in the dispute between schools and methods, the AID fed the fascination of the modern audience with new styles of movement. The lecture cycle on the »Techniques of Dance« regularly presented body techniques of »foreign« cultures in which, in addition to professional dancers from the countries involved, European dancers also performed, dancers who – like, for example, Charlotte Bara or the Sakharoffs – had been inspired by non-European dance traditions to create highly idiosyncratic interpretations. In addition to flamenco, the lecture-demonstrations showed traditional methods of popular Hindu dances, from Indonesian to Japanese, Balinese or Arabian dance. The AID moved in a terrain typical of the times, between exoticism and serious examination of non-European dance traditions. Its exceptional achievement lay in systematically linking together the various viewpoints that were available on movement cultures in the 1930s. This included, first and foremost, developing new ways of organising and arranging this knowledge in experimental classifications that combined and contrasted discourses which had up to that time rarely been associated or communicated with each other. In this way, comprehensive concepts emerged for collecting, researching and presenting movement cultures that provide interesting incentives for the current restructuring of the way we view knowledge.

Translation from German

---

18 | Ibid., p. 1.

References

Baxmann, Inge (ed.): *Kulturgeschichte als Körperwissen: Die Archives Internationales de la Danse (1931–1952)*, Munich: Kieser 2007.

Baxmann, Inge/Rousier, Claire/Veroli, Patrizia (eds.): *Les Archives Internationales de la Danse 1931–1952*, Paris: Editions du CND: 2006.

Corbin, Alain: *Pesthauch und Blütenduft: Eine Geschichte des Geruchs*, Frankfurt a.M. 1988.

Dua, Mikhail: *Tacit Knowing: Michael Polanyi's Exposition of Scientific Knowledge*, Munich: Utz 2004.

Hollier, Denis: »Préface: *La valeur d'usage de l'impossible*«, in: *Documents. Doctrines. Archéologie. Beaux-Arts. Ethnographie* 1 [1929] 1991.

Les AID, undated and unpaginated brochure, Bibliothèque Musée de l'Opéra (BMO Sign. Pro. 6.1).

Les Conférences des Archives Internationales de la Danse, Tribune de la Danse 3, 16 (March 1935).

Mauss, Marcel: »Techniques du corps«, in: idem: *Sociologie et anthropologie, précédé d'une Introduction à l'oeuvre de Marcel Mauss par Claude Lévi-Strauss*, Paris: Presses universitaires de France 1950, pp. 365–388.

Polanyi, Michael: *The Tacit Dimension*, New York: Anchor 1967.

Revue des Archives Internationales de la Danse, Paris, no 1/1932.

Schaeffner, André: »Des instruments de musique dans une musée d'ethnographie«, in: *Documents* 5 (octobre 1929), pp. 248–254.

Smoular, Alfred: »La Danse sacrée«, in: *Revue des AID* (July 1934), p. 86.

Tugal, Pierre: »La Position de la Danse dans la Sociologie«, manuscript *AID*.

Reception and Participation

Visitor Check-In at the BLACKMARKET FOR USEFUL KNOWLEDGE *AND* NON-KNOWLEDGE *by* Hannah Hurtzig, DANCE CONGRESS GERMANY 2006*, Photo: Thomas Aurin*

For a Participatory Theatre: Touching Instead of Fumbling

Felix Ruckert

Today's relationship between performer and recipients in the field of dance is reminiscent of the loveless interaction in a swingers' club. A nervous, and somewhat silly, forced encounter creating an illusion of freedom. A mind-boggling selection of hi-tech toys to conceal the lack of creativity. Feelings surface, only to be watered down with humour. Participants let themselves go physically, unperturbed by perversion or pain, but their hearts are not truly in it. What is going on? Contemporary stages are brimming over with fucking and shopping, but there is very little loving and giving. Communication theories are covering up for the fact that people have curiously little to say.

Apropos shopping: The successful dance product allows for greatest possible projections. It says a lot but means very little. It simulates altered perceptions instead of actually altering them. It offers us a choice of trivia. It sells us mere variation as innovation. Like all other superfluous consumer products, it simply creates an illusion of innovation and modification, without really offering anything genuinely new.

As with all other creative forces, the raw, subversive and healing power of dance is destroyed by the market. The system of academies and festivals, the alliance between the media, theoreticians and presenters filters out the primeval passion for movement, leaving only sterile artefacts destined for the gratification of a fickle elite of dance spectators. Consumer society. Although we dancers love the playful, irrational and fleeting qualities of our art, we are also trying to create marketable products and sell them for as much money as possible! We also have a tendency to believe that sales figures and consumer-friendliness are an indication of quality and so we ultimately yield to the demands of the masses. We deliver the goods in the required format and colour.

Theatres are dark ›non-spaces‹, designed to control everyday perception. They are artificial nights in which we try to focus attention on our message, with the help of complex stage technology. We have the same zeal as rocket scientists and physicists who use sophisticated technology to try to grasp the infinity of the universe or the subtleties of relativity. If the same efforts were applied to investigating the subconscious mind, our perceptual capacity, our own built-in software, how much more satisfying might the results be. But as long as winning concepts and consent are supported instead of uncertainty and provocation ...

One hundred years ago, when images of the steam locomotive first chugged towards cinema audiences, our grandparents ran screaming from their seats. Despite the poor picture quality and the obviousness of the illusion, the viewers could not trust their senses and were not able to suppress their need to respond physically to the ›danger‹. The more sophisticated movie effects have become, the more sophisticated is our perception. Today, we can easily distinguish between appearances and reality and happily sit in the cinema exposing ourselves to emotions such as fear, revulsion, pity and grief. Our acquired sensitivity as recipients is decisive in this context. If we are familiar with our feelings, then we will be aware of them. If we are used to expressing them, we will be susceptible to authenticity.

The magic, and also the impotence, of the silver screen lies in the ethereal quality of the pictures, made only of light. Because we know that it is not possible to experience them kinaesthetically, the most emotional channel of perception remains blocked. If this were not so, we dancers could become rich through selling movement itself, our core competence. But a medium for storing cinematic experiences has not yet been invented. What would it be like if the feeling of a triple pirouette or a floor relaxation exercise could be called up on a Walkman?

Film allows moviemakers to portray their wildest and most brutal fantasies without seriously threatening the emotional security of their audiences. The sophisticated eyes of today's viewers only allow the images to filter through to our bodies when we deliberately decide to switch our minds off. However, we are used to controlling our feelings in this context. Yet, while our eyes are over-stimulated and hardened, our physical sense, our skin, is soft and weak. We are largely unschooled in dealing with physical presence, closeness, intimacy, and only learn through private improvisation. Intense physical experiences such as hunger, cold, pain or fear of death are not immediately accessible; we have to deliberately induce them in order to appreciate them. This has opened up a new market for the more daring among us: the extreme sport and adventure holiday sectors are thriving. For more cautious types who find the cinema too commonplace but are too wary to tackle a bungee jump, dance is an excellent way to experience physical emotions.

The people who attend dance performances, the observers of our activities, are a very particular, and fortunately quite rare, species. They want to be close to the physicality, the carnality of the dancers, but keep their feelings hidden. They are gropers in the dark, voyeurs who seek to gratify themselves without getting involved. They have seen it all and are quickly bored, yet they are also easily unsettled or even feel cheated by the possibility of a discomfiting, embarrassing authentic experience or of experiencing a black hole of genuine sensations. Tricky customers. Contemporary choreographers are asked to create fear without being frightening, create shame without being shameful. Dancers must demonstrate control of their feelings, not the feelings themselves. This balancing act between the desired thrill and the required level of comfort produces nothing but hypocrisy.

Often only two options are left open. So-called conceptual dancers practice seduction through refusal. ›Post-modern dancers‹ are excellently trained, yet dance sloppily. They look fantastic, but are dressed hideously. They are sexy, but never sexual. Nakedness is absolutely okay, but it must be embellished with a concept. The ›dance dancers‹, on the other hand, rely on the good old formula of heroic pangs, self-harm, despairing virtuosity, suffering from the form: pent-up emotions which explode into life on the stage. Fortitude and self-sacrifice are reliable assets. This works for large, powerful companies in particular. They can give their dancers sufficient fame and financial security to compensate for the self-abuse they endure. They are good to watch and audiences applaud with a slight feeling of shame. In this orgy of simulation and/or simulation of an orgy, some theatres are becoming ever louder and more cynical. They are trying to avoid a descent into banality, while the audiences leave the halls – not slamming the doors in disappointment, but closing them quietly, in the knowledge that the exciting stuff is going on somewhere else anyway.

In the subcultures of physical work and play, alternative models are flourishing which are dedicated to obliterating borders. Dance is mixed with therapy, performance is feeding off psychodrama, the martial arts are becoming a form of meditation, and cuddling is turned into a party. Tantra groups organise orgies, fetish clubs hold permanent carnivals. The gay and lesbian scene invents a range of sexual identities beyond mere ›man‹ and ›woman‹. Interwoven connections. All over the place, watching and touching at the same time. Participation instead of reception. In the mainstream too, doubt is growing as to whether passive consumption can really bring fulfilment. The internet as a participatory, communicative medium is superseding television. Sports fields and courts are full. People want to go out and play themselves. Tango, Salsa, Hip-Hop and Contact Improvisation are becoming new forms of folk dancing and leisure rituals.

The body has largely been replaced as a means of production by machines and technology and has thus gained relevance as a means of expression. It plays the central role in this reorientation; it has become a statement, a project. Depending on taste, wallet, socialisation and neuroses, it is beautified, styled, adjusted, decorated, trained, instructed, pushed to its limits, analysed, reflected upon, tended and mended. Of course, it is also moulded into a product, something to be sold and marketed. And yet there is more to it than that: the clients of the proliferating dance studios, gyms, yoga schools, tattoo parlours, spas, Botox clinics, hair salons and other playrooms have one thing in common: the desire for beauty, well-being and company, and then, to be physically in touch with themselves and with others.

For over ten years I have been attempting to give my audiences a taste, a whiff, a sense of dance. I unsettled them individually with my solo dancers (HAUTNAH, 1995), I encouraged them to dance themselves (SCHWARTZ, 1997), I organised kissing and groping (RING, 1999). I massaged them in public (DELUXE JOY PILOT, 2000), I had them bound and whipped (SECRET SERVICE, 2002), and lured them into a collective cuddle (LOVE ZOO, 2003). I enticed them to join sex and tantra workshops (XPLORE 2004) and packed them inside plastic and iron (PLACEBO TREATMENT, 2005). Ultimately I clothed, cleaned and trained them and made them subject themselves to a megalomaniac (myself!) (UNITED KINGDOM, 2006).[1]

All these partly magnificent, partly ridiculous projects owe everything to the audience themselves. They were astonishingly willing to surrender themselves and clearly enjoyed doing so. Sensing an opportunity to experience something new, they were capable of overcoming inhibitions and apprehensions. All the monstrosities I have listed above, until now inconceivable in the context of theatre, arose through chance-collaborations (I mean through the coming together of different events, not through collaborations that came together by chance) in which the most daring and curious participants in my experiments and test arrangements were involved.

---

1 | UNITED KINGDOM is an interactive performance project with different degrees of participation. Based on the idea of creating an utopic society it functions on a corpus of laws and rules. It allows its members to explore different degrees of dominance and submission in the frame work of a fictional kingdom. The central mission of the kingdom is the elaboration of play structures that allow the authentic experience of emotions such as fear, pain, anger, aggression, sadness and weakness but also trust, strength, kindness, pleasure, connection and devotion to happen. These play structures may include choreography, scenario, role play, ritual and drama. Cf. *www.unitedkingdom-berlin.de* from 12 May 2007.

Guest and performer of the project
United Kingdom by Felix Ruckert at
Tacheles, Berlin 2006

Photo: Philipp M. Wittulsky

When reflecting on all these extraordinary events, three terms always come to mind: presence, permeability, transformation. If the French philosopher Jean Baudrillard was right, and art has replaced religion (everyone practices it but no one believes in it!), then these three terms could be deemed the equivalent of the Holy Trinity. However, just like with the miracles of old, these phenomena have to be experienced in order to be understood. And if neuroscience is correct, we must – put simply – act if we are to perceive. So we sprang into action. The overwhelming reactions inspired me to develop rules of play and composition tools so I would be able to respond more flexibly to unforeseen challenges. This knowledge could be applied to conventional stages remarkably well. I began to undermine the world of ballet, which suddenly seemed more open towards less traditional forms of stage performance (Tools and Tricks, 2003; Venus in Hanoi, 2004; Tokyo-Tools, 2005). The technical excellence and intelligent use of space and time, which I trained in these projects, could easily be converted into direct physical interaction with the audience, i.e. dancing strategies proved successful when they were to be applied to the bodies of spectators.

Guest and performer of the project
UNITED KINGDOM by Felix Ruckert at
Tacheles, Berlin 2006

Photo: Philipp M. Wittulsky

We clearly experienced the kind of liminal situation postulated by theatre researcher Erika Fischer-Lichte in her »Ästhetik des Performativen«[2], an experience which affected not only our audience, but the dancers, too. They started to develop empathic, psychological and therapeutic skills. This was, however, not a planned development, it was a spontaneous, organic growth, more of a mutation than a design, more of an avalanche than a snow cannon. Every new project arose out of the questions which the previous project threw up. Every new adventure the audience embarked upon was initiated, demanded, even provoked, by them. The borders between the actors and the reactors became fluid even at the design stage of the new projects. The power of the participation principle slowly became clear to us. The fourth wall collapsed.

This self-generating dynamism my projects acquired often overtaxed me. I changed, too. It seemed increasingly difficult to separate art from life, work from play, the private from the public sphere. Is this the longed-for re-enchantment of the world or an insidious insanity? Participatory theatre leaves all questions about meaning or content behind. It does not represent anything, it *is*, it *does*. It is pure movement. It is the choreography of the moment and of placelessness. It is everywhere and always,

---

2 | Erika Fischer-Lichte: *Ästhetik des Performativen*, Frankfurt a.M.: Suhrkamp 2004.

because it abrogates time and space. It consists of a series of impulses. It proliferates. It is called flow, ecstasy, meditation, communitas, liminality. Like all these phenomena, it can offer much more than mere entertainment; it can change lives. It knows no spectators, only participants. It is created wherever the will and readiness are there and disappears when it fails to keep its participants' attention. It cannot be enforced, it can only be practiced.

Participation is much more than just a peripheral form of theatre, a risqué ›no-go area‹ of the dance scene. It is a social desire. The removal of boundaries and differences and the acceptance of conflicts are part of a historical process of individual emancipation, democratisation and abolition of hierarchies. Participation is the fundamental strategy applied in the search for renewal, change and bonding.

Translation from German

References

Fischer-Lichte, Erika: *Ästhetik des Performativen*, Frankfurt a.M.: Suhrkamp 2004.

Online References

www.unitedkingdom-berlin.de.

On the Threshold

Aesthetic Experience in Performances

Erika Fischer-Lichte

Since the 1960s, a series of developments have questioned the very basis of our traditional system of arts and the concepts related to it. They have led to a constant overstepping of the boundaries between the various art forms as well as the boundaries between art and non-art – a transgression which was, in part, proclaimed and attempted by the historical avant-garde movements in the early 20th century. These developments also contributed to the erosion of the concept of the work of art, which is increasingly being replaced by the concept of the happening, the event. It is a shift in emphasis with far-reaching consequences for aesthetic theory. For while works are generally meant to be interpreted and understood, events are meant to be watched and experienced. Consequently, it is only logical that, since the 1970s, the concept of aesthetic experience has regained prominence.

It is a characteristic peculiar to the performing arts that performances can, in themselves, rarely be classified as works. They always are rather occurrences, or events. Since the 1960s, this characteristic has been emphasised and displayed in an almost programmatic way. Performances repeatedly explode conventional dichotomies such as those between actor and spectator, subject and object, art and reality, aesthetic and political spheres, as well as aesthetic and ethical values. It is no longer a case of ›either ... or‹ but rather one of ›both ... and‹. This opens up the space between opposites – an ›in-between‹ which has evolved into a favoured category. The boundary which separates one thing from another has become a threshold that brings them together.[1]

---

1 | Cf. Erika Fischer-Lichte: *Ästhetik des Performativen*, Frankfurt a.M.: Suhrkamp 2004.

It is in this way that aesthetic experience in the theatre can be considered a liminal experience. The concept of liminality – which is of central importance here – has its origins neither in art theory nor in philosophical aesthetics. Nor is it a new concept. It was developed in the field of research into rituals and was coined by the anthropologist Victor Turner based on the work of ethnologist Arnold van Gennep. In his study, »Les Rites de Passage« (1909), van Gennep used an abundance of ethnological material to show that rituals are linked to a highly symbolic threshold and transitional experience. Turner called the state created in the threshold phase a state of liminality (from Latin *limen* – threshold) and defined it, more specifically, as a fragile state of limbo »betwixt and between the positions assigned and arrayed by law, custom, convention and ceremonial«.[2] He explains that the liminal phase opens up room for experiments and innovations and how it does this: »in liminality, new ways of acting, new combinations of symbols are tried out to be discarded or accepted«.[3] According to Turner, the changes which lead to the liminal phase normally affect the social status of the person undergoing the ritual as well as the entire community.

If I describe aesthetic experiences created by dance, dramatic and musical performances or performance art as liminal experiences, it does *not* mean that I am equating artistic performances with ritualistic performances. Even if artistic performances (such as those by the artists Hermann Nitsch and Joseph Beuys, stage directors Einar Schleef and Theodoros Terzopoulos or choreographers Saburo Teshigawara and Felix Ruckert) have repeatedly questioned and sought to undermine such kinds of delimitation by emphasising striking affinities between both types of performance, at least two differences exist: while the change in status and identity effected in a ritual is irreversible and must be accepted by the community, the transformations which spectators may undergo during an artistic performance are generally temporary and do not require any form of social acceptance.

One cannot fail to notice that many artistic performances over the last forty years have developed and employed processes which create spaces capable of placing people in a state of liminality. Below I am going to provide examples of three such processes which I will outline and discuss: (1) role reversal between actors and the audience; (2) a particular use of rhythm and (3) the oscillation of perception between phenomenality and symbolism.

---

2 | Victor Turner: *The Ritual Process. Structure and Anti-Structure*, London: Routledge & Kegan Paul 1969, p. 95.

3 | Victor Turner: »Variations on a Theme of Liminality«, in: Sally F. Moore/Barbara C. Myerhoff (eds.): *Secular Ritual*, Assen: Van Gorcum 1977, p. 40.

Role Reversal between Actors and the Audience

Owing to the physical presence of both actors and audience, the *sine qua non* of any performance, the option of a role reversal is always there. It is an option which the choreographer Felix Ruckert decided to use in a very unusual way in his piece SECRET SERVICE (2002). The ambiguity of the title refers both to clandestine services such as those rendered in the business of prostitution, as well as the state-run secret service, whose operations range from monitoring the most private of acts to the use of instruments of torture.

The piece consisted of two parts. Before it began, a dancer explained the rules of the game to the audience/participants. All members of the audience were to remain blindfolded throughout the entire performance. Only the dancers could see. Conversely, the blindfolded audience became the actors. Throughout the performance they had the option of giving the dancers a sign that they wanted to stop playing. Visitors were asked to remove their shoes and socks. The dancer then blindfolded them, took them by the hand and led them into the performance room.

The theatre researcher Peter Boenisch described his experience of this performance in the following words:

After a while, a hand suddenly touched by chest, pushed me into the room, lifted my hand and let it go again. [...] Led by my hand, I ran round in circles. Suddenly my body is shouldered and spun through the room. And then I'm lying on the floor, feet stubbing at my body, pressing against me. Then someone is lying on top of me, rolling slowly over and off my body, grabs my toes and tickles the soles of my feet. The spectator becomes part of a precise choreography, which is visible to no-one apart from the actors themselves. [...] Who is the subject here, who is the object? It makes no sense to separate these roles, because I too am reaching out to touch another body, am pushing to the beat of the techno music, shoving and acting. And is this other person one of the dancers involved? Or is it just another member of the audience? And is it someone else at all? We cannot really hope to answer much more than the last question.[4]

The audience in this case experienced a radical example of a role reversal, but under very different conditions than those imposed in so-called »audience participation« events as introduced by Living Theatre or Performance Group in the 1960s. Their facial sense was eliminated. This not only meant that they now had to rely on their other senses, on their sense of hearing, of smell, and especially their sense of touch, but also on the actors who could see and thus control what was happening. The ›specta-

---

4 | Peter Boenisch: »ElectRONIC Bodies, Corpo-Realities in Contemporary Dance«, unpublished manuscript 2002.

tor‹ was thus put in a situation of extreme liminality, which presented them with an incredible challenge. On the one hand, they were forced to trust a group of wholly unknown actors, literally putting themselves in their hands, without having a clue as to what was going to happen. They were forced into a kind of passivity far beyond the peep-show passivity which the historical avant-garde had protested so vehemently against. But on the other hand, they were encouraged, or even challenged to influence the course of events through their sense of touch. By touching, pushing, kicking, stroking, cuddling up etc, they made each and every performance entirely different. Their reactions could neither be planned nor predicted nor controlled by the actors, despite their ability to see what was happening and keep an overview. In this piece, ›spectators/visitors‹ experienced something which they almost never experience in other performances, namely that they can physically influence the course of the performance, without, however, determining it. They experienced themselves as subjects, who are determined by the course of the performance while also contributing to shaping it, i.e. they were neither wholly autonomous subjects nor entirely controlled by others. They were subject and object at once. It was this experience which put them in this liminal state of »betwixt and between«, a more radical example of which is barely conceivable. It was a situation which, according to online feedback from the event, many spectators found extremely stimulating.

PLACEBO TREATMENT by *Felix Ruckert*

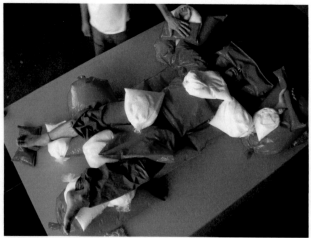

Photo: Philipp M. Wittulsky

Rhythm

A different process, which also aims to induce a liminal state in the spectator, is a particular use of rhythm. Different from beat and metre, rhythm is a principle of classification that is not based on evenness, but regularity. It is a dynamic principle, continuously creating and expressing itself according to certain patterns. Rhythm is produced by repetition and divergence from that repetition, through beat and break. Mere repetition would not produce rhythm. Rhythm could therefore be described as a principle of classification that depends on continuous, forward moving transformation.

This principle is already anchored in the human body itself: our heart beat, blood circulation and breathing all follow their own rhythm; we make rhythmic movements with our bodies when we walk, run, dance, swim or write with a pen; and the noises we make when we speak, sing, laugh or cry are also rhythmic. The movements created within our bodies, of which we are not actually conscious, are also completed rhythmically. The human body is tuned to operate to rhythms and this is why we are able to perceive rhythm as an external as well as an internal principle. Rhythm is, however, only able to affect us when we feel it in our bodies, similar to our own bodily rhythms, when we ›tune into‹ them.

Performances always combine several rhythmical systems – that created by the choreography or production and that of the different spectators. If the audience is successfully drawn into the rhythm of the choreography or production so that they ›tune into‹ the rhythm of the actors' movements, taking them ›out of themselves‹, they can be said to have entered a liminal state. The actors produce energy in such a way that the audience is able to feel it circulate through space, affecting them and energising them so that they, in turn, generate energy themselves and are thus transformed.

We should, however, bear in mind that every spectator is tuned to a different rhythm. Rhythmic coordination is particularly important for the interplay between intentionality and emergence during the performance. The interplay is brought about by people ›tuning into‹ each others' rhythms and, in this case, by direct, reciprocal bodily interaction between the actors and the audience.

The Oscillation of Perception between Phenomenality and Signification

A further process which aims to induce a liminal state among spectators consists of causing a constant shift in focus from the phenomenal corporeality of the actors and the characters they are playing. In order to achieve this, individual theatrical tools are often removed from wider contexts. They are no longer contained within a logical system of action or psychology, but rather seek to free themselves from any kind of causal link. The elements appear in the room in accordance with specific rhythmic, geometrical and other patterns, or entirely at random. They appear, stabilise for a varying amount of time, sometimes moving or in perpetual transformation, and then, as is so often the case in the choreographies of William Forsythe, they vanish with as little explanation as when they first surfaced. The elements that appear in this way seem to be emerging phenomena.

Emerging in this way, these isolated elements seem somehow de-semanticised. They are perceived in their particular materiality, rather than as bearers of meaning. But of course there can be no real question of de-semantisation. Although the respective movements and gestures may not be related to a particular story, emotion or mental state of a specific character, it does not mean that they are de-semanticised, but rather that they mean exactly what they do. Perceiving the theatrical elements in their specific materiality thus means taking them as referring only to themselves, as the simple phenomena they are.

If the spectator perceives the body of the actor as his particular body, he perceives it *as something*. We are not talking about a random stimulus here but the perception of something as something. Bodies and things mean that what they are, or what they appear to be. Perceiving something as something therefore necessarily means perceiving it as meaning something. In a self-referential state, materiality, the signifier and the signified become a whole. The body and the thing that is perceived to be something mean no more and no less than what they appear to be.

It is therefore advisable to distinguish between the phenomenal body of the actor and his semiotic body. For while the phenomenal body is perceived in its materiality for that what it appears to be, the semiotic body is interpreted as a sign for something else – for a character or another symbolic system. A mechanism commonly used since the 1970s, which causes spectators to enter this liminal state, is simply to draw their attention to the difference between the actor's phenomenal body (dancer, actor, singer, performer) and his semiotic body in such a way that they can no longer be kept congruent. In a classical ballet or a play based on the principles of psychological realism, spectators are mostly in a position to connect the bodies of the actors, their peculiar characteristics and different movements to the story that is being told and the situations, functions, characters and psychologies of the characters that are being represented, and thus perceive them as symbols which are to be interpreted in a certain way. But in this case too, the spectator's attention will focus on the phenomenal body of the actor from time to time, his mere corporeal being-in-the-world which will never be fully explained or contained in the character presented or any other symbolic system. This applies in particular to every kind of dance theatre – even classical ballet. For it is precisely the virtuosity of the movements performed which direct the spectator's attention to the phenomenal body of the actor. So even here, from time to time, the spectator's attention will oscillate between the perception of the actor as the character or other symbolic system he is representing and the perception of his phenomenal body that refers to nothing beyond itself and the nature of his coming-into-presence.

It is this alternating effect which produces the conventional dichotomies of actor/spectator, subject/object, signifier/signified which leads to an ›either ... or‹, or a ›both ... and‹. Performances that conflate these opposites create a reality in which the one can appear to be the other, an unstable reality, a shifting, blurred, multi-faceted, merging and limitless reality. The aesthetic experience of such a reality involves venturing onto such a threshold and lingering upon it; this is the definition of a threshold experience.

Translation from German

References

Boenisch, Peter: »ElectrONIC Bodies, Corpo-Realities in Contemporary Dance«, unpublished manuscript 2002.

Fischer-Lichte, Erika: *Ästhetik des Performativen*, Frankfurt a.M.: Suhrkamp 2004.

Fuchs, Georg: *Der Tanz*, Stuttgart: Strecker & Schröder 1906.

Turner, Victor: »Variations on a Theme of Liminality«, in: Sally F. Moore/ Barbara C. Myerhoff (eds.): *Secular Ritual*, Assen: Van Gorcum 1977, p. 40.

Turner, Victor: *The Ritual Process. Structure and Anti-Structure*, London: Routledge & Kegan Paul 1969.

The Politics of Collective Attention

Rudi Laermans

Imagine we are in a small theatre venue somewhere in Western Europe. It's 8.30 pm, the lights are dimmed, the performer steps in the direction of the proscenium, takes his or her place behind a lectern and starts talking. That's all that seems to happen in the eyes of all those present. Yet, something different also happens, and it is most of the time overlooked by those who are looking at a stage. Precisely because their sensory attention is absorbed by the action on the stage, those present do not notice that the attention of every single spectator disappears in a collective gaze (which of course includes ›a collective ear‹ when text or music is used). How to understand this gaze or, more generally, this *condensation of collective sensory attention?* As an autonomous social medium that is fundamental for every sort of live performing art, besides for instance the medium of text in the theatre or the body-as-medium in dance. This medium is per definition a temporary and contingent product that emerges again and again – or not! – during a performance.

Dance or theatre makers do of course anticipate public attention during the preparation and the rehearsals of a piece. They try to direct or steer this simultaneously desired and feared medium by means of the timing of a performance and all kinds of rhetorical devices (such as joking, insulting the public or just going on stage naked). Yet the simultaneously constitutive and contingent nature of the collective attention during a live performance cannot be simulated or controlled: the risk of ›going live‹ *is* the risk of being confronted with the black hole of scattered attention or a distracted audience. A proverbial attention cloud does or does not emerge, and when it does, it has only partially foreseen effects. Although this attention is anything but unmediated (a point to which I will return at the end of this essay), the condensation of the different individual perceptions into an autonomous quasi-reality is a temporal event in the strict sense: a passing moment in time. During a particular performance, this often happens several times, always with different outcomes, so that it is probably more appropriate to speak of a series of events and, consequently, of an inherently instable medium.

The social medium of collective sensory attention is not just the passive sum of the different individual perceptions, but an active, even transformative, quasi-reality. Evidently, the individual attention of every single member of the audience contributes to the emergence of a collective gaze (and/or a collective ear). The elements of the medium do indeed consist of individual perceptions, but their mutual couplings generate an autonomous surplus effect. It is reminiscent of the productivity of interaction effects in so-called complex systems, but one could as well refer to the semantic and rhetorical autonomy of a simple phrase in relation to the words that are its constituent elements. The media autonomy of collective attention is confirmed by its capacity to transform, for instance, some simple steps on a stage into meaningful movements, or to change a relatively long-lasting silence of the performers into a profound statement. Also, as every spectator knows, the momentary collective attention may greatly influence individual perception. Simultaneously, it is itself largely influenced by the overall way the audience behaves. Indeed, neither individual concentration nor the emergence of a collective attention is possible without the silence and adequate behaviour of those attending a performance.

We take it for granted that, once the lights are dimmed, the spectators become silent and attentive, thus transforming themselves into an audience. Actually, this crucial pact between performance and audience is a historical and social construct. At least in the West, it is the outcome – briefly speaking – of the bourgeois redefinition of the arts. Historical research indeed shows that during the first half of the 19th century silence and self-restraint did not yet predominate in theatre venues or during music performances. The expectation of genuine bodily self-control and a distanced, primarily mindful attention was only gradually imposed within artistic spaces, first and foremost by the new urban bourgeois elite. They did this because (partly coinciding with the first generations of new artistic professionals) they ›sacralised‹ those segments of theatre, music, sculpture or literature that were considered to embody »the best of mankind« – to use a famous phrase of the British poet and critic Matthew Arnold in »Culture and Anarchy«[1] (originally published in 1869). In this view, participation in the arts became synonymous with »the study

---

1 | Matthew Arnold: *Culture and Anarchy*, Oxford: Oxford University Press 2006.

of perfection«. The net outcome was a thorough purification of several cultural genres, resulting in the well-known distinction between high (or ›sacred‹) culture and low (or ›popular‹) culture. Thus an all too direct bodily or emotional involvement, for instance booing or interim applause and loudly ventilated encouragements, became taboo during artistic events. In order to contemplate the deeper meanings of a work of art, silence and concentration were a must: only in this way could Immanuel Kant's famous »interesseloses Wohlbehagen«[2] (disinterested pleasure) – the ›hallmark‹ of every aesthetic experience – be realised. This mode of participation generalised within the new sphere of high culture the modern way of reading a text as the basic model in encounters with works of art. The new bourgeois model initiated equivalence between the arts, silence and self-control, contemplation, and ›reading the meaning (or decoding the message)‹. In contrast, a more unrestrained involvement was allowed, even expected, during the attendance of the various forms of popular entertainment, such as the new genre of cabaret or of all kinds of sports events.

From a broader historical point of view, much can be said for the thesis that the 19th century redefinition of culture continued a much longer process in which first the aristocracy, then the bourgeoisie tried to distinguish itself from ›the people‹ by means of a high level of physical and affective self-control. Or, to paraphrase the famous study by sociologist Norbert Elias[3], the so-called process of civilisation that accelerated during the early-modern period within court circles was continued by the new social elite that took over economic and political power by the end of the 18th century. Yet, with becoming bourgeois in the civilisation process, the primary locus of self-restraint also shifted from the demonstrative showing off of good manners and a refined, highly elaborated public behaviour to the silent participation in the sphere of high culture. The well-known German notion of *Bildung* legitimised this shift; it was also in Germany that the new religion of Art achieved its first momentum with the *Gesamtkunstwerk* of Richard Wagner and the Festspiele in Bayreuth.

What happened to the bourgeois model of arts participation? Notwithstanding the discourse on post-modernity and the relative ›erosion‹ of the distinction between high and low culture, silence and self-restraint are still the rule in museums or during public artistic events. At a first glance, the basic parameters of this model are also respected by performance artists who joyously appropriate expressions of popular culture. To give just one example: in the first version of Jérôme Bel's much discussed THE SHOW MUST GO ON, the performers illustrate in a very literal way the

---

2 | Cf. Immanuel Kant: *The Critique of Judgment*, London: Dover Publications 2005.

3 | Cf. Norbert Elias: *The Civilizing Process*, Oxford: Blackwell 2000.

content of well-known pop songs. Although the number of public laughs elicited, to say nothing of their collective intensity, was much higher than during a regular theatre play or a straightforward choreography, the audience remained seated and did not start to yell along with the songs, let alone start up a party. Like many other artists, Bel crosses the symbolic distinction between high and low culture in his work, yet he conceives and presents this cross-over according to the overall lines of the dominant participation model of emotional self-control and a primarily text-oriented modus of perception and appreciation. One may therefore argue that the performing arts remain modern (not modernist!) as long as they rely on the medium of collective attention as the conditioning frame for the production and the reception of individual works.

Bel's performance work is often associated, and rightly so, with that of Marcel Duchamp, the doyen of avant-gardism. To a large extent, the history of the 20th century avant-garde has been an extended play with, sometimes even a fierce battle against, the passivity of the audience within the different artistic disciplines. This comes as no surprise in the light of Peter Bürger's influential account of avant-gardism.[4] For according to the literary theorist Bürger, who tries to create a common framework for Futurism, Dadaism, Surrealism and Constructivism in an overall way, the historical avant-garde questioned the autonomy of the arts in the name of the possibility of an emancipating merger of the arts and daily life. It is highly instructive that within the traditions of Dadaism and Surrealism, the various attempts to create more direct forms of public involvement again and again drew on popular culture genres, particularly cabaret and comedy. After their renewal during the 1960s and the early 70s, with the work of Living Theatre, which is probably still known best, both traditions went underground and made room within the sphere of the performing arts for more subtle forms of involvement with the overall passivity of the audience (witness Bel's THE SHOW MUST GO ON and many other examples).

Within contemporary art, the avant-garde dream of the politically liberating potential of a direct merger of art and daily life has become a marginal bet. Yet within the realm of the performing arts, contemporary dance has recently developed a striking reflexivity regarding audience participation and the medium of collective attention. Some artists still question the overall model of passive participation and aim at a more direct bodily involvement. Prototypical examples are the HIGHWAY project by Meg Stuart, the various excursions into the field of installation art by Boris Charmatz, or the performances within unusual public settings

---

4 | Cf. Peter Bürger: *Theory of the Avant-Garde*, Minneapolis: University of Minnesota Press 1984.

by Patricia Portela and the Deep Blue collective. In general, these and related projects try to punctuate the so-called fourth wall that distances the spectators from the performers and allows the audience to hide away in the dark. Thus, Thomas Lehmen in STATIONEN and Meg Stuart AUF DEN TISCH! placed the audience around a table. Lehmen even completely reversed the roles and asked members of the audience to talk about their professions. Yet the examples of a more direct involvement of the audience are relatively rare and do not illustrate the more general interest within contemporary dance in the medium of collective attention. Does this interest also have a wider political and societal relevance?

STATIONEN by *Thomas Lehmen*

Photo: Thomas Lehmen

In order to answer this question, I loosely rely on the recent writings of the French philosopher Jacques Rancière.[5] In his view, every political order implies an always specific distribution of visibility and perceptivity. Some social groups can, others cannot, raise public issues in a legitimate way. This power relationship implies the literal invisibility within the public sphere of various collective and discursive subjects that are not considered to be part of ›the community‹. In contemporary society, this imposition of a particular order of visibility, and even of public attention as such, is first and foremost the work of the mass media in their broadest sense (including advertising, for instance). Mass media communication constructs and reproduces a highly selective representation of life. What

---

5 | Cf. Jacques Rancière: *Disagreement: Politics and Philosophy*, Minneapolis: University of Minnesota Press 1998, and idem: *The Politics of Aesthetics*, London/New York: Continuum 2006.

is primarily left out of the picture, literally and figuratively, is the heterogeneity and anonymity of daily life. Both are precisely the subject of many contemporary dance performances, which tackle issues ordinarily unseen or ›made invisible‹ via various appropriations of daily movements and postures. Mass media communication negates the sheer anonymity of the body naked and clothed at the same time, of the complex feedback between the body as a nameless biological entity and its various articulations according to gender-specific, class-defined or ethnic cultural codes. Contemporary dance takes up this simultaneously generic and mediated body as its primary material, knowing that it is always already colonised, even in the ways it is looked at. This reflexivity necessarily involves specific concepts of representation and participation.

Looking at manifestations of the body overlooked within the spectacle society, this is how one could summarise the subject of those contemporary dance performances that take a more reflexive stance. Indeed, a quite important part of contemporary dance is the general concern to appropriate concepts of visibility or perceptivity and it regards itself, implicitly or explicitly, as belonging to a counter- public. Many contemporary dance productions do not just rely on the medium of collective attention but try to re-articulate it because it is inevitably ›infected‹ by the dominant ways that contemporary mass media communication uses to raise and direct sensory perception. A contemporary dance performance that takes into account this simple fact therefore develops various necessarily risky tactics to re-negotiate the socialised nature of sensory attention. Some of the better known procedures are the use of video cameras and digital images, the slowing down or – on the contrary – the speeding up of movements, the sheer repetition of poses or gestures, and the performance of nearly unperceivable micro-movements. These and related forms of ›public body work‹ try to destabilise the dominant modes of perception, which all of us are familiar with through contact with contemporary mass media. They do not question the bourgeois model of arts participation, but take it up as a possibility to create forms of collective attention that differ from the ones generated by television, Hollywood film, or glamour photography.

Contemporary mass media communication, in the broad sense, has become the primary societal frame for the production of public attention in all societal domains, including politics. This is not surprising, since to raise public attention and to create social visibility is the principal commodity of the mass media system. As such, this system equals an attention regime, a capturing machine that tries to raise, fix and frame sensory perception. The performing arts cannot avoid reproducing or disputing the dominance of the mass media since they work with the very same medium of sensory attention, albeit in a collective and so-called live situation. Yet it is not this »live« character as such matters, but the way one deals with the collectivisation of sensory perception – that is: with the principal medium of the performing arts. The decisive point is to take up, or not, the at once contingent and conditional collective attention during a live performance as the possible foreshadowing of *a community yet to come* – of a togetherness that may allude to *the shared visibility within a community without secrets.*

References

Arnold, Matthew: *Culture and Anarchy*, Oxford: Oxford University Press 2006.

Bürger, Peter: *Theory of the Avant-Garde*, Minneapolis: University of Minnesota Press 1984.

Elias, Norbert: *The Civilizing Process*, Oxford: Blackwell 2000.

Kant, Immanuel: *The Critique of Judgment*, London: Dover Publications 2005.

Levine, Lawrence (1988): *Highbrow/lowbrow. The Emergence of Cultural Hierarchy in America*, Boston: Harvard University Press.

Luhmann, Niklas (1990): »The Medium of Art«, in: idem: *Essays on Self-Reference*, New York: Columbia University Press, pp. 215–227.

Luhmann, Niklas (2000): *The Reality of the Mass Media*, Oxford: Polity Press.

Rancière, Jacques: *Disagreement: Politics and Philosophy*, Minneapolis: University of Minnesota Press 1998.

Rancière, Jacques: *The Politics of Aesthetics*, London/New York: Continuum 2006.

Smithuijsen, Cas (2001): *Een verbazende stilte. Klassieke muziek, gedragsregels en sociale controle in de concertzaal*, Amsterdam: Boekmanstichting.

Generating Space

HOOMAN SHARIFI IN DIALOGUE WITH BJÖRN DIRK SCHLÜTER

Björn Dirk Schlüter: How did audience participation evolve as an important aspect in your work?

Hooman Sharifi: A long time ago, when I was dancing Hip-Hop I did a show for an audience of 500 people and 100 performers distributed among the audience. These 100 performers started the performance by standing up, screaming and running to the stage.

So even without being part of the contemporary dance movement I was involved in the interaction between seats and stage and the question how to remove the boundaries between both sides. But at that point I was not consciously or theoretically involved. I was just dancing Hip-Hop, moving around, without having any theory underpinning it, or a direct goal.

During my dance education, I did a solo performance in a tent with 400 seats. On every chair I put a »reserved«-sign and then I asked the audience to come up onto the stage because the seats were reserved and people would be coming. But at the end of the show I told them that these people hadn't come and that the audience could take the seats. Then we watched the empty room become lighter and lighter.

In my first solo after dance education, entitled AS IF YOUR DEATH WAS THE LONGEST SNEEZE EVER, the chairs were not arranged in theatre style but spread across the room. The chairs each represented the idea of loneliness. If you wanted to sit next to someone you had to move to create a group of two. So this piece was about creating space where the audience can move. In the final twenty minutes, it is dark; not light enough to see and dark enough to hide. You cannot see clearly who is performing and who is not and we were encouraging people to move, getting the audience involved.

It did not start out as a clear idea to move the audience but in the meantime we worked with active audience participation in three productions and in two children's performances. There is always meaning behind it, a clear purpose, a clear idea of involving the audience. It is never directly about provocation. But I feel it is a way to communicate with them.

AS IF YOUR DEATH WAS THE
LONGEST SNEEZE EVER
by Hooman Sharifi, Glasgow 2003

Photo: Hooman Sharifi

How does the audience react when its expectations are not met?
The moment you get involved with an audience you deal with their expectations. This is something I always work with. The audience chooses to come and they have some information about what they can expect. This information evokes their imagination, which must be handled sensitively. You can have powerful discussions with an audience when you involve them, but when performers become too powerful, too manipulative – I mean there is always manipulation – this creates a big problem, because the audience can start reacting very strongly and control can be lost of the overall concept of the piece.

For example, the piece AS IF YOUR DEATH WAS THE LONGEST SNEEZE EVER is diligently made although it looks very raw. It takes place in two rooms and if the distance between the rooms is too great, we loose the feeling for the rhythm of the people. In a performance in Antwerp, for example, the room was too dark. It became a violent room, because the audience could not see anything and could not even find the exit sign, they felt imprisoned by people playing loud music. This means that they didn't move anymore, just went to the wall and sat down. So we carefully manipulate or create the conditions of the situation. We show the direction that we want to move towards. We play with expectations, but we also feed an expectation at the same time.

Could you describe your work with children, the expectations they have and how they behave when these are not met?

One piece is called WHO ARE THE ALIENS? The scene is set up like a café. You come in, there are chairs in groups with no clear indication of where the front of the space is. There is a black curtain in front of a window. During the performance the audience sits down and many of them start to turn their seats to face the curtain, waiting for it to open and the performance to start. In one particular show one of the kids walked up to the curtain, looked behind it and shouted: »There's nothing there!« Then the whole activity started. They started searching for the performance. Some of the kids were disappointed: »We expected someone to show up dressed as an Alien«. Interestingly, they are already aware of this concept of theatre. So they know it is not real, that it is fake.

When they started to move after approximately 20 minutes, we intervened: electronic music started, we took their chairs away, turned the lights down a bit, they shouted and ran around, the music became louder and they started to go more and more bananas. I walked around filming them with an infrared camera and then sat down, the music still playing and I imported this film into my computer. I used another soundtrack and while they were still running around, they saw themselves in slow motion on a video screen. Because of the infrared they had green faces and white eyes, so they became the aliens themselves. Some kids understood it right away and reacted accordingly.

How do you involve the audience sitting on a tribune facing the stage?

As far as audience involvement is concerned, in the best moments we are actually generating movement. But even by getting the audience around, the audience situation never changes. It is shaken, but it never changes. This disturbed me for quite some time. The audience remains the audience all the time. Of course, it's understandable because that is the deal. Why should it change? Why should someone come to the theatre to watch and suddenly start being part of its creation? I felt at least we were successful with this involvement, creating the conditions of the situation and allowing them to move around.

In this context we have to understand that there is something important about active involvement in a performance: we have to stop being judgmental. We have to allow people to dislike the performance, to not want to move. We never ask people to move twice. If they don't want to, they don't want to. We can just allow a performance to happen and allow things to appear. Here the notion of ›inclusion‹ comes into play. How to include? If there is no inclusion, there is no participation. So you have to include the »Nos« and the »Yeses«. It is more difficult to include »Nos« because you have a performance to put on. What does a »No« mean? Does it change the whole performance? No. The only thing you can do as a performer is to allow the »No« to exist so that this particular person does not feel uncomfortable or judged or focused on just because they don't like the show.

Considering these questions we developed a kind of ›audience drama-turgy‹ (I know it is a vague word). I am not talking about a storyline, it is rather about how this storyline is perceived. This is also the basic idea of MEETING WITH SOFIE. What does the audience expect when they come to see a solo by an eleven-year-old girl? Sofie is alone on stage for 35 minutes. She speaks, gives signs to the technician and is totally in charge of the whole space. She is dancing very raw and violently. She does not move like an eleven-year-old girl but assumes the movement style of the dancers of the Impure Company.[1] This show does hardly come up to the audience's expectations. Instead it raises questions: ›How is it possible that such a young girl has such a style?‹ So by activating the mind of the audience their own expectations become part of the performance.

Depending on the particular piece, I have different approaches to this kind of dramaturgy. In HOPEFULLY SOMEONE WILL CARRY OUT A GREAT VENGEANCE ON YOU, for example, we have a scene of three minutes of darkness. The dancers come in naked, talk and leave the room. Then the room goes dark. They come back with their clothes on, but you know they didn't really need this long to put them on. Some people think, ›I didn't come here to see darkness‹, and for others who love the dark-ness, something opens up for them. And in my last solo, there are fifty lights over the audience's heads and for the last twenty minutes, there are only these lights and no light on stage. The audience is completely illuminated and this light reflects on the stage. So I am in the dark but I am still visible.

You create a comparable situation in your piece No. The audience of one ›spectator‹ is with a single dancer and gets a text to read. But you leave it up to the audience how to work with it and also go a bit further. I sat in one performance where the dancer even touched me, which usually doesn't happen. Do you also expect the audience to go further than it usually does?

I believe that we treat them with respect when we touch them. But the moment we break rules, we have to make it clear that it is okay for the other side also to break rules. We are not trying to control the audience, we are trying to control the situation. We are trying to show the audi-ence that we are not there to harm them or to threaten them in any way,

---

1 | The Impure Company was founded in 2000 by Hooman Sharifi.

even when it is dark and the dancer is moving very raw. We give signs to the audience that we will cross one boundary but not another. And maybe that's why we have never come across anyone who has gone totally bananas in that room and disrespected what we were doing, because we did not disrespect them. There should be a certain sincerity in the work. Honesty is a difficult word in theatre so I won't use it. Sincerity fits better: It is what it is and we don't pretend otherwise.

Another important aspect in your work is ›cultural participation‹. Does your Iranian-Norwegian biography play an important part in your work and in the perception of your work?

It is very difficult for me to talk about perception of the work because I don't really know. I don't see a direct link between my concept of audience involvement and my cultural background. I sometimes don't even see what *my* culture is because my way of working (or producing) is affected by the Western European culture. I studied European contemporary dance, which has nothing to do with Iran. I cannot even speak in Farsi about my work because in that language I don't have the words to talk about it. I grew up in a country which has a different smell and a different method or system of being than European countries.

What does it mean to be Iranian? I don't know and I didn't go into it. I know there was a certain period when I listened to music with some patriotic idea or some memories, which are specifically from Iran, which came into my head and still come into it when I'm dancing. But there is no direct link. Sometimes I read my background into my work and it is explicit in a performance. But now I feel more and more comfortable talking about it directly, because I have the emotional distance which enables me to reflect on it.

For me it is more interesting what I see when I travel – in Brazil or Beirut or in Kosovo: how do artists produce there, what do time, money, capital, activity mean and how do the people keep themselves active? These observations have taught me a lot about ways of producing and about protecting the arts, which I can also link back to what I know from my childhood or Iranian culture.

So I have a slightly different understanding of culture: Since we perform in many different places, there are many different cultures that we meet and there are different kinds of behaviour. In Brazil for example we had the feeling that during the performance the people were moving much faster and that they were touching us as performers much more then anywhere else. But I really don't know if that was a fact or not, as we were first and foremost busy making our show. It could also be our preconception of Brazil. It is such a free country, so sensual and so sexual, but maybe it is not. Maybe people are the same in the theatre there as they are here.

Kosovo, Pristina 2003

Photo: Hooman Sharifi

For me culture has always been interesting, but not as something to hold on to, but as a means of existence: how do people choose to exist, what is their method of surviving? So I was never interested in culture in the sense of cultural heritage. Culture is my family, it has nothing to do with my country. I don't know my country. I know what my mother gave me, or my father, or what my friends give me. So in this way it is traceable for me. But I don't know what it means to be German, Norwegian or Dutch. I've never been interested in this question. That's why I've always dealt with my personal culture, not general culture. I mainly use general culture symbolically in the work to comment or contextualize it in a wider sense.

I hope that a certain duality of culture is present in my work, so it is not this one or that one. It is always moving between the two. So I never manage to define my own culture. I refer to it. I am part of it but not completely. It is a personal culture, a culture of migration, of moving, of nomads, of not belonging. So I try to involve the public in this non-belonging, in my personal experience.

I can link it, perhaps not to my culture, but to my history. In the sense that I moved away from my friends and my family when I was 14 years old – from what I knew once as something that was mine. I came to somewhere where I didn't even know if I felt it was mine. I just started to become part of it. So I am part of it now and it is part of me. Maybe this experience affects the work. When I meet an audience, I really would like to look them into the eyes and I really would like them to watch me, to see me, to see what I am doing because it then becomes ›us‹ at a certain point, to create this ›us‹, this space which is made by us.

I determine the space, because that is my job. But still the audience is willing to accept the conditions and to work within them as an audience. That makes you a participant and this participation will take time, becomes shared time and shared space. It is still determined by me, so the question is whether or not they are willing to accept these conditions.

I've always been busy watching the audience at the beginning and the end of the piece – how people sit, how they look. What is the look on their faces when they come out of the No-project after 20 minutes? They either like it or they don't like it. If something has happened to the way they look, the way they sit, maybe something has changed the space.

Critique versus Critical Practice?

The Impossibility and Possibilities

of Contemporary Dance Critique[1]

Constanze Klementz

I work as a dance critic. Not only, but also for this reason I have a justifiable interest in the critic as a socially placed player not to become obsolete. Much, however, seems to indicate that this is the case. The critic's subject, art, of all things perpetually undermines his authority and places him under justification constraints, which do not reflect his self-perception in the media. Because if art turns towards political and aesthetic fundamental conditions, which enable and accompany our perception, it also indirectly makes the critic's perception its theme. The critic becomes drawn into the art while watching it. He can ignore it. However, if he tries not to ignore it then the problems start.

The service that the critic is expected to provide and for which he is generally paid, is in the opinion of many readers, editorial staff and specialist colleagues the capacity to observe art professionally from a so-called »critical distance«. What resonates in this expectation is the assumption that a neutral, unbiased – some even dare to say – objective form of critique is, if not possible, however worth striving for. Now a whole series of works in contemporary choreography reveal the body as a violation, which is always subjected to specific applicable and effective balances of power. They call for a redefinition of active and passive moments, but also the general scope and relevance of aesthetic experience as such. The French philosopher Jacques Rancière, for example, defines aesthetics as the basis of the political. He refers to the fact that in no sphere other than the aesthetic sphere decisions are made regard-

---

1 | This contribution is based on a lecture given in the context of »Unfolding The Critical«, a symposium organised by the Belgian platform for dance critique, »Sarma«, as part of the DANCE CONGRESS.

ing LE PARTAGE DU SENSIBLE[2] (the distribution of the sensible), i.e. into the visible and invisible, the presentable and unpresentable, whereby a mapping of the political room for manoeuvre and scope of experience is also provided.

Why should we deny it – the notion of what the critic, whether a journalist or a theorist, entertaining feature writer or rigorous analyst, should have accomplished a long time ago, and what he believes he can accomplish in accordance with his traditional self-image, is currently not reconcilable with artistic practice or with the majority of its theoretical discussions. Art as well as theory are calling more and more vehemently for a turnaround, which is shaking the foundations of the critic's field of work. Art historian Irit Rogoff[3] calls this a shift of definition and sphere of action of the term critique in three moves, the last of which we are now at the point of taking a chance on; from Kant's criticism to postmodern varieties of critique like in the case of Derrida to what Rogoff calls »criticality«[4] and describes as inclusive instead of exclusive and intrinsic instead of remote access to the domain of the critical. Hence critique is not a third party perspective on processes, which it compares with privileged perspectives, while at the same disconnecting itself from them, and grasps separation through them. It develops in fact from experience generally understood as potential and critical practice, from practice or: from practices in the cultural domain itself and is in a changing vegetative relationship with it.

Ideal Paths and Wrong Tracks

With such thoughts in mind this raises the question of whether the critical thought can only be conceived without or also and perhaps directly in relation to the critic as a person.

The critic's job description goes back to an institutional (institutionalised in the person of the critic by means of a competence transfer) understanding of critique, which – and I quite deliberately present my case from a subjective and not a generalising perspective – barely has

---

2 | Cf. Jacques Rancière: Le Partage du sensible. Esthétique et politique, Paris: La Fabrique 2000.

3 | Irit Rogoff works at Goldsmiths College in London and is responsible for developing a scientific discipline for »visual culture«, which ranges from contemporary art to theoretical analysis and discusses culture with the focus on cultural difference and performativity as a space for participation.

4 | Cf. Irit Rogoff: »WE. Collectivities, Mutualities, Participations«, in: Dorothea von Hantelmann/Marjorie Jongbloed (eds.): I promise it's political. Performativität in der Kunst, Köln: Museum Ludwig 2002, pp. 126–133.

any relevance to my personal approach to reality and the participation in this reality in art and society. That critique is nevertheless ubiquitous as an ideal path to analyse and assess the world (or art) in accordance with a general set of binding categories which have precedence over this world (or art) is something the critic knows better than anyone else. The critic is expected to follow a standard pattern in almost all areas of the publishing professions, in my case this means the journalistic profession: i.e. analysis, interpretation, passing judgement against the backdrop of specialist knowledge and with the help of a conceptual structure that is as complete as possible, which embraces its subject matter in order to open up its hidden meaning. Or, the critic is reduced to his product, critique as text. If the belief in a ›truth‹ of art that can be revealed wanes, then the willingness to take account of any responsibility – whatever form this responsibility may take – on the part the critic often dissipates too, if not for, then with regard to his subject matter. Then the task turns into creating diversion, brilliance, rousing polemics, an entertaining piece of prose.

The feature pages represent a format in which art has its place in the information medium of the daily press. It sees itself as a mirror of current significant events and discourse in the cultural arena. Allowing selected representatives to have their say creates this image. A connection is constructed between their relevance for the disentanglement, understanding and assessment of reality contexts and their privileged access to the public through the medium, which works as follows: the representativity of the selection of representatives equals the representativity of the overall image. The critic is a representative because he is to represent not just anybody, but a particularly educated, experienced and relevant spectator. Installing the critic as an independent, incorruptible authority acting in the service of an editorial department, ensures that the editorial department retains its respectability and competence and the critic in turn is assured of the same.

How moments of individualisation and objectivisation of the critic's perspective combine in a problematic way in this dual setting up of the critic as authority and what kind of distortion of self-perception may ensue was demonstrated in Germany not so long ago by the bizarre drama surrounding theatre critic Gerhard Stadelmaier. He was verbally attacked from the stage during a premiere by an actor, who was clearly infuriated by disparaging comments made by the critic, and had his notebook snatched from his hands. It was not the provocation and violation of a spectator's privacy by the actor, who had stepped out of his role, which induced Stadelmaier in the days following the event to conjure up a scandal in the newspaper Frankfurter Allgemeine Zeitung. It was his being compromised as a critic through an »attack on my body and my freedom, which is nothing less than the freedom of the press.«[5] This is where ideal paths and wrong tracks meet: at the moment when he no longer wants to or can no longer differentiate between his persona and his role, his own strategies and the strategies of the system in which he moves, the critic disconnects himself from his contemporary professional reality.

Freewheeling, Collapse, Disturbed Rhythm

While sitting at my desk, I never understood the fact that you should never identify your work with the system in which it takes place, but that at the same time it has to work actively and incessantly against the mechanisms and implications of this system; in the theatre I did, though. Just like Kant's criticism which withdraws into itself with the system of human thinking and understanding, the black box has survived for as long and as well as it has because as a system, which follows the nature and quality of our perception of the world like a template, it has placed itself next to or above this world, but not in it.

Seating arrangement on the square facing the Vatican, Rome

Photo: Pirkko Husemann

I gained my first experiences as a critic at the end of the 1990s. During this period dance began to see, not just those on one side of the fourth wall as its players, but all those present in the theatre. It became inter-

---

5 | Gerhard Stadelmeier: »Angriff auf einen Kritiker«, in: *Frankfurter Allgemeine Zeitung*, 18 February 2006.

ested not just in the dancers, but also in the spectators as the converging point of movement, dynamism and meaning. Productions, which do not allow the theatre to serve or to castigate as a hierarchical, authoritarian, anachronistic machine, which it certainly is in many respects, have made a striking impression on me. Instead they persisted in getting moments of freewheeling, collapse and disruption of rhythm from this machine by deliberately blocking individual wheels or letting them overheat. These works did not amount to the demonstrative showing of function misfiring, but stood like open pores and waited to see what I might do with them. In these moments I as an observer – and only to the extent that every critic is simply an observer, also as a critic – was forced to address myself and my role in this play. I was not a representative, and not an authority, but a kind of accomplice, and at the outset with my then definition of critical distance in the back of my mind this caused me the problems indicated. At some time, however, whether I wanted to or not, I had to stop defending a territory that did not belong to me.

What I would now describe as my view of critique as critical practice, I developed in a milieu of objects of study, which compelled me to the view that my subject matter is not a subject at all. Not a work that I could use or damage in my specific role, but a communication process open to both sides. If this communication, to which each meeting of art and observer leads, is described as a dialogue, it cannot be the case that the critic asks the questions and art replies, nor vice versa. Rather this discussion is like an unpredictable, inspired, infiltrated conversation with oneself. Each of the critic's reflections about a performance is to a large extent self-reflection.

Nice for the critic, you could say and ask, for whom this self-reflection would still be of interest, if the critic has dismissed his function as role model and role as super spectator. Critique can develop new potential at the moment when the critic allows the reader to see him ›only‹ as another observer with a different perspective, where the reader has every right and no choice other than to absorb the text he is reading as attentively as the play he is watching. This happens as in the theatre via gaps which remain unfilled and simply prevent the machine from running smoothly.

I do not have a master plan and I know from experience that in nine out of ten cases one will fail in this at first glance possibly pretentious attempt. Nevertheless, only if critique not only articulates criticism, but also permits and even creates blurred areas within its own system, can it run the risk, which choreographic practice has long been exposed to. These blurred areas are not an invitation to the author to become vague or imprecise in his approach to a production. On the contrary, they are produced only through extremely precise observational and written work, not with the aim of putting the system critique perfectly over an object, but of allowing its edges to fray. As an alternative to critique I therefore plead the case (not purely for reasons of self-preservation) not for no critique at all, but for critique that is prepared to declare itself out of order.

The well-known Beuys dictum that everyone can be an artist does not make the artist generally redundant as an artist. There is just as little reason for me as a critic feeling robbed of my right of existence when voices like Irit Rogoff demand that critique must no longer be acquired by licence and defended as a domain, but, emotional as it may sound, released, shared and given full expression. On the contrary, what was right for contemporary choreography: declaring its position and the system from which it comes, not from a distance, which is always reserved for ›other people‹, but from right in the heart of its practice can and should be right for critique, too.

Translation from German

References

Rancière, Jacques: *Le Partage du sensible. Esthétique et politique*, Paris: La Fabrique 2000.
Rogoff, Irit: »WE. Collectivities, Mutualities, Participations«, in: Dorothea von Hantelmann/Marjorie Jongbloed (eds.): *I promise it's political. Performativität in der Kunst*, Köln: Museum Ludwig 2002, pp. 126–133.
Stadelmeier, Gerhard: »Angriff auf einen Kritiker«, in: *Frankfurter Allgemeine Zeitung*, 18 February 2006.

Professional Education

and Retraining in Dance

Reading exercise in BOCAL *by Boris Charmatz, Photo: Nicolas Couturier*

Performing the School

Boris Charmatz in dialogue with
Jeroen Peeters on Bocal[1]

Between July 2003 and July 2004, the French choreographer Boris Charmatz and the association edna conducted the project Bocal within the
framework of a three-year residency at Centre National de la Danse. A
nomadic and temporary school, Bocal sought to develop the idea of a
contemporary dance school by inventing the modalities of their own
education. Charmatz and fifteen participants with different backgrounds
investigated issues of pedagogy within an artistic project outside the existing institutional school context.[2] Negotiating the relationship between
education and the arts field, Charmatz aimed to inscribe Bocal in a
context provided by fourteen residencies in different European cities.[3]
The single idea to undertake a school project entailed questions about the
transfer of knowledge, the performance of education, critical positioning

---

1 | This is an abridged version of the interview »Performing the School«, which
is available in its entirety on »association edna's« website. Cf. *www.ednaedna.
com* from 11 Mai 2007.

2 | Bocal's participants were Félicia Atkinson, François Chaignaud, Nicolas
Couturier, Maeva Cunci, Eve Girardot, Gaspard Guilbert, Joris Lacoste, Elise
Ladoué, Clément Layes, Barbara Matijevic, David Miguel, Bouchra Ouizgen,
Frédéric Schranckenmuller, Natalia Tencer and Nabil Yahia-Aïssa.

3 | Apart from Centre national de la danse (Paris/Pantin), which was visited
six times throughout that year, it concerns the venues and coproducers
ImPulsTanz (Vienna), Le Quartz (Brest), Bonlieu Scène Nationale (Annecy),
Les Subsistances (Lyon), Espace Malraux (Chambéry), and Art radionica
Lazareti (in an abandoned hospital) in Dubrovnik. Several residency places
were visited more than once.

and reflection upon context. Bocal did not result in a school model, but rather became a container brimming with ideas, concepts, methods and exercises, all between performance and education, art and pedagogy, practice and theory. Meeting with Boris Charmatz in March 2005 for a conversation, the question was: What stays? Which elements of Bocal still resonate in his artistic practice?

I Am a School

If you ask me when Bocal started, I can only say that Bocal was already there at the official launch and it's still going on, eight months after its closure. Bocal didn't have a real starting point, since the idea of a school was already inside us. But Bocal was a new school that we didn't know yet, so there was a lot to be discovered. Claiming that »Bocal is a school« or »Bocal is a performing group for one year« elicits completely different preconceptions and expectations.

To connect Bocal with the idea of a school brought up all kinds of memories and nightmares having to do with obtaining your diploma or not, experiences with teachers, and so on. And of course you already have ideas of knowledge, ignorance and learning. You tend to think of school as a period in your life, which actually encompasses much more than just school: you think of mathematics, philosophy and sports, but also of fights with others, sitting on a chair for hours, your first kisses, how you perceived yourself as a boy or a girl. It's also a period of your identity formation and sexual education. School is part of your phantasmal world, your thoughts and inner landscape. Rather than starting and finishing a school, you incorporate it throughout your life – the way it functions, how to learn, and so on. I really think I am a school.

Saying »I am a school« also means that you are teaching yourself all the time. Your brain is active, you are correcting yourself, you are learning. You observe other people's behaviours. You transmit something when you are talking or when you touch someone. You share information that will be interpreted by others. All this happens in a single gesture. The idea »I am a school« says that education doesn't have to happen in the classroom, but can happen everywhere and anytime you have the conscious idea that a school is inside you. John Cage and others said that you already know a lot but don't express it, because you are told that you are not educated yet. It is a good practice of inner observation to think that you are a school and explore the potential of what is already there inside you.

Immersed in the Smell of Dance

One of the starting points of Bocal was the decision not to invite ›real‹ teachers. Instead, we would extract our lessons from watching performances and from books, video, audio archives and other documentation. So the act of looking at performances became part of our school. This attention to performances has been part of my story with dance all the way. For me, the most important incentive to start dancing was seeing a performance by Jean-Claude Galotta when I was still very young, in which people of about 45 years were eating sandwiches in a train station in Paris and performing among the people waiting for the trains. I was trained in several techniques in the Paris Opera School and elsewhere – but that's only part of the thing. Watching performances or Andrei Tarkovsky's films, reading poetry or discovering the world of choreographer Dominique Bagouet: all these experiences were as important for my education as ballet classes.[4]

The idea to bring the cultural field inside Bocal prompted us to go to the ImPulsTanz festival in Vienna for one month in July 2003 for our first residency. We found ourselves amidst an array of workshops with 90 different teachers, and each night we would see one or two performances. Some of the Bocalists had seen very few performances in their lives or were taking their very first dance class: Vienna promised total immersion, being surrounded by a smell of dance, although it's a limited smell. You might not find your ideal teacher there. Or you might have to divide your time, so you end up mixing a cocktail of techniques, while it might be better to pursue one track or invent your own practice. How do you not get bored with seeing one performance a day, or get sick of taking classes among 3,000 dance students without a single theoretical class? That's a fact in Vienna.

Still, dance is a physical practice, but the way speech is used in physical practices was one of our focal points. There is talking and discourse everywhere: instructions in a yoga class, parables and metaphors in Elsa Wolliaston's African dance class, but words are also in the dressing rooms, in the corridors and so on. The way teachers use language in their teaching makes them also move in a certain way. Teaching through oral explanation while demonstrating, you may go deeper into a movement, understand it better, sometimes even perform it better. The way teachers talk or don't talk to a group, the way they teach themselves through explanation and demonstration: we were observing teachers to find out how their use of speech informed their own minds and bodies. How does

4 | For an extensive discussion of Charmatz' dance education, see: Boris Charmatz/Isabelle Launay: *Entretenir. À propos d'une danse contemporaine*, Paris: Centre national de la danse/Les presses du réel 2002, pp. 50–56, 70–72.

the talking transform the movement and the gesture? How is it possible that a teacher seated on a chair is able to make thirty people shake in one second? So we saw performances, took and observed workshops, observed teaching and the aesthetics of pedagogy as if it were performance: that was all part of our education.

How Should a Young Artist Be Educated Today?

This was the theme of a roundtable we did in Vienna after a few weeks there. The result was striking: it wasn't just an exercise or class, but no less than a performance organised by and for ourselves. Each of us had to speak in the name of a teacher or an artist from the festival, like Zvi Gotheiner, Elsa Wolliaston or Anne Teresa de Keersmaeker. There was a risk of irony in it, but our aim was not to fool around with faking icons or trying to catch their attitudes. Some of the teachers were not even known at all. We were looking for a way to connect ourselves to the work of others. In dance, we privilege a direct relationship with the artist for a learning process, but then how can you explore the world of the late choreographer Dominique Bagouet? Do you just leave him aside out of a lack of contact, or do you try to guess, to sense something of his universe? At the roundtable the teachers were not present, we had worked rather little with them, sometimes not at all. Yet this absence or removal of contact didn't keep us from working with the resources we could find in ourselves to explore their ideas. The roundtable revolved around the urgency to digest classes, it was a performance set up to make us move and think, to twist our brains.

Suppose that you took one single class of African dance with Elsa Wolliaston, could you imagine what she would answer to the question of how to educate a young artist today? You could say that you don't know. But if you start from the one simple exercise you know, there is a lot to be discovered: one class contains a whole world of aesthetics, philosophical statements, you are pondering the question what you want to do or not with all this. One class is a starting point for reconstructing a universe, which is inevitably a phantasmal work in progress, but it prompts you to think, guess and smell what lingers in that one gesture. What is the philosophy or ideology behind it? What does the movement say? How is the movement taught? How is the relationship between men and women organised? You have to make it your own. If you approach the class of Wolliaston as a tourist with an exotic interest, then you stay where you are and Wolliaston stays where she is. But if you try to find out what she would answer to the question – by trying to teach African dance yourself – in the end you are really taking it in and thinking about it, you are moving in the foreign world of Elsa Wolliaston. It's not her actual world and it's not ›real‹ African dance, but it's a very good point of departure for a learning process.

Predicting a Performance

We saw 31 performances in one month and we visited museums and exhibitions in Vienna. In order to survive this daily practice of looking, I proposed to organise a ›prediction‹. A prediction means you use movement and speech to predict what the performance that you will see the next day will be like. But before we went into the actual descriptions of performances we hadn't seen yet, we first had to discuss the nature and interest of the exercise, were even guessing and analysing what the exercise would be like. Is it possible to predict what will happen? What about improvisations and premieres? When you predict what will happen, don't you destroy the performance in advance? Doesn't the ideal spectator enter a performance with an open mind and a neutral point of view? How do you deal with your expectations?

There are lots of things that you know in advance: the title, the rumours, the program text, some pictures perhaps, someone might have shared an opinion with you, you might have seen the company before. In fact, you already know a lot, and formulating your preconceptions makes you become a highly active viewer. You are obliged to formulate what you like and don't like, what you understand, what you know about the theatre and the kind of audience etc. Strangely enough, what you describe frequently comes about because you often predict stereotypes that can be easily matched. Also, because you see what you want to see, predictions probably tell you more about the way you are structured than about the way a performance is. In essence, you are working on yourself – your opinions and preconceptions – not only predicting an artist's work.

Books in the Studio

Since we decided not to invite teachers for BOCAL, an alternative was to work on books and documents, for which we compiled a library that travelled with us to all the residencies. The travelling library contained a selection of both new books and works contributed by Bocalists to share and read together. Just reading the book titles gave you an idea of the domain we were aiming to explore: the field of dance, arts, pedagogy, aesthetics and sociology. The books were used a lot during BOCAL. Building a culture around them was important for us.

Reading exercise in BOCAL *by Boris Charmatz*

Photos: Nicolas Couturier

We had recurrent discussions on Laban and dance history, read poetry by Christophe Tarkos and Gherasim Luca, worked with statements on education by artists like Robert Filliou and John Cage etc. Jacques Rancière's »The Ignorant Schoolmaster«[5] spurred our reflection on education: it's a parable around the idea that anybody can teach you writing, even if that person cannot write himself. But if you know how to compare things and to encourage correct results, then you are able to teach. This means that a school can also happen in a family context or elsewhere: the idea of a school outside the school was a shared interest of research in BOCAL.

Reading was a nice and simple way to enter research. In dance schools, the library is not always actively consulted; books are certainly not used in as lively a way as we did. We tried to bring books into the studio and invent exercises with them, so training got mixed with the act of reading. This came from the banal observation that you are working all day long in the studio as a dancer and when you come home you're too tired to read. As if reading and dancing do not go together. Why not reverse this situation and bring reading into the daily practice?

The Book Is Your Ground

We invented warm-up exercises while reading. For one exercise we took out all the reading furniture and spent time reading on the studio floor, without cushions or anything. After a while you start to discover strategies to hold your book, which are very interesting little choreographies. The positioning of the hand, the body postures. Can you sustain a certain position or not? How many different postures do you use? It's a behavioural study.

For another exercise you just stand and imagine that your book is able to move. So, not unlike the »Alexander Technique«, you adjust your gaze and your neck in the right way to read the text. Then you try to move the book a little bit, and after some time, you find out that you don't lose the text. You can move and at the same time continue reading. Out of this

---

5 | Jacques Rancière: *The Ignorant Schoolmaster. Five Lessons in Intellectual Emancipation*, Stanford: Stanford University Press 1991.

principle, we developed duets: one reads, the other slowly moves the book. In the end, you invent trajectories to bring the reader to the ground and up again, continuously moving. It allows you to study how your gaze is connected to your spine, to what extent you can be precise with it, what kind of landscape it creates, which are possibilities and impossibilities.

One exercise was to consider the book to be your ground. Put the book on the floor and get on top of it, touching only the book, and then read it without touching the floor. Obviously it's easier to start with a large book, but after stretching and looking for the right balance and precision in the movements, you discover hundreds of possible postures to do this exercise, which combines physicality, balance, concentration, consciousness etc. It's nothing less than a modern dance exercise. And at the same time you are reading: even if you read only ten or twenty pages and might not remember everything, it's at least something. After the warm-up, you are ready to enter the workshop and spit out the experience, you are physically warm and have reading baggage. To share the knowledge of our reading warm-up and reading sessions, we moved as duos, with one asking the other questions about the reading.

With this basis, you can develop increasingly complex exercises or do any dance exercise, add a book to it and see what's possible. How much space is there to improvise when you are holding or reading a book? How do bodies enter into contact while thinking about something else? In Bocal we aimed to make the training space more complex and not only focussed on a single activity, simply because in daily life and human activity it is customary to be connected to several things at the same time. Reading while moving was a way to achieve this, with sixteen different teachers, different books, movements, ways of approaching each other … all in one single class. And yet you are the only one responsible for what you are doing, to observe your activities, find the right balance, see how much you can digest: you are your own teacher. The notion of multitasking is also close to improvisation: there is the space and you have your own ways to use it, but you need to have an awareness of what is going on around you. Reading while moving is an exercise that equals the complexity of what is happening on stage nowadays.

References

Charmatz, Boris/Launay, Isabelle: *Entretenir. À propos d'une danse contemporaine*, Paris: Centre national de la danse/Les presses du réel 2002.
Rancière, Jacques: *The Ignorant Schoolmaster. Five Lessons in Intellectual Emancipation*, Stanford: Stanford University Press 1991.

Online References

www.ednaedna.com.

Building a Common Language

THOMAS LEHMEN IN DIALOGUE WITH PIRKKO HUSEMANN

Pirkko Husemann: Your two most recent projects, LEHMEN LERNT *and* LEHMEN MACHT, *addressed issues of learning and teaching. As a result, you've received a number of invitations to participate in conferences and symposia on topics relating to dance and cultural education. How do these topics relate to your own work as an artist?*

Thomas Lehmen: One of my interests is the potential inherent in all people. My basic assumption is that everyone has something to teach someone else. My goal in these projects was to discover what people are able to teach each other. This kind of social learning is a treasure trove of knowledge and of communication, but as a form of learning is slowly dying out.

Whenever a person is asked, ›What do you know that you could teach to others, or show others how to do?‹, there's always an answer. It might be something amusing, something academic, or something banal. That's what I did with the visitors to the Haus der Kunst museum in Munich: I asked them to explain something to me, or to show me something, or to write something down, or to cook something in the kitchen nook. Just about everyone had something to share, and this resulted in a beautiful collection presented in an exhibition.

What was the significance of the fact that this transfer of knowledge occurred in an artistic forum rather than in a domestic or educational setting?

I think that this expanded the awareness and perceptions people had of their own actions. Their ideas were being taken seriously and were being put on display. People realised their small, apparently trivial product would be put on display in a museum. And their work was accorded the same status as Allan Kaprow's Happenings, which was on display in the same room. So people were able to participate with small offers in an artistic context, and to perceive themselves as artists. During the work process people were aware that they were actually creating art. In other words, their activity was transformed into art by the process as well as by the setting of their creation.

In LEHMEN LERNT, you allowed others to teach you the things that you wanted to learn how to do. Did the people who were teaching you clown performance or flying know that you were going to use these images of learning for a theatre performance?

Yes, they knew, but I don't think it made any difference. In LEHMEN LERNT, the learning process was filmed. In this sense, the process of medialisation played an important role. The participants were not themselves inside the image, but rather were behind the camera, filming my learning process. Their perspective was thus the perspective of the camera recording my actions.

Your project STATIONEN was different in this respect. In this work, the actors and the audience sat together at a table, and the dancers stood on stage alongside ›individuals from all professional walks of life‹. This configuration made it clear from the outset that the dancers and workers were there to demonstrate daily work processes. For this reason, they did not simply reproduce their actions, but rather staged them. In contrast, the process of learning and teaching in LEHMEN LERNT and LEHMEN MACHT took place prior to the performance or the exhibit.

That's true, but the basic idea behind the two projects was the same. Unlike learning in an academic or school context, I'm interested in making it possible for everyone to participate in exchanging information of all kinds in a shared setting. Teachers and learners are accorded equal status in this process. The teacher also learns from the students, and from other teachers. The most important aspect of the process is the form and the mode of communication that takes place. For example, imagine the classic example of a university lecture: at the front of the class stands an old and wise professor, who delivers the lecture to the students. Suddenly, a student asks a question, and at first the question makes no sense, because it just sounds silly or banal. But the professor listens to the question, and thinks about it for a while. And then the professor begins to explain, and suddenly the apparently silly and banal question makes a lot of sense. In other words, this isn't the classic model of communication, the model of sender and receiver. Instead it's a model of communication based on the reduction of complexity, on recontextualisation, and on mutual understanding.

But communication is based on difference. Everyone knows something, but not everyone knows the same things. By this I don't mean necessarily a hierarchical difference, but rather a qualitative one. Everyone has different opinions and experiences. This is true whether you're interacting with another artist or with non-artists. In your work, you always manage to create situations in which there is a collision of different perspectives, opinions, and experiences. Do you find working with these spheres of tension and contrast especially interesting?

Yes, of course. Meaning is created through difference. But I'm especially interested in the way in which the sphere in which these differences meet and collide must always be reconceptualised and reworked. In order to make this happen, it is first necessary to locate the common denominator to cultivate the common ground.

For quite some time, you have been conducting workshops at schools of dance across the world. Would you say that you are creating situations in these workshops in which a common creation of meaning can take place? Meaning, something different from the ordinary concept of instruction, in which the teacher instructs the student in what he or she thinks the student ought to know?

The students have a lot of questions, they challenge me and ask a lot of me, and they all have different needs. On the one hand, they seek information, meaning knowledge in the simplest sense of the term. For example, they ask questions like ›who did what, and when, and how?‹ With situations and questions like this, the teacher has to have enough knowledge in order to provide the students with answers, or at least to be able to help them locate the answers. But the students are also always situated within different phases of their lives, and different stages of development. So they all have their own smaller, individual problems, and their own different communicative needs. Sometimes a student simply is not in a position to take advantage or make sense of an opportunity that I provide in a workshop, simply because he or she doesn't speak the necessary ›language‹.

For this reason, I try to engage in an individual dialogue with each student. This means that we build a common language. That's a trick I was taught by a translator some time ago, someone I asked for advice when I was working with a group from China. In that workshop, the opportunities for verbal communication were extremely limited, and we also were confronted with cultural differences. At the start of the workshop, we couldn't understand or make sense of each other at all. Every word, every utterance spoken by the teacher was misunderstood by the workshop participants, and the reverse. At the time, the translator suggested to me that we work to develop a kind of third language, a language entirely different from our own languages. This third language could be developed by referring to a concrete object or process, and could only function when we all assumed a position or a stance in which we know nothing. In other words, we had to create an equal and mutual dialogue using the work that we were engaged in as the object. Only in this manner were we able to arrive at a point in which we were able to work together.

How do you accomplish this? Is there any similarity to the performances in which you work with universal themes such as work, death, cooking, fucking (sic!), laughing, or crying? Or similarities to the systems in which you work with fundamental rules and instructions? What tools do you employ in your workshops?

In general, I work by proceeding from a basic premise or topic. For example, last week I conducted a workshop in Amsterdam using the topic of the ›function of the hero‹. Heroes are always transgressive. The workshop participants were asked to develop a heroic figure, someone who uses his or her special qualities to solve problems, or to engage in political activity, or simply to help an older woman cross the street – for example, perhaps simply to create something.

The hero is thus a kind of container which can be filled with certain kinds of ideas or experiences?

Yes, that's what I would call a fundamental function. The repertoire of functions that I employ has expanded over time. Right now, I am working with the function of learning.

Do you employ different functions for different ›students‹? In the near future, you will be engaged as a guest professor at the University of Hamburg, working with students in the department of performance studies. Does your ›third language‹ approach also work with people who have a theoretical and academic background and approach?

It almost always works. In my experience, I've always been accorded respect for my function as an artist, even when there is a gap or difference between art and theory. After all, the point is to create meaning using this difference.

In other words, you have discovered an open method, a method that works independently of context?

The method that I use is simply that I take seriously everything that people say to me. If I want people to experience art, then I first have to allow them to participate in a value-free manner. That's why I don't set limits upon what they may do. Everything that they do is accepted – at least as far as their participation in the workshop or the performance is concerned. In other situations, for example in my brief ›informational workshops‹ (which are more like introductory courses), I follow my own interests more closely. And in this case it is sometimes helpful to have only a few hours of time to spend together.

In other words, first you allow everything, and then you look to see what can be created within the larger artistic context from the variety of small skills?

No, at that point, it's already art. At the very moment when I begin to interact with people within an artistic framework, this involvement is already a form of artistic creation or work. We engage in a creative process to cultivate and process their material into something new, something that didn't exist previously.

That's an intriguing understanding of material. As a choreographer, what role do the body and movement play for you? Do you work with a specific kind of material, or is everything your material, in a sense?

Yes, I do work with movement, but not necessarily only with physical movement. While I work with physical movement, my real concern is the mental movement – within people, and between people. Something is in flux, something is in motion. In this sense, movement is not limited to the body.

LEHMEN MACHT by Thomas Lehmen

Photo: Thomas Lehmen

But you create situations in which this kind of mental movement also becomes visible. You can see that the participants are thinking or reflecting upon something, and communicating about something. More precisely, I can see a museum visitor who is reflecting upon what should be learned, or I can see an actor on the stage who has received an instruction and is thinking about how this instruction can be put into motion. In other words, the process of thought and the transfer of thought into motion become visible. This action might be a physical motion, but it isn't necessarily or always physical.

In the case of a theatre performance, I take care to ensure that this process happens in a concrete form and is immediately transformed into movement. What movement is appropriate? What movement supports the demands placed upon it? How is a movement transformed depending on the topic or theme? But my fundamental concern is the participation of the audience in the creative process of reflection – in the process of reflecting upon their own observations. This process of reflection is always at the same time a process of construction.

You just said that you were interested in the ways in which altering certain factors or preconditions in turn may influence movement. Now let's ourselves make a mental leap. What changes would you make within the parameters of dance education in order to bring movement into dance as a concept?

My position on dance education is that I come to a school as an artist in order to conduct a workshop. When I do this, I'm not interested in questions of pedagogical correctness. When I conduct a workshop, I work with the participants to expand upon my (and ideally also their) ideas. I can't simply set aside my perspective as an artist just because I'm conducting a workshop. This was particularly apparent during the period in which I was working on STATIONEN and FUNKTIONEN, where I spent many hours explaining systems theory to the workshop participants, and to myself. It was often fascinating, especially when I was forced to admit that there were gaps in my own knowledge, or that problems exist when working with choreographical systems. The participants thus did not perceive and experience me as a teacher providing instruction, but rather as an artist engaging in his daily work, facing the same kinds of problems that they face themselves.

This reminds me of a sentence from your text, »Ich bin ja kein echter Lehrer-Lehrer« (I'm not a real teacher-teacher anyway): »Transmitting art from the perspective of an artist, allowing others to participate, seems to me to incorporate the knowledge of lack of knowledge, of being able to work with not-knowing [...] it's at those points where there is no standard procedure to call upon to solve a problem that we become creative.«[1]

Not-knowing is inherent to art because in art we work with things that we don't know. After all, the essence of art is to allow something to be realised, or to set a process in motion, or to make something apparent, or to materialise something, or to think thoughts that haven't yet been expressed, or can't be expressed, or can be expressed only with difficulty. One of the central functions of art is creating a space for this realm of non-knowledge. Conveying and communicating art thus always entails working with and experiencing something that is unknown or not yet known. There's no simple recipe for this process. Many of the parameters of a process can be unknown, including its result.

For this reason, I think it is extremely important that art retains a kind of freedom, a freedom in which no attempt is made to predefine the method and process of art. My goal is to resist any attempt at predefinition. This is also something that is important to keep in mind within the realm of dance education. It's essential that the educational structure and the instructors always take care to enable and protect this essential sphere of freedom and possibility. Dance education is always also a kind of artistic involvement, which ideally may also be transmitted by artists within a particular framework and setting.

Art is often instrumentalised. For example, artists were called upon

---

1 | Thomas Lehmen: »Ich bin ja kein echter Lehrer-Lehrer«, in: Cornelia Albrecht/Franz Anton Cramer (eds.): *Tanz [Aus] Bildung. Reviewing Bodies of Knowledge*, Munich: epodium 2006, p. 215.

to bridge the gaps during the eastward enlargement of the EU. Now artists are being asked to develop projects on the topic of learning and cultural education. The artists are told that they must precisely formulate their plans and actions, explain exactly how it is that they work, and precisely what it is that they will produce. This is nothing but an absurdity. This is how art is killed – by establishing definitions and limits upon its function and meaning. The purpose of art is not to reproduce something beautiful, something expected, something known. Rather, I believe the purpose of art is to challenge our thoughts through perceptions, and to develop them further. I don't expect this of my students, but if someone were to place a beautiful bouquet of flowers on the stage during class, then I might well ask: So? What now?

Now we've come full circle. You said that you are often invited to events or to dialogues in which the topic is an exploration of what artists can teach us about the topic of learning.

Yes, precisely. And as a result, I am always looking to create new spaces, spaces that are not already occupied with something that already exists. I believe that it is my role to insist that the ›How‹ is a question that simply cannot be answered in a definitive fashion. The only thing that is possible is to create the conditions and the parameters that ideally will provide space for the development of artists, artists who will produce something meaningful. But that's something that is impossible to predict. We have statistics about how many people who study art ultimately work as artists and create art. Unfortunately, the number is very, very small.

Translation from German

References

Lehmen, Thomas: »Ich bin ja kein echter Lehrer-Lehrer«, in: Cornelia Albrecht/Franz Anton Cramer (eds.): *Tanz [Aus] Bildung. Reviewing Bodies of Knowledge*, Munich: epodium 2006, pp. 213–218.

On Considering a Comparative Approach

A Model for Classification of Dance Techniques

Kurt Koegel

What if we could increase our capacity to look beyond stylistic considerations in teaching, making and criticizing dance? In what ways can we expand our frame of reference, see similarities between styles, approaches and techniques, and discover more cooperative ways of sharing knowledge and information? How might a course of study in pedagogy prepare one to teach not only existing methods, but encourage the development of new approaches, new techniques, new methods of teaching?

Over recent years, with growing disappointment, I have noticed that although there are good programs in place for educating teachers in pedagogic process, and many excellent, progressive systems available for educating dancers, there exist few programs that promote innovative, *contemporary approaches to teaching and guiding movement research.* One of the obstacles I perceive is the difficulty to recognize and, hence, classify what is fundamental to various contemporary styles. It is a challenge, therefore, to determine which pedagogic principles and methodologies may advance more effective training of contemporary dancers.

Towards this end I have been considering ways of comparing various types of movement research and listing essential attributes according to shared qualities or characteristics. One such attempt I call SCAPE (SYSTEMS FOR CLASSIFICATION AND ANALYSIS OF PARTNERING EXPLORATION). It embraces the great variety of partnering forms and looks for points of similarity and distinction, grouping these elements into categories useful for sharpening one's observational skills in the service of teaching and decision-making while dancing or composing. Extending this line of thought, one might envision a model that could be used to discern characteristics of various forms of contemporary dance.

Rationale, Benefits and Proposed Starting Points

Since dance has no single codified technique, and the range of technical considerations grows every day, we may benefit from designing a language of patterns for contemporary dance. This »pattern language« might begin as a list of attributes and categories that could be used to determine which components are included in a style or technique, facilitating an understanding of the range of concerns within different fields of dance research. Such a model would provide: a ›neutral‹ framework with which to stimulate discussion and feedback by focusing on the nature of the materials; a tool for naming effective aspects of one teacher's pedagogy and showing how these methods might be applied to other approaches; and a scaffolding for stimulating new developments and hybrid techniques.

This paradigm is not conceived of as a way of judging movement material based on a set of rules, but rather as a method to further pedagogic reflection on the research occurring today. It is discouraging to be in a lesson of someone who has developed an interesting aspect of movement research, only to find the lesson so awkwardly structured that the method itself creates a barrier to receiving the gift. Perhaps the chances of this happening can be reduced. The intention is for this »pattern language« to function as a constructive instrument for teachers: encouraging innovative pedagogic research; improving the structuring of lessons and curricula; transforming group and choreographic processes.

An Example from Experience

During the past years, I've been developing arrangements of information to help enrich the process of learning partner dancing, and to break down the largely artificial distinction between Contact Improvisation and other »Partnering techniques«. This has involved finding recognisable patterns, identifying basic principles and classifying these into lists or *palettes* that can be used to facilitate assimilation and creative application of knowledge and skill. I am attracted to the word ›palette‹ for the imagery it evokes. It evokes the rich colours of oil pigment, the smell and texture of the material, the manner of mixing and blending the material with a sensitive eye and hand at close range. I also like the reference to graphic design computer applications such as Photoshop, as the palettes in these programs help the artist maintain an overview and an active responsiveness to a wide array of design parameters. It does this by organizing visual principles into workable groupings (see Fig. 1).

Figure 1

Ways of Being Supported		
Different types of body tone and structural organization while being supported in top-loaded positions
(There exists a complementary palette of corresponding guideposts for the supportive role.)		
	Image	**Characteristics**
	Sack of Potatoes	Body as collection of unorganized weight units. Low muscular tone. Body mass feels heavy. Difficult to control degree of friction at contact surface. All paths lead down.
	The Frightened Cat	Very high tone. Muscle fibers firing quickly. No precise sense or reaching directions. Feels light but out of control. Produces acceleration especially when supporting surface also moves.
	Light as a Breath	A light controlled tone radiating out from center. Able to make contact surface more precise and defined. Able to reduce size of contact surface to allow rotational shifting ("Scratching").
	Rooting and Reaching	Calm, extended tone. Connection from periphery to center and energy reaching out from center out past periphery. Body mass feels light and controlled. May utilize oppositional pushing into floor or partner (torque) to assist extension into space. Very effective for developing a sense of confidence and range of movement potential in any given situation
	The Clinging Vine	High friction at contact surface. High body tone. Utilizes contraction or constriction. May feel secure, or conversely, may feel limiting.

My approach is also influenced by the work of the architect Christopher Alexander. He has developed what he calls a »pattern language« of architecture based on human living patterns rather than visual conceptions of form. For example, let's say an architect's client is a writer for whom it is customary to sit at morning coffee and write. Instead of conceiving of a square space called a ›kitchen‹, the architect might imagine a cluster of environmental patterns – a view on a quiet garden space, a transparent wall to let sunlight filter indoors, cosy seating with accessible shelves – to use as inspirational guidelines for designing a living/working space that responds to the unique lifestyle of his or her client.

As Alexander explains in the book »A Pattern Language«[1], each pattern describes a problem or situation which occurs in our environment, and then describes the solution to that problem, in such a way that this solution can be used repeatedly, without ever doing it the same way twice. Alexander is interested in what makes certain places work both spatially and psychologically, and has developed a theory for identifying indigenous patterns of use. I think of these patterns as *traces of use*. Imagine for instance the southwestern corner of a refuge in the mountains; people regularly go outside to sit under the eave to drink something hot on rainy afternoons. Someone puts a log there to sit on. Another adds a bigger cut stump for a table. Eventually a wood stack extends the wall of shelter. A pattern is recognised that might then be shaped further by design. Alexander's theory offers an approach to creating appealing, liveable architectural solutions that blend the basic instincts we have about place making with an orientation towards intentional design.

Working from this sort of perception, I wished to understand what was essential in a dance between two partners. I began to recognize patterns in contact improvisation and catalogue them, creating charts that established a vocabulary and graphically illustrated a spectrum of working relationships between partners. This method resulted in dancers sharpening their observational skills and experimenting further with new methods of dance making.

To hone these skills I often use a variety of *observation scores*. One of these scores involves two duets working together. Two of the four dancers choose to witness first, and are given contrasting tasks for directing their perception. One person will watch for images, emotions, and elements of story, the other watches for physicality, mechanics and techniques utilized in the dancing. The two witnesses are viewing the same dance, but observing through different filters. They sort their impressions according to different palettes. When they share their impressions with the dancing couple or the group there is delight in hearing the same phenomena described from different perspectives and with different language. This practice also stimulates the compositional process while dancing. Dancers report a sense of ease and clarity in making choices as well as the feeling of being creative and communicative at the same time.

Creating recognisable lists or palettes to define the work can also be used in developing new methods for researching or teaching. I had been hearing dancers profess the fundamental precept that Contact Improvisation was about sensing weight, gravity and the freedom between partners; however, what I often saw was manipulation, inefficient holding patterns and lifting weight against gravity. I searched for a way to encourage actual

---

1 | Christopher Alexander: *A Pattern Language. Towns, Buildings, Construction*, New York: Oxford University Press 1977.

freedom between partners. In my search through the German language, there arose a clear impulse from the word ›*Unabhängigkeit*‹ (›non-co-dependency‹, or literally: ›not-down-hanging-off-of-ness‹). I pursued this research for several years, structuring sessions with limitations that did not allow holding or touching with the hands and feet, and began to develop skill patterns that supported this way of partner dancing. Students were discovering that they learned more effective techniques for supporting when they understood the nature of the surface they were offering. They began realizing that they could fly more efficiently when they used their hands and arms for reaching into clear vectors and controlling the surface friction rather than holding on to their supporting partner in an unconsidered manner. In all, the dancers became excited at the new range of movement possibilities opening to them through this clarifying limitation.

Off balance secure exercise: »Once a principle is understood, it can be applied in more complex situations with choreographic effect.« (Kurt Koegel)

Photo: Susanne Bently

In later years, when I began exploring »Partnering« exclusively *with* the hands, I postulated that the primary division for classifying partner dancing is whether a ›roled‹ or ›non-roled‹ principle is in effect. The non-roled exploration may be referred to as »non-leading« and »non-following« or with a phrase the novelist William S. Burroughs coined: »working with the third mind«. The roled exploration I refer to as »Mover/Partner«

or »influence and response« research. Participants in my classes are presented with techniques, principles and guidelines in both types of practice, leading to the facility of blending them with clarity. The palettes of principles and techniques they learn serve to keep the expanding syllabus of information grouped in a way that makes it accessible for use in the dancing.

Working with students in Universities and intensive four-year courses or with large companies, the dancers are often facile with learning and changing patterns – but also over-saturated with new information from many directions. Furthermore, in these environments time is always at a premium, and I discern the necessity to be more efficient in the guiding process. These factors led me to search for pedagogic methods that would *accelerate the learning process.* I began to structure the lessons according to different scales of information. A palette of patterns often has an accompanying list of tips: strategies that can facilitate ease of learning – and a parallel list of traps or pitfalls to avoid. After the session, I often put up a large sheet of paper that lists and graphically illustrates the material we cover that day.

This coherent, graphic organization of the material assists the dancers with absorbing the principles rapidly and integrating them effectively in relation to their own choice making. They improve in their capacity to observe the choices of others and make informed responses. Their problem solving becomes less personal and more objective. For example, they might ask themselves: Why am I getting tangled up in the limbs of my partner? Why do the transitions between weight-sharing moments seem heavy or awkward? Why does a moment of flight feel reckless or unstable? This method provides a tangible tool for identifying problems in physical terms and developing practical solutions in the dance.

This pedagogic method is demonstrating its effectiveness for assisting dancers to integrate »Partnering skills« in their choreographic research and performance work in an articulate, intelligible, and safe manner. They begin to realize a wide spectrum of working possibilities and choices with one side of their awareness – the questioning, reasoning mind that, somewhat counter-intuitively, needs to be engaged in order to be quieted. This leaves the playful, creative, other side of the brain open to be in the moment and engage in the subtleties of movement interaction.

Another attractive outcome, due to the organic foundation of the approach, is that, as a teacher, I have more access to an intuitive guiding process during a class. I feel more open to shift spontaneously from one principle or pattern to another and discover innovative pathways into the material. I find a more enjoyable balance between clarity and mystery in my teaching. I allow myself more licence to swing between field-tested approaches and letting the group delve into their own creative interpretations of the material. In the best sessions, the dancers are constantly in the process of dancing. There are no timeouts for mental analysis or reflection. Evident in the way they practice and, after the session when they speak about the work, it is apparent that their conceptualisation of the material is embodied in their dancing. They experience a fluid, intuitive realm where body-learning takes place; and submerged within it, though essential to its ability to exist, is the skeletal framework of the design that underlies the research of each session.

New Directions

The above example relates to my teaching of »Partnering«. It does not address the issues or concerns I confront when planning and giving technique classes. In these I find a different set of concerns at play. This led me to imagine that there might be a way to integrate concerns across diverse sets of technical approaches.

To apply this line of thought to a broad range of approaches and techniques, I am interested in proceeding with a collective process of discovery. I have begun to make a listing of components of a contemporary dance training. The list addresses different attributes that a technique class might address and begins to group them into categories. This is not proposed as an exhaustive list of constituent elements for contemporary dance training. Rather, it is in development as a working model with an intention towards usefulness and universality. One idea is that in designing a series of classes, or a curriculum, each component may not be addressed in every session, but in a course lasting several days or weeks one might strive to integrate a particular set of these elements in each session to create an effective syllabus for the sequence.

I am excited to begin working with this model as a basis to stimulate discussions about *comparative methodology in dance pedagogy*. These discussions addressing different ways to observe, analyse, plan and present lessons will be one of the cornerstones of the new Masters program in Contemporary Dance Pedagogy at the Hochschule für Musik und Darstellende Kunst in Frankfurt a.M.[2]

---

2 | Cf. *www.hfmdk-frankfurt.de* and *www.kurtkoegel.com* from 12 May 2007.

References

Alexander, Christopher: *A Pattern Language. Towns, Buildings, Construction*, New York: Oxford University Press 1977.

Online References

www.hfmdk-frankfurt.de.
www.kurtkoegel.com.

Break-Up: New Paths in Dance Education

INGO DIEHL

As head of educational projects at »Tanzplan Deutschland«[1], I am interested in incorporating innovative, practice-oriented educational models and interdisciplinary exchange projects within the field of dance into the entire German educational landscape. This report summarises developments in discussions with state dance education institutions and the status of joint planning between January 2006 and March 2007. However, this report should not be regarded as a by-product of exhaustive debates on the issues. Rather, it is intended to provide an overview of a work in progress within a sphere in which results generally are not made available to the public until after proposals or final plans have been settled.

The goal of »Tanzplan's« educational programme is to conduct a debate on tradition, innovation, and transfer of knowledge with specialists in the field. The aim is to develop concrete strategies that will secure improved professional development opportunities within the realm of professional dance for the dancers of tomorrow. New learning and teach-

---

1 | »Tanzplan Deutschland« is a five-year initiative of the Federal Cultural Foundation that aims to achieve lasting improvements in the working conditions and the social position of dance by the year 2010. Under the title »Tanzplan local«, the project is promoting nine forward-looking model projects in a number of cities. In Berlin, Dresden, and Frankfurt, the model projects focus on the development of new educational programmes and courses of study. In addition to »Tanzplan local«, »Tanzplan's« educational programme are the second key area of emphasis. »Tanzplan Deutschland« has received funding in the amount of 12.5 million Euros. Cf. *http://tanzplan-deutschland.de* from 10 May 2007.

ing models, which emerge across national boundaries in dance practice and in theoretical discourse, must be made visible in and through dance education. Plans to reform the German dance education system are being developed in cooperation with educational institutions. These plans are intended to strengthen the traditions and the specific profiles of each individual institution.

Photo: Linda Moritz

The participants in this discussion include the eight colleges of dance[2] and the three state vocational colleges[3] in Germany. The eight colleges of dance exhibit a range of focal points within classical, modern, and contemporary dance. Several of them also offer continuing studies in dance pedagogy and choreography. The three state vocational colleges, in turn, make a decisive contribution to classical dance education in Germany.

This 18-month span of dialogue, which included three intensive meet-

---

2 | These include the Folkwang Hochschule in Essen, the Department of Dance of the Cologne Hochschule für Musik, the Palucca Schule Dresden – Hochschule für Tanz, the Hochschule für Musik und Darstellende Kunst in Frankfurt a.M., the Staatliche Hochschule für Musik und Darstellende Künste in Mannheim, the Heinz-Bosl-Stiftung-Ballett-Akademie in Munich, the Department of Dance at the Hochschule für Schauspielkunst Ernst-Busch in Berlin as well as the Co-operative Dance Education Centre Berlin-pilot project Tanzplan Berlin.

3 | The Staatliche Ballettschule Berlin/Schule für Artistik, the John Cranko Schule – Ballettschule des Württembergischen Staatstheaters and the Ballettschule Hamburg/Ballett John Neumeier.

ings with educational institutions, has resulted in a unique exchange of perspectives in dance education. In February 2007, this dialogue culminated in the »Dance Education Conference«, which included representatives from the many different interest groups.

The DANCE CONGRESS GERMANY of 2006 provided an ideal platform for organising the first meeting of the educational institutions. Previous discussions with the colleges of dance had demonstrated a pressing need for debate on the upcoming restructuring process to Bachelor and Master degree programmes.[4] On April 19 and 20, 2006, two representatives from each of the Essen, Frankfurt, Dresden, Cologne and Berlin colleges of dance met under the working title »BA/MA as Opportunity?« The institutions presented projects demonstrating new work forms. During the presentations, it became apparent that a great need exists for mutual exchange and ongoing cooperation. An important aspect of the meeting was the naming of common interests and dilemmas:

- the transmission of dance theory and dance history,
- further education measures for teachers (for which »Tanzplan« has already proposed a financing plan),
- and the need for dialogue on the status of programme restructuring into Bachelor and Master degree models.

The colleges are currently all at different phases in the restructuring process. To date, there is little consistency in the duration of the BA/MA programmes or in the process of mutual recognition of degree work among the German federal states.

In addition to discussions on accreditation, compatibility and transparency of course work, a further topic of intense debate was the status of modularisation.[5]

In late November 2006, the Hochschule für Musik und Darstellende Kunst in Frankfurt hosted the second meeting of educational institutions. Following an invitation issued by »Tanzplan's« educational programme, a number of experts in the field and 44 directors, professors, lecturers, and students from nine colleges and vocational schools met at the two-day conference in Frankfurt. Two representatives of the European ELIA network were also invited – Lars Ebert,

---

4 | In accordance with the so-called Bologna Agreement, by 2010 the programmes of the colleges and universities are supposed to be transformed into Bachelor's and Master's degree programmes in order to align courses of study across Europe. This reform is not binding for colleges of art.

5 | In the future, instruction will be grouped into thematic modules. »Credit points« will be granted for the course of study and for preparatory and follow up work; the credit points are intended to provide comparable and measurable data.

project manager at ELIA (European League of Institutes for the Arts), and Jan Zobel, artistic director at the University of Antwerp. Ebert and Zobel provided insight into developments in other European countries resulting from the »Bologna process«. According to their report, representatives of various European colleges of dance will be working on a Tuning Template paper within the framework of INTERARTES, one of ELIA's key projects, until summer 2007. The TUNING TEMPLATE results paper, which will summarise the key competencies to be ensured by dance education, will be presented to decision-makers in Brussels to help strengthen the role of dance. The paper will include descriptions of the learning outcomes to be achieved, as well as descriptions of new developments and differences within the various types of dance education programmes in the European educational sphere. German dance education institutions are not yet participating in this process.

During follow-up discussions, the participants displayed a range of opinions regarding the utility, necessity, and practicality of programme restructuring, and regarding the facts and the demands to be documented in the TUNING TEMPLATE.

The question whether the new call for comparability and compatibility within dance education might harm the unique identity and the independence of dance colleges already arose at the DANCE CONGRESS in Berlin. Indeed, some fear that this new call for compatibility might, in the worst case scenario, result in a kind of unification and standardisation among educational institutions. In a lecture entitled »Compatibility versus Identity«, Vincent Assink, managing director of Rotterdam Dance Academy, described the procedure undertaken by the institutions for dance education in the Netherlands. At the start of the restructuring process in the Netherlands, the educational institutions met to jointly determine the learning outcomes, or the competencies to be acquired during the educational process, at the national level. After a two-year process of negotiation, each college undertook the restructuring of its course of study in a highly individual manner. According to Assink, the process of restructuring in the Netherlands promoted institutional individualisation by contributing to the development of specialised educational programmes.

Among German institutional representatives, there is general agreement that the educational institutions should not simply continue to react to the demands placed upon them. Instead, German educational institutions should become active contributors to key cultural committees and take the lead in introducing upcoming innovations. Following a constructive and lively debate, the representatives decided to present a united front on educational concerns from now on, under the motto »One Voice for Dance Education«.

A working group on the topic of »dance theory and history«[6] undertook an initial inventory of the field. As a result, the working group issued a joint demand that theoretical subjects should be accorded higher status in the future, and should aim for more intensive cooperation in content and methods. The working group also developed practical suggestions on how dance theory might be better integrated into dance education.

Alongside the two work groups on »dance education« and »dance history and theory«, the first joint further education programme for professors, lecturers, and students in departments of classical dance took place in Frankfurt under the leadership of the internationally active training director and choreographer Javier Torres. The practice-oriented training course addressed the topic »Different Points of View in the Communication of Classical Dance«.

The Staatliche Ballettschule hosted the third meeting organised by »Tanzplan«, held in Berlin in February 2007. At this meeting, a joint lobby group for the German educational institutions, entitled the »Ausbildungskonferenz Tanz« (Educational Conference Dance, Working Group of the State Educational Academies for Dancers in Germany – BA/MA/Diploma/Final Stage Examinations)[7], was formed. The goal of this initiative is to optimise professional dance education in Germany by creating the best possible conditions for (pre)education, strengthening cooperation among the colleges and universities in the field of further education of dancers and instructors, and establishing networks with international partners. Future cooperation will require concluding an agreement on common goals. In previous meetings, agreements have been reached on the following projects and measures:

*Further education:*At the juncture of theory and practice, a continuing education programme will be offered at different educational sites for lecturers and professors twice a year. Instructors in the various departments will meet with internationally renowned experts (for example, Gill Clarke, Laban Centre London) to exchange new ideas and work methods.

Mobile module: »Tanzplan Deutschland« is one of the co-producers of MOTION BANK, a new multimedia project by William Forsythe. It is an analytical method for choreographical structures based on the choreography of ONE FLAT THING, REPRODUCED. In the course of the discussions, a general agreement was reached that »e-learning programmes« as well as other learning tools and teaching materials will be made available for educational facility. These modules will be designed for simple and mobile implementation at institutions and will be made available on demand.

---

6 | This work group is comprised of departmental instructors from the various institutions.

7 | Cf. *http://tanzplan-deutschland.de?tanzhochschulen.php?id_language=1* from 12 May 2007.

Videotape library and archive: Within its plan to make instructional materials available, »Tanzplan« will cooperate in establishing and expanding videotape libraries and archives at educational institutions. Video material will be selected to strengthen theoretical, historical, and practical engagement with contemporary choreography. In order to tailor the offerings to users' needs each of the educational institutions will first conduct an inventory of existing holdings, and assess their wishes and needs. However, the actual establishment of the archives will depend upon the acquisition of usage rights.

Biennial of the educational institutions: The »Biennial Dance Education Project« (working title), a major meeting of students and teachers at the national educational institutions, will over the long term serve to provide a platform for presenting college and university projects and works by students to a broad audience. It will also provide a platform for experimentation and work with William Forsythe's MOTION BANK, which will then be complete. In addition to a workshop programme, the project will also organise an expert conference. The pilot project will take place this coming year at the Hebbel am Ufer theatre in Berlin during the »Context« festival. The achievements of the pilot project will be further developed by a work group comprised of representatives from the educational institutions, the Hebbel theatre, »Tanzplan Deutschland«, and the Forsythe Foundation.

International exchange: »Tanzplan« will promote and expand contacts with educational institutions, partners, and networks (for example, ELIA and INTERARTES) within Europe and beyond, as appropriate.

Ausbildungkonferenz Tanz: The dance education conference entitled »Ausbildungkonferenz Tanz« is active in the area of early and professional education certification. It is also promoting debate on the topic within the sphere of culture and policy. Its selected speakers will participate in relevant discussions and debates on educational issues. In addition, there is a plan to implement regular meetings.

If the many participants involved in this process succeed in jointly strengthening individual educational institutions, the coming years will produce important developments in dance education.

Translation from German

Online References

http://tanzplan-deutschland.de.
http://tanzplan-deutschland.de?tanzhochschulen.php?id_language=1.

Dance Careers in Transition

A Field of Action for Dance in Germany?

CORNELIA DÜMCKE

Dance art in Germany has only been under the microscope in terms of its social background and institutional existential forms for a short time and translated into new approaches for dance within the bounds of art policy.[1]

However, contemporary concepts of action for dance should not ignore its economic dimensions, nor for that matter, the aesthetic or legal issues. The correlation between dance and the economy in Germany – much like the neglected connection between dance and law – has unfortunately only been touched on as an issue and has barely been investigated or researched. The latter is also true of the field of action »dance careers in transition«.

Dance – an Economic Perspective

There is clearly a social interest in dance with its broad, varied range of aesthetic appearances and performance practices as well as the different forms of production it involves. This increased interest also makes dance an interesting economic prospect. It is, for example, an integral part of the cultural and creative worlds which are accredited with growing development potential throughout Europe. Current studies show that in England the ›dance industry‹ employs around 30.000 dancers, choreographers, dance teachers, technicians and managers. Added to this number are those working in completely different production and service fields loosely connected to dance (music, design, medicine, therapy, wellness etc.).

---

1 | Cf. *www.tanzplan-deutschland.de* from 12 May 2007.

Here in Germany, no comparable information or sustainable data are available that could evoke a different public perception of the economic significance of dance. A press release issued on 4 February 2005 by Deutscher Bühnenverein (the German Theatre and Orchestra Association) on the state of dance in Germany indicated that around 1.500 dancers were under full contract at about 70 dance companies in city or state theatres. This means that large areas of the dance field are not accounted for in the public, non-profit and commercial sector. A practice that masks the depth of the dance field in its political and ultimately also its economic perception does not do justice to the developments currently taking place in dance.

Economically speaking, dance as an occupational field and as gainful employment has its peculiarities. From a social and individual perspective, dance is a special ›field of investment‹. Unlike other occupational groups, dancers have to rethink their career after just a relatively short active time on stage. For this reason, every professional dancer is confronted with the issue of retraining or further training sooner or later. Consequently, »career transition«, as the problem is called in the English vernacular, is an unavoidable, integral part of any dancer's career anywhere in the world.

Nonetheless, there appears to be an unwritten law dancers follow, because the perception of the dance profession is based on other demands and criteria than the size of income or length of employment.

NO MONEY, NO LOVE by Jochen Roller, DANCE CONGRESS GERMANY 2006

Photo: Thomas Aurin

Career Transition Models Derived
from International Practices

Unlike Germany, the interest internationally in the multiple dimensions of structuring career transitions in professional dance and in the social potential of dancers has grown. At the same time, the general awareness that dancers acquire valuable competencies in the course of their career such as discipline, perseverance, ability to work in a team and foreign languages has been raised in general. These competencies can easily be transferred to other occupational fields.

Both the high-profile nature of the so-called transition centres in Canada, England, Holland and the USA that specialise in fostering the retraining and further training of dancers have helped to achieve this, as have the initiatives of the umbrella organisation International Organisation for the Transition of Professional Dancers (IOTPD) based in Switzerland.

Worldwide, four organisations exist today that are dedicated exclusively to the retraining and professional reorientation of dancers:
- The Dancer Transition Resource Centre (DTRC), Canada[2]
- Dutch Retraining Program for Professional Dancers (SOD), Holland[3]
- Dancers' Career Development (DCD), England[4]
- Career Transition for Dancers (CTFD), USA[5]

Together, these organisations offer certain core services such as consultancy and financial support. However, they differ in terms of their funding models[6] and the rights of dancers to avail of the services of these organisations.

Transition centres make a significant contribution towards improving the general conditions for putting dancers' potential to use in society. This is backed up by the findings of a three-year international research project conducted by aDvANCE entitled »Making Changes, Facilitating the Transition of Dancers to Post-Performance Careers«.[7] The study

---

2 | Founded in 1985, cf. *www.dtrc.ca* from 12 May 2007

3 | Founded in 1986, cf. *www.kunstcultuur.nl* from 12 May 2007

4 | Founded in 1974, cf. *www.thedcd.org.uk* from 12 May 2007

5 | Founded in 1982, cf. *www.careertransition.org* from 12 May 2007

6 | In the federalist countries of Canada and Holland, for example, the organisations receive funding from a variety of sources: public funds, membership fees, profits from funds as well as private funding (associations, foundations, individuals).

7 | Cf. William J. Baumol/Joan Jeffri/David Throsby: *Making Changes, Facilitating the Transition of Dancers to Post-Performance Careers*, The aDvANCE Project, Research Report, New York 2004.

was conducted on behalf of the IOTPD and examined the processes of professional reorientation and the retraining of professional dancers in a total of eleven different countries.

According to aDvANCE, progress in this field is not only a question of the social esteem shown to the dancers and their artistic performance. It is rather of fundamental importance for the vital development of dance as a self-contained art form: »Can we continue to marginalize and ignore the issue of career transition when it has such an obvious impact on the long-term health of the field?«[8] There is clearly a need on an individual country basis for varied, i.e. adapted, models for the different areas and/or phases of a dance career.

Historical Background in Germany

In Germany, too, initiatives have got off the ground over the past few years aimed at drawing attention to this peculiar feature of the dance world. Approaches have been developed to some extent, which largely originated from standing companies or standing engagements. At the same time, the needs of free-lancing dancers went largely unconsidered; the actual need in this field is virtually unknown. What's more, the initiatives and proposals have only produced concrete offers for dancers in selected areas.

The country report on dance in Germany[9] included in the aDvANCE report leaves many issues unresolved since it contains significant, fundamental gaps in the representation of socio-economic data, institutional structures and both social and legal framework conditions. The majority of data used for dance in Germany is based on estimates.

A so-called »minor interpellation«, a written question put to the government in writing in July 2001[10] in the Bundestag, Germany's lower house, on the subject of the special occupational standing of dancers in Germany heralded for the first time that the training and education, retraining and covering of the social security needs of dancers had become an express subject of a parliamentary debate. It is a fact that, in the replies to the relevant questions, references had to be made to a lack of information and base data: »No extensive studies have been submitted to the Federal Government on the training, education and career paths

---

8 | Ibid., p. 15.

9 | In addition to the country reports on dance in Australia, Canada, England, France, Hungary, Japan, Mexico, Netherlands, Switzerland and the USA.

10 | Cf. »Minor interpellation« to the government on »Education and Training, Retraining and the Covering of Social Security Needs of Dancers«, Bundestag printed papers 14/6693 and 14/6493.

of dancers.«[11] This lack of information was justified with a reference to the fact that the German states and local authorities were responsible for this task.

In a »major interpellation« to the Bundestag in December 2003 on »The economic and social development of the artistic professions and the arts industry in Germany«[12], dance is largely overlooked. With respect to the field of dance question 21, which deals with the possible retraining measures for artists, refers to the answers given in the »minor interpellation« on dance in Germany in July 2001.

Until now, the situation has barely changed even though there is an even more pressing need for debate on this issue, given the current developments on the labour market. For the time being, the dance field sees itself confronted with the changing framework conditions applied by the Bundesagentur für Arbeit, Germany's agency responsible for the country's unemployed, to promotion of jobs and training, and especially by the Central Stage, Television and Film Agency (ZBF) and the local job centres.[13] At present, too little is known or said about the impact that such changes will have on how dancers build their career transitions. What's more, attention needs to be given to the general trend towards cutting back on the cultural job market for salaried employees inside the scope of the national insurance system while, at the same time, the number of self-employed, free-lance cultural professions is on the increase.[14] Dance is especially affected by this development.

Over and above this, there is the problem that dancers usually only have a recognised college degree. This significantly impairs their attendance of a university course in dance or arts-related professions.

---

11 | Bundestag printed paper 14/6693, p. 48.

12 | »Major interpellation« on »The Economic and Social Development of the Artistic Professions and the Arts Industry in Germany«, Bundestag printed matter 15/2275.

13 | The limitations placed on welfare benefits as well as the range of consultancy and job finding services have increased following the restructuring of and implementation of austerity measures at the Bundesagentur für Arbeit.

14 | The largely positive market forecasts for cultural work in the cultural and creative industries need to be counterchecked far more exactly in terms of their concrete conditions. This includes the often gloomy economic situations found in a large number of the so-called cultural and creative professions and the fact that a large portion of the self-employed artists and artistic professions struggle to make ends meet or to make arrangements for their retirement (especially those who are unable to join the social security scheme for artists).

A Transition Model for Dance in Germany?

It was against this background and knowing the findings of the research project conducted by ADvANCE and the »Tanzplan«-initiative, a national initiative for dance in Germany that representatives of the dance scene from at home and abroad met at the DANCE CONGRESS[15] to discuss the status quo and the prospects of structuring career transitions in the dance profession taking the following issues into account:

Does the issue of »structuring career transitions in the dance profession« have to be viewed holistically and become an integral part of the strategies for dance in Germany? Have the institutional, structural and legal framework conditions for the training, education and retraining of dancers in Germany, in their status quo, actually been sufficiently analysed and made known? What needs to be done in Germany to hone the arguments and, if necessary, to develop and implement alternative concepts based on international experiences?

One of the »Dance careers in transition« discussion findings was to call for a model to be developed for dance in Germany that adapts the experiences made by existing transition centres internationally, tailors them to the conditions in Germany and establishes a level of sustainability that extends beyond the »Tanzplan Deutschland« that has been mapped out until 2010.

To achieve this requires, on the one hand, the continued use of sensitisation processes among those players and institutions responsible for dance. On the other hand, knowledge of the actual needs and current state of affairs needs to be improved in order to further hone the arguments. The impulses for this must continue to come from those players involved in the dance scene.

Translation from German

---

15 | Cf. Panel »Dance Careers in Transition« as part of the DANCE CONGRESS involving the following participants: Linda Yates/Anja Dobler, Director/ Development Officer of the Dancers' Career Development Centre (UK); Paul Bronckhorst, Director of the Retraining Program for Dancers (NL); Reinhild Hoffmann, choreographer (D); Maja Langsdorff, dancer and author (D); Sabrina Sadowska, Assistant Ballet Director, Theater Vorpommern Stralsund/Greifswald (D); Claudia Feest, dance teacher (D); Günter Pick, until 2005 Head of Department Dance at the Central Stage, Television and Film Agency (D); chaired by Dr. Cornelia Dümcke.

References

Baumol, William J./Jeffri, Joan/Throsby, David: *Making Changes, Facilitating the Transition of Dancers to Post-Performance Careers*, The aDvANCE Project, Research Report, New York 2004.

Deutscher Bundestag: »Major interpellation« on »the Economic and Social Development of the Artistic Professions and the Arts Industry in Germany«, Bundestag printed matter 15/2275.

Deutscher Bundestag: »Minor interpellation« to the government on »Education and Training, Retraining and the Covering of Social Security Needs of Dancers«, Bundestag printed papers 14/6693 and 14/6493.

Online References

www.careertransition.org.
www.dtrc.ca.
www.kunstcultuur.nl.
www.tanzplan-deutschland.de.
www.thedcd.org.uk.

Dance Pedagogy and Cultural Work

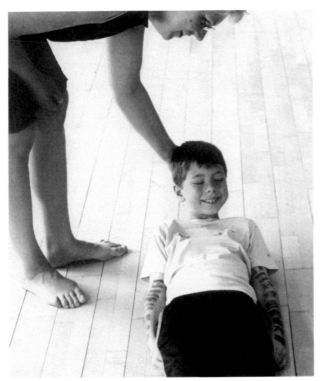

»TanzZeit – Zeit für Tanz In Schulen« (DanceTime – Time for Dance in Schools), Berlin 2006,
Photo: Marion Borriss

Working on Experience

ROYSTON MALDOOM IN DIALOGUE WITH EDITH BOXBERGER

Edith Boxberger: You prefer working in small groups. But since your work has attracted more attention through the film RHYTHM IS IT! You have choreographed a number of large-scale projects. Are you still doing this today and what is the reason behind it?

Royston Maldoom: Yes, together with a variety of assistants, I'm mainly involved in extensive projects this year – in Luxemburg, for example, as part of the Cultural Capital Programme, in Saarbrücken, Vienna, New York. The size of the projects is dictated by sponsors and orchestras wanting to do large-scale projects usually because small projects are far more difficult to fund. I am concentrating on the possibility of working on larger scale projects that can combine many different small-scale ones, along the lines of the Community Dance Project[1] in Hamburg last year where I myself was working with a small group of eighteen men.

The idea behind acquainting Germans with my work was to establish structures and create space and frameworks.

I still consider the bulk of my work to be in promoting the *idea of dance for everybody*. Major projects tend to attract more attention from the general public, sponsors and politicians. It is my hope that through these large-scale events smaller, ongoing projects will emerge like the

---

1 | In the summer of 2006, five choreographers developed productions with a variety of different social groups as part of the project »Can Do Can Dance«, held workshops and presented their work at a symposium. Royston Maldoom worked on the project – which was funded, among others, by the Federal Cultural Foundation – with a group of young male adults and was responsible for the overall artistic direction.

»TanzZeit«-project in Berlin[2] or a project in Marl which has since produced several dance groups spanning a wide age range and who are
supported along from several sources. Nearly all of the projects I have
been involved in have come about because of the commitment of the
sponsoring organisations to continue and develop the work. My job is
either to draw attention to the existing work to solicit support for its
continuation, or to help a new initiative get off the ground.

Dance project DANCE 4 LIFE: *Royston Maldoom with pupils of
Gesamtschule Ost (a comprehensive school) in Bremen 2006*
Photo: Volker Beinhorn

What is the main difference between working with small and large groups?
First and foremost, the way in which the choreographer and the participants interact. The more intimate and this relationship is, the more
intensive the flow of information and dialogue. With a large group, you
have to take a more disciplined approach, take more control, because
the time constraints and expectations are greater. I know from my own
practical experience that, while this can still be a transforming experience for the participants, concessions need to be made in terms of the
intensity of the work.
*Can you give us an idea of the kind of dialogue that goes on in a small
group?*

2 | »TanzZeit – Zeit für Tanz in Schulen« (DanceTime – Time for Dance in
Schools) was initiated in 2005 by dancer and choreographer Livia Patrizi
with the aim of bringing pupils at primary schools in Berlin closer to contemporary dance through regular dance lessons, developing performances
and attending dance performances. Cf. *www.tanzzeit-schule.de* from 10 May
2007.

Clearly, it's not only about a verbal exchange but a dialogue within the creative process and the piece. You can *delve* deeper, work on a more individual basis, and the participants have a stronger involvement. The ultimate experience for me is being able to accompany a group over an extended period of time. This is something that is currently happening with the group of young men I worked with last year as part of the Hamburg Community Dance Project, for example. They are continuing the work with other choreographers but still keep in touch with me, and we are currently discussing how I can best support them as mentor and choreographer in the longer term.

Working with this group wasn't easy. Where did the difficulties lie?

The participants had to develop and acquire skills in a very short period of time. That was a huge challenge and people often wanted to give up. Because they are accustomed to failure, it was more comfortable to give up whenever something did not work the first time. They resisted doing things that they thought didn't make them look good or even made them look ›handicapped‹, which is an interesting statement in itself. This was understandable to an extent because they had to move in a way that was alien to them. They found the movement difficult at first because they were more used to expressing themselves physically in a more confrontational manner. They evidently felt that their self-image, their perception of their body and themselves as men was in jeopardy. There was always an air of failure in the room because it was so difficult for them to withstand the tension that emerges when something doesn't work the first time round.

So is there a positive side to failing?

Failure, coming up short, not being able to do something the first time round – these are all foundations for success. The entire process in this work is actually based on failing – day in, day out; hour after hour and you can't avoid it. If you cannot fail, you cannot learn and develop as a person. Failing in this sense however isn't really something negative but positive. It's not the end but the beginning. It's the way we grow and move forward. Every dancer, every artist knows this all too well. We rehearse, abandon, practice, refine. This nourishes us, motivates us and drives us forward but many young people are really afraid of failing. Maybe they don't get enough encouragement.

In your experience, does this apply to different social classes?

There can undoubtedly be differences, but I've worked with pupils from grammar schools, and to me no other group appeared to have more problems and be more afraid of failing than they did. They were very well taken care of but they had very little sense of personal identity.

How do you deal with fear? How can it be turned around to enable experiences and knowledge to emerge?

The key element in the entire process is to believe in others, to believe unerringly in people's potential – and by this I mean every single person. This is what gets you through the entire process. As soon as you lose that belief and think that people are incapable or not worth the trouble, you cannot achieve anything. You must communicate this belief to the people you work with. When the work is done, I hear the same thing time and time again: »I didn't really want to do it. It was so difficult at times. If it had been up to me, I would have given up, but I couldn't, because you were so sure, so convinced that I could do it.«

In doing this, you're going beyond the leap of faith that is the foundation of all interaction. As a prerequisite to learning, you anticipate the potential that first needs to manifest itself or become known. How does that work?

Somehow the participants seem to sense it as soon as I enter the room. The young men in Hamburg told me that they had repeatedly tried to provoke me to make me give up like everyone else had, but that they didn't succeed. Instead they felt themselves becoming drawn into the work ever more closely until they couldn't give up. I've heard that kind of assessment on a number of occasions; in retrospect, people do understand why they did things the way they did.

Dance project DANCE 4 LIFE: *Royston Maldoom with pupils from Gesamtschule Ost (a comprehensive school) in Bremen 2006*

Photo: Volker Beinhorn

In other words, you assume in your work that everybody has the potential, a universal, creative potential that needs developing.

We all have the potential to do something greater than we are. Even people who have already achieved a lot in their lives so far have not exhausted their potential. Many of us do not even realise that we have such potential. I really believe this. If I didn't, I couldn't carry on, because this work is difficult, sometimes depressing, stressful and very demanding. It can be very hard to lock in on this potential: you can see that people have, but they either don't or won't recognise it. There is a fine line between being incapable of taking a chance and refusing that giant leap forward in terms of ability and trust that can occur if participants would just go that extra mile. The choreographer needs to think hard – and I can usually come up with something that helps but sometimes it's very hard. The turning point, when a dancer makes that leap forward, is a moment of pure joy. You see it in their face, in their body, in the participants' entire posture, and they may say strange things like »I'm flying« because they don't have the right words to express the feeling.

In your work, what role, if at all, does not accounting for the participants' situation play?

I've often been criticised in England, but also here in Germany, for the fact that where people come from, what they do and how they live plays no role in my work whatsoever. It is true. That is my approach. I believe this approach is not common but it can be a truly liberating experience for people in difficult situations.

The choreography is always completely in your hands. In what way are the participants involved in the creative process?

There is a big misconception that developing the steps is the only creative part of the work. It's true that I create rather stringent structures. But on stage, the audience first and foremost sees the people who are interpreting this structure, and in their own way as individuals. I'm very critical at work, not because someone can't perform the right step or doesn't get a leg position right, but whenever the motivation and dedication is lacking, when there is a lack of respect for the work, themselves and for others. I attach the greatest importance to these things. I don't criticise movement. I work on the person's commitment, on how the individual takes on the process by being prepared to look at themselves differently. It's about experiencing the transformation.

You stress the specific nature of the experience, a transforming experience, as you put it. What role does talking play in this?

Talking is a very significant part of my work which I also like to see as a process of sharing. I share my experience as a person, as a teacher, as a choreographer. That's why I talk about a lot of different things, for example my life, nature, history or friendship during the process, I address everything that has an effect on the work directly and unequivocally, and I try to explain things directly to the participants. There are long periods where all the energy concentrates on physical work. This is a very important aspect of the work and though it is sometimes not easy, I will interrupt the process and talk till everyone has understood what is really important.

Is there a certain approach, a type of method to this work or should there be one, if only to pass on knowledge and experience?

I don't think much of that idea of method. I don't think about methods and nor do any of the »community choreographers« whose work I most admire. We would say it's about a philosophy, a perception of people and the world which is positive. Of course, this does not mean that you should be naive about what is going on in the world – on the contrary. You have to accept that there are a lot of bad things in the world, learn how to get to grips with this fact and still love people. It is my belief, born out of experience, that people have a naturally strong desire for excellence. If you don't have this fundamental conviction or don't develop it, you can learn any theory you like and still not have anything to give. This is *the attitude I work with*, you can develop your own theories naturally through practice. It allows me to work with everybody, and I mean everybody. I think the time to start to acquire theoretical knowledge is after spending some time doing practical work. And first, you have to learn not to see yourself as an educator, but just as a person working with others. You have to learn how to deal with other people, how to open up and how to share.

Does this mean that the decisive factor is the nature of the relationship, a slightly hierarchical relationship between the artist/teacher and the participants?

There's no doubt that I have the authority in this process. Someone has to take decisions and assume responsibility so that a piece can evolve. A leader is needed but the decisive element is *how* you perform this function, not condescendingly but in a way that the others feel recognised and supported and see their own contribution valued. In the course of working, I have, of course, learned to share. But it is better to recognise from the start that the key to this work is a real desire to share your knowledge and experience.

What does this sharing process look like?

You have to be in a position to reflect on your work, your life and your experience. This is one of the most important parts of this work. I tell young people that it's not so much your experience as your ability to reflect on that experience that is decisive for personal development. With reflection you may discover how you can use your own experience when working with others.

How do you pass on your knowledge?

I invite those interested to get involved in the work process and be as open as possible so that they can perceive and feel what is going on in the room. I encourage them to reflect on the process and to talk with me about it. Rather than writing as much down as possible, it's more important to be at the heart of the process. It is not so much about what I do, rather recognising why I do it, how I do it, how I go about it and what happens in the process. They may draw quite different conclusions; but the important thing is to find their own standpoint.

Can you give us some examples of this approach?

There are many: how I introduce something; at what point I decide to express criticism, at what point to lend support; how I criticise – in other words so that the criticism is accepted – how committed I am during the process; how fixated I am on myself or free to perceive things around me and respond to them; how I help individuals feel they are involved even if I don't address them directly; whether and how I manage to have everyone feel they are making a valuable contribution without being patronising. All of these things are very important for the process.

If ›how‹ things are communicated is the key, how do you enable people to do this?

I've come up with very many exercises for all kinds of purposes to structure the work, and develop movements, movement sequences and forms, to help people relax or to overcome inhibitions. Everyone can adapt these for themselves or develop something different from them. The most important thing here is not to slavishly stick to the exercises you have planned but go with the flow of the situation. You shouldn't expect that you will be in control all of the time but even risk losing it and be aware that control over what is happening in the room is often more in the hands of the people you are working with. When working with children, I address this issue head on by explaining to them that I may appear to be in charge, doing all of the shouting, but that, above all, I am only trying to wrest some control from them.

This means that the risk is spread equally across the participants and the choreographer – both enter into an unknown, open process.

It is about not knowing exactly what you will do so that you are open for new experiences. After all, it's exactly this experience of working together that is reflected in the piece that you are developing. If you have a certain approach, plan or method, there's a danger that you won't dare to deviate from it and take a risk. You might even say that sticking to one approach is a way of reducing the risk – but usually there is a high price to pay for this.

Where should the emphasis be placed when training for this work?

Looking at the projects, my impression is that the quality is improving. Above all, this is linked to enabling practical work. To my mind, this is the key to further development. As far as the issue of quality assurance is concerned, I would tend towards extending the opportunity for practical work. To do this, however, would require taking a somewhat un-German approach – I sincerely hope that this is taken the right way – in other words of not introducing endless theory based training courses but inventing as many practical opportunities as possible for potential artists/teachers: internships, mentoring programmes, practical experience with competent people. I did the piece Sacre du Printemps with 250 children. Maybe it would be a good thing to stage the piece with 250 dance teachers.

In your opinion, how should the development continue, within schools or even outside them?

Having artists work in schools is a good idea as long as they can remain artists. Working artistically is a crucial experience for children. But if too many conditions are brought in to cater to the school day – severe time limits, for example – the question is whether the result will still be art. The system has its restrictions and cannot be changed easily. I would therefore prefer to see a more concerted move into the surroundings, in other words where the children live. The range of leisure possibilities for young people there are usually scarce and other problems arise more easily as a result. Besides you can reach out to other social groups in the wider community.

Are there moves or signs of a move in this direction?

Until now, there have only been a few one-off projects because we don't have the infrastructure for them. This is not quite so much a problem in parts of the UK, but in Germany the connections to schools seem to be the preferred choice. I, for my part, am leaning more and more towards an artist-based development that brings different people together and enables them to learn in different social areas – kindergarten, sports clubs, community centres etc. I can certainly imagine the »artist in residence«-model taking off where an artist wanting to share his or her work with others could also invite other artists to do so. In concrete terms, this would entail employing an artist or even a company to work on behalf of a local authority to develop and implement ideas, within an agreed time, for a dance culture in the sense I mentioned above for a certain area – be it a part of town, a small town or a rural region.

Online References

www.tanzzeit-schule.de.

Learning Unconsciously

Linda Müller in dialogue with Silvia Stammen

Since 2003, sports scientist and physiotherapist Linda Müller from the NRW Landesbüro Tanz (Regional Office for Dance in North Rhine-Westphalia), Germany, has been running the »Tanz in Schulen« (Dance in Schools) project. Although she has already gone a long way towards achieving her goal of making dance a permanent feature of lessons in all-day state primary and secondary schools, there is still a long road ahead. Linda Müller talked to journalist Silvia Stammen about how her work is progressing.

Silvia Stammen: In 2003, when you launched the »Tanz in Schulen project«, you were considered one of the pioneers of the initiative in Germany. How did your vision of »Tanz in Schulen« come about?
Linda Müller: The call for dance to be established in schools has actually been around for one hundred years, and many groups and institutions have offered dance in schools since time immemorial. Back in 2003, our main concern was to broaden the base and to bring together all people with experience to jointly consider how dance in schools could be expanded to a broader base to avoid everything always relying on certain individuals. Experience has shown that dedicated individuals have got fantastic projects off the ground but that the project also dies once these people move on. I'd like to see these initiatives sustained.
In your estimation, how far do you believe you have come?
We've definitely made inroads inasmuch as, on the one hand, we have made many dance makers aware of this line of work. On the other hand, it has also been necessary to make schools aware in the first place that something like dance actually exists. Without doubt, the film RHYTHM IS IT! has helped a lot. In NRW, we have also benefited from a state

government that is highly committed to cultural education. As a result, over the past three – almost four years – many dance makers have been able to acquire experience in teaching at all-day primary schools. This is something that can be built on.

Is it conceivable that dance will perhaps soon be taught as a separate subject?

We're a long way from that just now. The models currently in place here in NRW are mainly work groups run in the afternoons or project-related working methods, often integrated into sports or music classes. Children who have opted to go to a so-called *Ganztagsschule* (open all-day school) can choose what they want to do in the afternoon.

How has demand for dance classes developed since the project was launched?

Schools have to fund the tuition fees themselves. For this reason, when I did my first stint back in the spring of 2003, I only found one solitary school willing to pay 35 euros for a 45-minute class. As a result, we looked for other funding sources. Together with the »Landesarbeitsgemeinschaft Tanz in NRW« (Regional Association for Dance), we developed a model that funds taster courses at schools; in other words, we first had to inform people on what dance and creative dance education can actually achieve. The response to the project was tremendous – with a lot of word of mouth advertising. In the meantime, over 150 schools now offer dance, and in the past year secondary schools have also come forward with their own ideas of how to integrate dance into mornings. One grammar school in Cologne has even been offering dance as a special subject for a year now.

What is the selection procedure for dance educators?

We look at who has experience in teaching children and perhaps even at schools. What kind of artistic career has that person had? We offer the people we place with the schools a monthly training course on a variety of subjects such as the use of music, choreographies with children or even development psychology.

This is a wholly new situation for dancers, too: suddenly finding yourself in front of a group of children who have never had any contact to dance until that time.

Sure. It's not that easy. To do this, you need certain tools of the trade. Even dance educators who did their training in Holland, where the aspect of dance at schools is integrated, at times have great difficulty coming to terms with the situation in Germany because there simply isn't the same level of acceptance for artistic education here yet.

What other problems exist in the interaction with schools?

There are often reservations because neither side knows much about the other. School is often perceived to be an archaic system even though much has changed there in the course of time. And schools often have no clue about what to do with dance education. During this academic year, for example, one father told his son's teacher in no uncertain terms that »my son does not dance«. This type of reaction, of course, is a reflection of fear at the sensuous nature of dance, or because people have this image of pink tutus, and some fathers are afraid that their boys will turn gay if they dance.

But the main problem continues to be how to finance the dancers' fees. Although open all-day primary schools have a budget for courses that can be used in part to pay for dance lessons, I believe that the adequate fee is a lot of money for schools. Other alternatives to this are to ask parents to make a financial contribution and assistance from funding organisations, or we need to jointly find third-party funds from sponsors or foundations.

We also have to submit a new application to the »Ministerium für Generationen, Frauen, Familie und Integration« (Ministry of Generations, Family, Women and Integration) every year for our own Euro 60.000 budget for the organisation. Although we receive an additional Euro 16.000 from the »Kulturabteilung der Staatskanzlei NRW« (Department of Culture at the State Chancellery of NRW), a certain degree of uncertainty still remains.

What positive experiences and encounters motivate you in this situation?

First and foremost, only those conducting the courses get to see how each child actually develops in the class. My role is merely that of an intermediary. Nevertheless, I am constantly inspired by the look of joy in the children's faces when they're on stage presenting what they've come up with as a group. We also have academics accompanying the programmes writing dissertations and PhD theses, and it's always good to hear children being interviewed expressing exactly what we had hoped for, namely that they are far more self-confident now, can approach others more readily and that they simply enjoy dancing. That these children learn so much in the process is something that they don't really notice. Another constant source of motivation for me is seeing the project develop as a whole. Year in, year out, I have noticed that communication with the schools is improving and that the dance educators feel much more at home in the third year. Things are moving forwards.

How many lessons do the artists normally give at the schools in addition to pursuing their own artistic work?

As a rule, they spend about two hours per week at a school and on average each dancer goes to two or three schools. Needless to say, they sometimes find it difficult to coordinate their ongoing work at the schools with the time demands that their artistic project work places on them. That's why it's important to have a pool of artists who can deputise for one another when called upon.

We see our primary task as that of an interface between the school and the artists whereby we advise both sides and mediate on any everyday problems that occur. The contract itself, however, is concluded directly between the artist and the school.

How long are the programmes offered as part of »Tanz in Schulen« designed to run?

If it were up to me, then for a long time. Many schools have been working with our dancers for three or four years non-stop throughout the academic year. What I'd really like to see is that each child is given an opportunity to dance if he or she wants to.

What prospects do you see for the future?

The »Bundesverband Tanz in Schulen e.V.« (Federal Association for Dance at Schools) was founded this past February. Here, we want to work together to establish quality criteria for dance in schools. The idea is first to determine what is needed, how dance projects should be run, what abilities the teachers need to have, what content is important, or even what should be integrated into dance instruction in the future to enable dancers and choreographers to start preparing for work in schools during their studies. We want to jointly work on finding answers to these questions at national level – and we still have a long way to go – so that we can guarantee that the projects running today will be sustained.

Translation from German

Art Is Not a Luxury

Livia Patrizi in dialogue with Silvia Stammen

As a dancer, Naples-born Livia Patrizi worked with such famous choreographers as Mats Ek, Pina Bausch, Joachim Schloemer and Maguy
Marin. Since 1990, she herself has been a free-lancing choreographer
with engagements in Naples, Stockholm, Paris and Germany. Yet, two
years ago, she embarked on something completely new and initiated the
»TanzZeit – Zeit für Tanz in Schulen« (DanceTime – Time for Dance
in Schools) project in Berlin which she has run ever since. Journalist
Silvia Stammen spoke with her about how the idea was born and how it
has developed since.

*Silvia Stammen: The »TanzZeit« project has been running in Berlin since
2005. What motivated you as a dancer and choreographer to take such a
passionate interest in this area?*
   Livia Patrizi: Prior to this, I had just choreographed my first piece for
children with children entitled What is dance? and was very surprised
at the result: the children, even the boys, were immediately gripped by it
and wanted to carry on dancing. What's more, a large number of people
came up to me spontaneously and asked if it wouldn't be possible to
do something like this in schools, too. (I had previously given lessons
privately at schools and was amazed at how many prejudices children in
the 3rd form upwards displayed against dance). At the time, I had also
heard of the initiatives in North Rhine Westphalia (NRW) and invited
the person running those, Linda Müller, to attend a panel discussion.
Afterwards I though ›okay‹, maybe it was time to try something like that
in Berlin, too. What's more, I had got to know the British choreographer
Royston Maldoom, who immediately offered to help, as did Renate Breitig,
adviser for drama at schools from the »Berliner Senatsverwaltung für

Bildung, Jugend und Sport« (Berlin Administration Department for Education, Youth and Sport). Over 200 teachers replied on the spur of the moment to the initial circular we sent out to schools, and 80 schools registered, which meant that we even had to pare the number down to 40 classes before finally beginning the pilot stage.

Livia Patrizi in »TanzZeit – Zeit für Tanz in Schulen«

Photo: Marion Borriss

How did you win over the dancers to your idea at that time?

I also made a conscious effort to incorporate people from professional dancing. Kids and youth dance are often strictly separated from professional dance, which is something I have always seen as a problem. I'm not a dance educator but have, out of my own personal interest, taught on numerous occasions over the past eleven years – most of them were pros, but some were also adult or youth laypersons. For this reason alone, I have always believed that this project should only be run in conjunction with professional artists. Having been able to convince the Dachverband »Zeitgenössischer Tanz Berlin e.V.« (Umbrella Organisation of Contemporary Dance Berlin) to act as the supporting organisation, its members immediately became aware of the project.

Could you sum up the project based on the first two years?

We're now at a point where, as far as I am aware, we can offer the biggest project in Germany that concentrates on dance in schools during morning classes. This is a decisive point for me because we now get an entire class to dance, including those children who didn't want to at first. When you get big classes with around 30 children in them, this isn't an easy task at all at first. That's why we came up with a concept of having two dancers holding a lesson, one ideally with more extensive experience with choreographies and another who has more knowledge in dance teaching so that they complement one another. On the other hand, we also place a lot of emphasis on working together with the teachers. I think that, in the past, many things have failed because this aspect had been underestimated. Right now, there still isn't an official place for dance in normal morning classes at school. At the moment, teachers are voluntarily giving up music, arts or German classes to allow dance in. This is easier in all-day schools, of course, because children have to stay in school until 4 p.m. All in all, I was amazed that, with the type of risk involved – for most artists, teaching classes in the mornings was a wholly new experience – there have been no disasters but that it has always worked out somehow.

Were there any initial reservations on the part of the schools or individual parents?

For this to work, the entire class has to take part. This also exerts a certain amount of pressure on the parents, but somehow they've always managed to resolve it.

What are your primary objectives?

We want to convey art. We'd also like to bring art to those who wouldn't otherwise come into contact with it. That's enough reason for me. There are also pleasing socio-pedagogical side effects, but we don't see these as the main reason for doing something like this. Indeed, there's even a certain risk of always falling into this justification trap because art is still perceived by society as a luxury. We do, of course, sometimes have other reasons for doing what we do depending on the target group, but it's first and foremost about conveying art and that alone should be sufficient.

As an artist, I also naturally find it very exciting when someone succeeds in getting some of these young people started on the way to a professional career. Until now, hardly any Turkish, Arab or Lebanese pupils or students of immigrant origin have attended German dance colleges or universities even though there are, of course, numerous foreign students from Europe or the rest of the world. The same selection procedure takes place at dance colleges and universities as at other colleges and universities. Yet a young Turkish choreographer who has grown up here could talk of a very different life in Germany. If we can manage to take one of these young people out of the circle of street violence – I'm picturing a real case in question right now – then we will have also fulfilled a social task, of course. But I mainly do this because I see that the young man has talent and because I believe that he can succeed. Later on, these people would, of course, be the best candidates for contributing to our project as teachers themselves because they have gone through similar experiences themselves.

Do you also choose the schools according to their social environment?

We always try to incorporate enough schools that are social hotspots, but this is precisely where we need more money to be honest. Our only financial aid of Euro 48.000 comes from the Department of Culture of the Berlin Senate and we have to reapply for it every year. The artists' fees therefore have to be paid through the schools and the parents of the children there can't support such a project all that long. That's why, as part of our overall funding requirement, it would also be very important to have funds for schools in social hotspots which should be provided by Berlin's Department of Education.

Do you see any concrete chances of finding this kind of money?

The big problem here in Berlin is that the Departments of Culture and Education don't cooperate. Not only is there no prorated funding but the two sides don't even communicate with each other. We are trying to inspire dialogue because our project is stuck right in the middle. It would be wrong for only the Department of Culture or only the Department of Education to contribute some money. A new concept needs to be developed.

What problems exist apart from the financial ones?

In terms of content we are working in different areas: We founded a curriculum-working group, for example, to develop models on how to anchor dance more firmly in the curriculum in the future. Together with Prof. Gabriele Brandstetter from the Freie Universität Berlin, we're planning evaluation projects, and we're working together with the »Bundesverband Tanz in Schulen« (Federal Association for Dance in Schools) in numerous work groups that deal with quality assurance, structure, organisation and networking as well as further training and education. These days, doctoral candidates from a variety of fields of study accompany us. Only recently, we were even invited to perform a lecture demonstration at a psychology convention.

For me as an art director, the main problem lies in the fact that I can't do all of my project-related tasks any more because the organisation takes up so much of my time. There's a discrepancy between the amount of public impact and acceptance that the project has since achieved, and the degree to which it is funded. Until we can get relief on the organisational side, we can only move forwards in terms of content to a limited degree. If we want to continue on the same scale as last year, we need more money, otherwise we'll have to make cutbacks to allow us to concentrate more strongly on the content of the project again.

What types of lessons – process or product-orientated – work best in practice?

After six months, there's always a public presentation, but we leave it up to the artists to decide whether they want to work in a more process or product-orientated manner, in other words: the presentation doesn't have to be a choreography; it can also be a lecture demonstration. This is also very popular because parents or the other teachers often have no idea about how dance lessons work.

A major presentation is also held every winter which involves half of all of the classes. This year we were able to use the Berlin theatre Hebbel am Ufer for four days. Children often don't really notice the difference between a choreography and a lecture demonstration. If they know that an audience will be there, they even see it as a performance. In the majority of cases, however, children really just like performing anything, regardless of the type.

Where do you get the motivation to go on?

My own career as a dancer went very smoothly, with engagements in major companies. Of course, it was strenuous, but also very sheltered at the same time. It was only while working as a free-lance choreographer that I realised how small this dance world really is and how limited its impact is. Even when I was young, something was always missing in that respect. I knew I loved doing what I was doing; it's my passion, but you give little to society and since I grew up in a very political environment, it was important to me to combine these things. At a time when the major social utopias have more or less died, you can see, for example, that many artists are also beginning to bring non-artists onto the stage, simply from a need to re-establish a connection between art and society.

This raises the question of what significance art has in society. We can no longer afford to devote all our efforts exclusively to art. Without wanting to give up the freedom to use art for your own purpose, I do see that it possesses an immense power to affect things in a positive sense.

Translation from German

The Students Have to Come First

Hanna Hegenscheidt and Jo Parkes
in dialogue with Elisabeth Nehring

The »Tanz in Schulen« (Dance in Schools) project, in which choreographers and dancers visit schools during the morning lessons in order to introduce students to contemporary dance, has been a great success nationwide. Artistic work meets education. Journalist Elisabeth Nehring met with the Berlin-based choreographers Hanna Hegenscheidt and Jo Parkes to discuss what artistic and educational work have in common.

Elisabeth Nehring: As choreographers, you both have experience in community work and have taught dance at schools, abroad and as part of the »TanzZeit« project in Berlin. What is the motivation behind your educational work and how does it relate to your work as artists?

Jo Parkes (JP): I've always been fascinated by people and their stories. I'm interested in working with people from all walks of life and in how art, and dance in particular, can make a difference in society and in people's lives. My projects always have two goals: the first is artistic, i.e. telling a story or exploring a topic. The second has to do with the people involved: it's important to me that they gain something from our working together, that they take something with them. That's equally true of our work in schools. Each student is at a different stage of development, and I find it very exciting to find out where each individual stands and how we can help them grow.

Hanna Hegenscheidt (HH): I always love working with young students in schools because I feel it opens up worlds to me I'd never get to know otherwise. I meet people I wouldn't normally meet; I go to parts of town I don't usually visit. So, first of all, it expands my horizon. My motivation is quite selfish: I need to feel that my work is meaningful beyond merely ›creating pieces‹ that are only seen by a certain audience, that the knowledge I've gained over the years can be used in communicating with other people. And it absolutely can.

But it also has a lot to do with the fact that I'm just very interested in people. I really enjoy meeting the students and observing them. I'm curious to learn what they think, what interests and motivates them, what they have to say. That fascinates me. If it didn't, there would be little sense in my doing this sort of work.

You're primarily artists, and being creative makes up a large part of your work. How does that fit in with teaching? Are there parallels between artistic and educational work, and if so, what are they?

JP: Pedagogical work is central to my work as an artist. I don't see the two as separate – art on the one hand, teaching on the other – at all. For me, they're both connected and blend into each other. As an artist, I'm primarily interested in finding a way to approach something new, exploring unfamiliar territory. Creating a piece about something I've already understood would be boring. For me, it's all about discovering and learning something new – like at school. The kids trust that you know what you're talking about. As an artist, you can show them that even adults don't always have an answer to everything, but are sometimes at sea, too, and that they want to learn something themselves. That way you can set an example and help them realize that learning is an ongoing process.

Jo Parkes with students

Photo: Nick Gurney

HH: My interest in observing carefully is rooted in my work as an artist, but it stands me in good stead when it comes to teaching, as well. I always try and see what qualities, what ideas they bring with them. When I go into a classroom and see something that interests me, as an artist I have the luxury of being able to say I'd like to focus on this or that aspect, of course. That enables me to respond spontaneously to what's happening.

There's another parallel to my work as an artist that I find more difficult to put into words: Sometimes I'll have a certain idea or goal in the artistic process, but at that moment, I'm not quite sure where my strengths lie. Often I only discover later that they're actually somewhere quite different than I had thought, and that might reveal more about me than something I did consciously. That's what I love about my work as an artist and also about working with kids. Sometimes when a project is coming to an end you suddenly see that you've really created something new, or that it contains much more of you than you realized while you were working on it. Ultimately, you can never completely control exactly what is manifested in your work, whether artistic or pedagogical, anyway.

Parallels notwithstanding, there are surely also many differences between artistic and educational work. What are they?

JP: For example, when I'm working in a school, there's less time to observe and figure out what I really want to do. Normally I ask a lot of questions and we try out various ideas until we find something that we want to go with. I can take the time to take a step back and watch and just think about it for a while. You can't do that so much when you're teaching. Often the children would ask, »What are we going to do next?« Sometimes I'd answer, »I don't know yet, I'll have to see.« Or: »We'll have to find out together what works.«

How did the children react to that?

JP: At first they weren't quite sure what to make of it, but then they really enjoyed it and started making suggestions themselves. We tried out a few of them and incorporated them into the piece, but other times I said, »I don't like that idea, so let's keep looking.« There are times when the choreographer simply has to make certain decisions. Sometimes that was hard for the students to accept, but once we'd done it a few times, they understood why. Afterwards we would look at the result together and discuss the decisions.

HH: I've found that when I'm at a loss, I can tell the children and they respond very positively. Sometimes I explain that that's a normal part of the rehearsal process and we discuss how to go on from there. The kids usually react quite positively and come up with ideas of their own. Of course, you can't just retreat to the sidelines and spend hours mulling over something. You have to keep a close eye on everyone and try to be aware of what they're doing and what they want. That aspect has more to do with teaching, of course.

But I think there are other differences, as well. When I'm working with a class, for example, I'm not necessarily as focused on one topic. When I'm working on a piece, I want to concentrate on a specific issue or theme, and everything is based on that, from the research to the conceptual formulation to the way I adapt and treat the material. However, working with children and young people has made me realize they have to be my main focus. When working in schools, my goal is to familiarize students with a certain vocabulary, a certain language, and introduce them to certain qualities, spaces and principles of composition. I try to integrate the input I get from the students with what I know and want to convey. That way I can offer the children something that fits in with their needs and interests and covers certain topics. Then I see how they respond to that. It's a process of give-and-take.

JP: There's another difference. The pieces I create with students are often quite unlike my other work. I make different choices in a school project than I would make when working with professional dancers. For example, if I've already rejected several ideas proposed by a particular child, I'd probably accept whatever their next suggestion is and then develop and implement it with the group. I don't want to discourage any child, and I think it's wonderful that every child has the opportunity to suggest an idea and later see it realized on stage.

HH: Yes, sometimes it seems like a contradiction to me: when I go into a classroom, I do so as an artist, not as a social worker – but at the same time, of course, what I do *is* social work, absolutely. It may not be my goal to do social work, yet the students must always be my primary concern. When I go to a class, I always remind myself that while I may be an expert at what I do, they're the experts when it comes to their lives.

Would you say you need to work with a teacher for this kind of instruction to work?

JP: I would say yes. In the »TanzZeit« project, the relationship with the teacher was very important to me. The teacher whose class I worked with had a very good rapport with his students, and we really made an effort to work well together as a team. I specifically asked him to participate actively. Besides, that way I didn't constantly have to maintain discipline – he took care of that. After all, a teacher usually has a relationship with a class that has developed over a number of years, and it makes sense for me to draw on that. One of the great things about this artist-teacher combination is that it opens up the child-adult relationship in a classroom setting. Sometimes the teachers dance along with the students – and let them see that they don't always know everything and that they, too, are apprehensive at having to perform in front of others. They reveal a vulnerable side of themselves students don't normally get to see.

HH: I've had some really positive experiences working with teachers. I prefer them to participate in the entire program, but if they'd rather not, they can just watch. What I'm not so keen on is when they try to teach along with me and do things like ›correcting‹ students' movements, for example. Sometimes it's as if they're afraid their class might not present itself in the best light or might compare unfavourably with others. But in my experience, the teachers are usually very supportive and are actually

quite happy to let someone else take the reins for a while. That's important, because otherwise you constantly feel you're being monitored.

*Do you ever feel you're too ›specialized‹? Do you find it difficult to get
across what you want to convey?*

HH: Yes, I do, actually, but I'm all right with that. Of course many of
the students have no experience with dance and aren't on the same level
as professionals, and so naturally I have to approach them differently and
use a different vocabulary to reach them. In my artistic work I'm freer to
›grope around in the dark‹ and try out different things. With children you
have to be much more clear and direct, even when you make mistakes or
don't know something. Maybe that's the biggest difference.

JP: In my last project it wasn't always easy for me to get across what
I wanted. I tried many different approaches. Sometimes I used words,
sometimes music, and other times I demonstrated the movements myself.
I think each child learns in its own way, has its own way of understanding things. You have to try a variety of approaches to get through to all
of them.

*How do your work with students and the personal encounters you have
with children on a personal level, both brief and over the long term, affect
your work as artists?*

JP: For me the main thing is that I get to know people I normally
would never meet. In East London, for example, I worked with students
from all over the world, many of whom were from refugee families. The
experiences they had made in their lives were totally different. At the
time, I decided to make a film about the stories of three immigrant families. We worked on it for six months. So sometimes it's a very immediate
thing: you meet someone and you're inspired by them right away. Other
times, it's more like an idea is planted in your mind like a seed, and it
takes a while for it to flower. And sometimes I find myself thinking of a
child or young person for a long time, and in some cases the relationship
develops and we'll stay in touch.

HH: I find that it affects me more indirectly, in the sense that working with children changes who I am as a person and thus also influences
my work as an artist. What I like best about this kind of work is that it
puts everything into perspective – what's important to you, maybe even
what you're interested in. My interest in the children has grown steadily
since I've worked with them. I could no longer say what's more important
to me. That didn't use to be the case – I would have unhesitatingly said
working as an artist is what matters most to me.

Hanna Hegenscheidt in »TanzZeit
– Zeit für Tanz in Schulen«

Photo: Marion Borriss

Did you have any positive or negative experiences in the course of teaching that changed how you see yourselves?

HH: I can think of one, in particular, from which I learned a lot. I worked with three youths from Serbia-Montenegro who have been in Germany for many years, yet live with the constant threat of being deported. We were supposed to create a piece on the themes of »compassion« and »opening your home to strangers«. The young people knew that, but in the course of our work, it became clear that they didn't want to constantly have to deal with the issue of »tolerance« and so on. They complained about always having to talk about deportation, when what they really wanted was to assimilate into society here. Suddenly I found myself torn – on the one hand, there was the topic I had chosen them for; on the other hand, it really went against my grain to force them to do something they didn't really want to. In the end we came up with a pretty good solution, and that really awakened me to the fact that, in this kind of work, the young people really have to come first, and that it's presumptuous to think you have to prescribe a topic to them. If you approach it thinking ›I know what's good for them‹ or ›this is what they should learn‹ – then you really have a problem.

JP: When I teach students, I actually learn a lot about myself. Frequently those are not things I like about myself, but rather things I need to work on. I'm a very impatient person, and when you work with kids – especially with a large group of kids – you have to have a lot of patience.

Another thing I've learned is how to do many things at once. When you work with professionals, you can say ›They chose to do this of their own accord, so it's okay if it's a bit uncomfortable or boring at times‹. With students it's a different matter. I always feel like I'm juggling ten balls at once in order to keep all the kids engaged. You have to have your eyes everywhere at once and you have to think on your feet – and that's great. By nature, I'm actually a person who plans a lot and likes to think every rehearsal through. I always go into a lesson with a plan, but I hardly ever end up doing what I planned. I use it as a point of departure, but then I usually take things in another direction, depending on how the students respond. When you're under a lot of pressure and are supporting so many people in their work at once, some really interesting ideas can surface from your subconscious.

In other words, the diversity and complexity of working with children, that they're so unpredictable, plus the fact that you have to work in overdrive, so to speak, actually unleashes new reserves of energy and creativity?

JP: Absolutely! It's a totally different kind of work and a really explosive energy. There's little time to reflect on things, and the resulting piece has that energy in it, as well.

HH: Ideally, I'd like to get to the point where I don't need to prepare for lessons at all, but have enough experience to make those decisions spontaneously. At the moment, I still prepare quite a bit, but I often end up throwing my lesson plans overboard. What you do is largely dictated by the situation.

What fascinates you most about working with children?

HH: It surprises me again and again how deeply these kids touch me. It's really quite overwhelming how fond I am of them.

JP: When you finally perform a piece in front of an audience, with students – as with other amateurs – you often really sense this strong drive to be present, to be there on stage. That's the moment that fascinates me most. So much is on the line, they're really going out on a limb and taking the risk of exposing themselves to ridicule in front of their families and friends. You don't have that with professional performers. It's impossible to describe the feeling when you watch kids pull that off – it could almost make me cry.

Translation from German

Notes on Contributors

Alexandra Baudelot is joint chief editor of »Mission Impossible«, a magazine for contemporary art. As an art critic, she writes about contemporary dance and performance for such periodicals as »Mouvement« and »Parachute«. She is a curator and consultant to international festivals and lectures in contemporary performance at various art schools. Most recently, she has published an essay on the work of Jennifer Lacey and Nadia Lauro entitled »Dispositifs chorégraphiques« (Les Presses du Réel 2007).

Prof. Dr. Inge Baxmann has, since 2001, been a professor for theatre studies (focusing on dance studies/dance history) at the University of Leipzig, and is Director of Tanzarchiv Leipzig. She did her doctorate on the subject of »Die Feste der Französischen Revolution. Inszenierung von Gesellschaft als Natur« (Beltz 1989) and qualified as a professor for cultural studies on the subject of »Mythos Gemeinschaft. Körper- und Tanzkulturen in der Moderne« (Fink 2000).

Jason Beechey is president of the Palucca Schule Dresden – Hochschule für Tanz, and is the general coordinator of the D.A.N.C.E. (Dance Apprentice Programme aCross Europe) study programme. Since 2004, he has also been the artistic adviser to the Ballet National de Marseille and the École Nationale Supérieure de Danse de Marseille. After graduating from the National Ballet School of Canada, he began his career as a solo dancer with the London City Ballet. Following this, he was a dancer and training director for Charleroi/Danses.

Henk Borgdorff is an art theory and research professor at the Amsterdam School of the Arts. Together with professor Marijke Hoogenboom, he chairs the research group ARTI (Artistic Research, Theory & Innovation). Borgdorff lectures on the theory of science and artistic research as part of the practice-based doctoral programme in music, docARTES. His research interests include the critique of metaphysics, philosophy of music, and epistemology of artistic research.

Edith Boxberger studied social sciences in Munich after completing a two-year newspaper traineeship, then joined the Drama Department of New York University for one year and has been writing about dance ever since for German daily newspaper »Frankfurter Allgemeine Zeitung« and for »ballettanz« among others.

Prof. Dr. Gabriele Brandstetter has been a professor for theatre studies at Freie Universität Berlin since 2003. From 1997 to 2003, she held the chair for Modern German Literature at the University of Basle prior to which she was a professor at the Institute for Applied Theatre Studies in Gießen from 1993 to 1997. Her main areas of research are performance theory, body and movement concepts in scripture, image and performance as well as research into dance, theatrality and gender differences.

Boris Charmatz is guest professor at Berlin's University of the Arts (Hochschulübergreifendes Zentrum Tanz), where he is also involved in creating a new curriculum for dance. He co-authored the book »Entretenir« (Les Presses du Réel 2003) with Isabelle Launay and will be publishing a new book in 2007: »I am a School«. Charmatz founded the Edna Association with Dimitri Chamblas in 1992 and co-created with him the pieces À BRAS LE CORPS (1993) and LES DISPARATES (1994). Charmatz has produced a series of pieces from AATT ENEN TIONON (1996) to RÉGI (2006), which have toured extensively. Besides he continues to dance for other companies, including Odile Duboc, Fanny de Chaillé, Pierre Alféri and Meg Stuart.

Julia Cima studied jazz, classical and contemporary dance in Cergy-Pontoise and Paris. Since 1995, she has worked continuously with Boris Charmatz. Cima has also danced in choreographies by Myriam Gourfink, Alain Michard, Laure Bonicel and Elisabeth Schwartz. She has participated in various education and improvisation projects and collaborations with visual artists. In 2005, she created her solo VISITATIONS.

Bojana Cvejic is a performance theorist, dramaturge and performer. She teaches performance theory at P.A.R.T.S. (Brussels) and is the author of two books including »Performative practices beyond musical work« (IKZS 2007). Cvejic is currently writing her PhD on »Performance Theory as Event« at the Centre for Research in Modern European Philosophy at Middlesex, London.

Ingo Diehl has run the education projects of »Tanzplan Deutschland« since 2005. From 2000 to 2005 he worked as a ballet master and choreographic assistant at the Wiener Volksoper, the Luzerner Stadttheater, the Island Ballet in Reykjavik and at the Staatstheater Oldenburg. From 1988 onwards, he had national and international engagements as a dancer at various theatres and has also worked as a choreographer in film and theatre since 1995. Prior to this, he studied dance in Hanover and New York as well as performance dance pedagogy in Cologne.

Dr. Cornelia Dümcke works as an independent cultural economist and project developer. In 1991, she founded Culture Concepts (www.cultureconcepts.de). She provides a variety of national and international organisations with research and consultation services as well as project developments at the interfaces between artistic and cultural production to economic and social processes. She has written numerous scientific publications as well as studies and reports on the economics of performing arts among other areas.

João Fiadeiro lives and works in Lisbon as a dancer, choreographer, researcher and teacher. In 1990 he founded Cia. RE.AL (www.re-al.org), a hybrid production structure for contemporary dance. He is a teacher at and consultant to various international institutions such as Forum Dança in Lisbon, ex.e.r.ce in Montpellier, Tanzquartier Wien and the new MA programme »SoDA« (Solo/Dance/Authorship) in Berlin.

Prof. Dr. Dr. h.c. Erika Fischer-Lichte is professor for theatre studies at Freie Universität Berlin. She is a member of the Academia Europaea, the Göttinger Akademie der Wissenschaften and the Berlin-Brandenburgische Akademie der Wissenschaften. She has been a guest professor at numerous universities in Europe as well as in Russia, the USA, India, China and Japan. Some of her most recent publications include »Ästhetik des Performativen« (Suhrkamp 2004) and »Theatre, Sacrifice, Ritual. Exploring Forms of Political Theatre« (Routledge 2005).

Sabine Gehm has been the artistic director of the international festival TANZ Bremen since 2002 and project director for the DANCE CONGRESS GERMANY 2006. She works as a freelance curator and culture manager (including Jagniatkow – Move the Mount 2005, Veronika Blumstein – Moving Exiles 2006). Between 2001 and 2005, she coordinated the international network for performing arts »Junge Hunde«. A graduate of cultural studies, she was a dramaturge at Hamburg's Kampnagelfabrik from 1994 to 2001. Between 1988 and 1994, she was responsible for organising the International Summer Theatre Festival/Hamburg.

Rebecca Groves has been executive director of the Forsythe Foundation since 2004 where she initiates interdisciplinary research projects and publications exploring the embodied knowledge of the dancing body and the structures of innovative choreography. In 2002 she began working with choreographer William Forsythe as dramaturge for the Ballett Frankfurt. Groves did her graduate studies in theatre and art history at Columbia University, New York, and at Stanford University.

Dr. Yvonne Hardt is a dancer, choreographer and graduate of dance and theatre studies. She is an associate research scholar at the Institute for Theatre Studies at Freie Universität Berlin. Having earned her doctorate on the political dimension of expressionist dance, she has increasingly devoted her attention to dance and the media as well as the exchange between theory and practice. She also continues to develop choreographies for her own dance company BodyAttacksWord on an ongoing basis.

Hanna Hegenscheidt studied dance, Laban movement analysis and Klein technique in Hamburg and New York. Since 1998, she has taught the Klein technique and contemporary dance in New York, England and Berlin. She has worked as a teaching artist at the Lincoln Center Institute for Aesthetic Education in New York and is part of the »TanzZeit – Zeit für Tanz in Schulen« project in Berlin. Her own choreographies have so far been performed both in New York and in Europe. As a dancer/performer, Hanna Hegenscheidt has worked with Reinhild Hoffmann, Robert Wilson, Achim Freyer and Martin Clausen/Two Fish, among others.

Dieter Heitkamp is a professor for contemporary dance, director of the Department for Contemporary and Classical Dance as well as dean of the Faculty for Dramatic Arts at the University of Music and Performing Arts in Frankfurt a.m.. Between 1978 and 1995, he was one of the artistic directors at Tanzfabrik Berlin. Since 1977 he has been deeply involved with studying, teaching and performing Contact Improvisation. His choreographies have been presented throughout Germany and Europe, in Canada, the USA, Japan, Hong Kong, Brazil and Russia. He has also choreographed for Ballet Frankfurt, the Ballet of the Staatsoper Unter den Linden Berlin as well as for theatre and television.

Marijke Hoogenboom has been a professor at the Amsterdam School of the Arts since 2003 where she runs the interdisciplinary workgroup »Art Practice and Development«. Besides this, she co-developed the new interdisciplinary master's course »Artistic Research« and is a consultant for foreign cultural policy to the Dutch Cultural Council. A graduate of theatre studies and dramaturge, she co-founded the postgraduate course DasArts and was a member of the artistic board until 2001.

Pirkko Husemann was associate researcher for the DANCE CONGRESS GERMANY 2006. She graduated in drama, film and media in Frankfurt a.m. and wrote her dissertation »Choreography as Critical Practice« on Xavier Le Roy's and Thomas Lehmen's choreographic modes of work. A former assistant to the artistic director at Künstlerhaus Mousonturm, Frankfurt a.M., she has worked as a production manager, dramaturge and performer with Kattrin Deufert and Thomas Plischke, Xavier Le Roy, Thomas Lehmen, Prue Lang, Nik Haffner and Christina Ciupke.

Prof. Dr. Claudia Jeschke has held the chair for dance studies at the University of Salzburg since 2004. The main focus of her research work lies in dance history with an analytical approach to movement and practical orientation. The connection between history, theory and practice can also be seen in her numerous reconstructions of dance phenomena of the 18th, 19th and 20th centuries. She studied theatre theory and German literature in Munich and underwent dance training in Munich, Philadelphia and New York.

Prof. Dr. Gabriele Klein is professor for sociology of movement, sport and dance at the University of Hamburg. She is the director of the »Institut für urbane Bewegungskulturen« and runs the MA course in performance studies (www.performance.uni-hamburg.de). The main focal points of her research work lie in social and cultural theory of the body, movement and sport, dance and performance theory, the cultural and social history of dance as well as urban movement cultures and popular dance cultures.

Constanze Klementz has been a dance critic and freelance author since 1997 for journals and daily newspapers as well as the Internet platform Sarma. She is a graduate of ballet at the Berliner Tanzakademie and read theatre studies, philosophy and German literature in Berlin.

Kurt Koegel is professor for contemporary dance pedagogy at the University for Music and Performing Arts in Frankfurt a.M.. He has worked in Europe, teaching at festivals, schools and dance companies including Ultima Vez, Rosas, P.A.R.T.S., SNDO, EDDC, SEAD, and the Korean National University of Arts. His work is influenced by architecture, theatre, the visual arts, Feldenkrais, Pilates, Yoga, and BMC. Koegel graduated in his self-designed degree programme for Dance, Design and Communication at the University of Minnesota.

Rudi Laermans teaches sociological theory at the Catholic University of Leuven. He is also a regular guest teacher at P.A.R.T.S. in Brussels. His current research work deals with social systems theory, post-Foucauldian critical theory and contemporary art theory.

Scott deLahunta works as a researcher, writer and organiser on a wide range of international projects, combining performing arts with other disciplines and practices. He is an associate research fellow at Dartington College of Arts and member of the Art Theory and Research and Art Practice and Development Research Group at the Amsterdam School of the Arts. He serves on the editorial boards of »Performance Research, Dance Theatre Journal« and the »International Journal of Performance and Digital Media«.

Thomas Lehmen studied dance and choreography at the School for New Dance Development in Amsterdam. His productions, such as DISTANZ-LOS, MONO SUBJECTS, SCHREIBSTÜCK, BETTER TO ..., or LEHMEN LERNT are performed around the world. Lehmen gives numerous workshops in Europe, including those at the SNDO and the University of Hamburg/ »Performance Studies« where he teaches how to deal with choreographic systems that aim to achieve individual artistic compositions.

Susanne Linke learned the ropes with Mary Wigman and at the Folk-wang-Hochschule in Essen. Between 1970 and 1973 she was a dancer at the Folkwang Tanz Studio under the artistic direction of Pina Bausch. She soon gained international acclaim for her own solos and group performances. In the early 1990s, she founded the Company Susanne Linke. Together with Urs Dietrich, she formed a new company in 1994 at the Bremer Theater. From 2000 to 2001 Linke was a founding member of the Choreografisches Zentrum Essen and its designated artistic director. Since 2001 she has been freelancing again as a choreographer and dancer.

Waltraud Luley, conservator of the choreographic heritage of Dore Hoyer, was educated in dance by Beatrice Vigners in Riga. In 1943 she moved to Germany and graduated at the Lola Rogge Schule in Hamburg as a teacher for amateur dance. From 1955 to 2001, she ran her own dance studio in Frankfurt a.M.. Between 1987 and 1995 Luley taught creative dance at the University for Music and Dramatic Arts in Frankfurt a.M.. Since 2001 she has acted as a consultant on occasion and was involved in dance reconstructions, for example.

Royston Maldoom has been actively involved in various social contexts around the world for over thirty years – working not only with school children but also prisoners, exiled citizens, the physically and mentally challenged and other marginalised or excluded groups. The English choreographer made a name for himself in Germany above all through his almost legendary documentary RHYTHM IS IT! about a project involving the Berlin Philharmonic and school children from Berlin. He has been awarded numerous international prizes, among them the O.B.E. from the Queen in 2006 and the German Ehren-Tanzpreis 2005.

Linda Müller has headed the »Tanz in Schulen« project of the »NRW Landesbüro Tanz« (Regional Office for Dance in North Rhine-Westphalia) since 2002. She has developed concepts for establishing dance in schools along with project-related quality assurance measures. Müller finds experienced dance teachers to teach in schools, organises symposiums at regular intervals for all those involved in the model project and raises awareness and public attention for the project. A graduate of sports science and physiotherapist, she studied theatre-music-dance/movement theatre as well as elementary dance at the Deutsche Sporthochschule Köln.

Martin Nachbar is a dancer, performer and choreographer. He writes for various European dance and theatre magazines. He underwent training at the School for New Dance Development (Amsterdam) and at P.A.R.T.S. (Brussels). He was a co-founder of the collective B.D.C./Plischke for which, among other things, he reconstructed the dance series AFFECTOS HUMANOS by Dore Hoyer. In 2005 he organised the symposium entitled »meeting on dance education« (modeo5) together with Ulrike Melzwig and fabrik Potsdam. In addition to his solo choreography work, he is working together with other artists such as with Jochen Roller in MNEMONIC NONSTOP.

Dr. Elisabeth Nehring studied literature and theatre studies as well as classic and contemporary dance in Berlin. She works as a dramaturge and dance critic and is a freelance author for several German radio stations such as DeutschlandRadio Kultur, Deutschland Funk and WDR, as well as for periodicals such as »Tanzjournal« and »ballettanz«. One of the main focuses of her work is reporting on the dance scenes in Eastern Europe, Israel and the Arab nations.

Alva Noë is professor for philosophy at the University of California Berkeley (USA). He is the author of »Action in Perception« (The MIT Press, 2004) as well as numerous articles in different areas of philosophy. His work focuses on perceptual consciousness.

Jo Parkes is a freelance choreographer, teacher and filmmaker. She is a specialist in dance in educational settings and in integrated dance.

Parkes is co-founder of »People Moving«, a UK-based national training programme for professional artists. She has co-written curricula for schools, colleges and universities and taught at Newham Sixth Form College for five years.

Livia Patrizi is the initiator and artistic director of the Berlin project »TanzZeit – Zeit für Tanz in Schulen«. She underwent her training as a dancer at the Folkwang Hochschule, Essen. Patrizi was followed by dance engagements with the Cullberg Ballett, Pina Bausch, Joachim Schlömer and Maguy Marin among others. Since 1990 she has also been freelancing as a choreographer. 2006 was the world premiere of her production WER HAT ANGST VOR TANZ? – a stage documentary for young people and adults.

Jeroen Peeters studied art history and philosophy. He is currently living and working in Brussels as a writer, dramaturge and curator in the field of dance and performance. He has written articles about dance and art theory for various media and co-runs the critique platform »Sarma« (www.sarma.be). As a dramaturge, artistic collaborator and performer he has contributed to performances and research projects by, amongst others, Paul Deschanel Movement Research Group, Frankfurter Küche, Anne Juren, Thomas Lehmen, Vera Mantero, Martin Nachbar, Lisa Nelson, Meg Stuart and Superamas.

Felix Ruckert is a choreographer, dancer and, since 2004, also a curator of the self-initiated festival »xplore – sinnliche extreme/extreme sinnlichkeit«. In March 2006 he opened his own performance venue »schwelle 7« in Berlin. Above all, it is his interactive works such as HAUT-NAH (1995), RING (1999), DELUXE JOY PILOT (2000), SECRET SERVICE (2002) and PLACEBO TREATMENT (2005) that have given him and his company an international reputation. As a dancer, he has worked with the likes of Wanda Golonka, Mathilde Monnier and the Wuppertaler Tanztheater/Pina Bausch.

Björn Dirk Schlüter is the co-director of the contemporary Brazilian dance festival »Move Berlim«. As a curator he has worked for the festivals »Shanghai Dance« and »In Transit«, among others, and as a freelance dramaturge with Takao Kawaguchi and Hooman Sharifi. Between 1996 and 2003 he was a member of the artistic board of Theater am Halleschen Ufer in Berlin.

Norbert Servos has been working as a freelance choreographer and author since 1983. The co-founder and long-standing editor of the periodical »Ballett International«, he has published numerous books on

Pina Bausch and the development of German dance theatre. His most recent publications include a book entitled »Schritte verfolgen – Die Tänzerin und Choreographin Susanne Linke« (Kieser 2005). In addition to all his other activities, he has been the artistic director of Dance Lab Berlin since 1993 for which he has developed numerous performances (including DRINK, SMOKE – MADE IN HAVANA 2004) and is teacher for contemporary dance and choreography.

Hooman Sharifi is a choreographer and performer. Since 2000 he has created ten performances for children and adults with his Impure Company, made several installations and published three magazines. His first experiences with dance came with Hip-Hop and Street Dance. At the age of 21, he began learning classical ballet and modern dance. In 2000, he graduated from the National Academy of the Arts in Oslo after studying choreography there for three years. Sharifi was born in Iran and moved to Norway when he was 15 years old, where he has lived since 1989.

Irene Sieben is a Feldenkrais Method teacher and, apart from lecturing at institutes like the Berlin University of the Arts and Tanz Tangente, also offers private lessons. As a contributor to »ballettanz« and »Tanzjournal«, she primarily writes on the subject of somatic learning. Sieben studied dance and dance education with Mary Wigman and a variety of movement research methods.

Peter Stamer has been working as a dramaturge, author and curator in the field of contemporary dance and performance since 2002. In 2001, he joined the newly founded Tanzquartier Wien as the curator for theory. Between 1999 and 2002, he was awarded a PhD grant from the German Research Foundation. While reading theatre studies, he worked as a dance dramaturge at the Nationaltheater Mannheim from 1993 to 1998. He is the co-editor of a book entitled »incubator« (Passagen 2006) which was written on the choreographic project of the same name developed by Philipp Gehmacher. Among other things, Peter is currently working on publishing a book on the discursive performance series he created himself entitled »Personale«.

Silvia Stammen read theatre studies, German literature and philosophy in Munich and Freiburg. As a freelance journalist, she writes for »Süddeutsche Zeitung«, »Neue Zürcher Zeitung«, »Theater heute« focusing mainly on theatre and dance.

Meg Stuart, a choreographer and dancer, made her debut in 1991 in the piece DISFIGURE STUDY. Together with her Brussels based company

Damaged Goods, she has collaborated with artists such as Bruce Mau, Gary Hill, Ann Hamilton, Chris Kondek, Benoît Lachambre, Hahn Rowe, among others. REPLACEMENT (2006) was the first production made in Berlin since Meg Stuart & Damaged Goods started a partnership with Volksbühne am Rosa-Luxemburg-Platz. Her two most recent works are IT'S NOT FUNNY (2006) and BLESSED (2007).

Hortensia Völckers has been a member of the Executive Board and artistic director at the Federal Cultural Foundation of Germany since March 2003. Between 1998 and 2002, she was the director of the Wiener Festwochen and in charge of the fields of dance and interdisciplinary projects. From 1995 to 1997, Völckers was a member of the artistic board for documenta X. She was a fine arts consultant to Siemens Kulturprogramm in Munich, and was artistic director of the Munich Festival »Dance« from 1991 to 1995. She studied art history and political science while, at the same time, completing her dance education.

Dr. med. Eileen M. Wanke is a plastic surgeon, sports doctor, dance doctor and acupuncturist, and also works for the Sports Medicine department at the Humboldt Universität Berlin. Her main area of (research) interest lies in preventing injuries to dancers. An author of numerous studies, she has been invited to speak at numerous national and international dance medicine and sports medicine congresses. She also lectures at the Berlin University of the Arts, among other institutes, where she runs a dance medicine consultancy service.

Katharina von Wilcke was project director for DANCE CONGRESS GERMANY 2006. In 1995, she founded the production office DepArtment which works in conjunction with artists from the fields of dance and theatre. In addition to this, she is cultural manager and curator at festivals, theatre academies and other project-series like »Volkspalast« and »ErsatzStadt«. Between 1986 and 2000, she was part of the organisation team of the International Summer Theatre Festival Hamburg. She graduated in German and Spanish linguistics and literature at the Hamburg University.

Gabriele Wittmann works as a freelance dance critic for radio and television broadcasters (including German TV station ARD), is the author of numerous books and contributor of articles to the periodicals »ballettanz« and »Tanzjournal« among others. A graduate of American literature and musicology, she is a lecturer of dance criticism and dance history at the University for Music and Performing Arts in Frankfurt a.M..

Norah Zuniga Shaw works as dancer, multimedia-choreographer and dance theorist. She is assistant professor at The Ohio State University Department of Dance and Advanced Computing Center for the Arts and Design. Her research interests are dance and technology, interdisciplinary composition and critical theory of the body. Zuniga Shaw is co-editor of the online-magazine »Extensions: The Online Journal for Embodied Technologies«.